BUYING &
SELLING A
HOME

Kiplinger Books Also Publishes:
KIPLINGER'S INVEST YOUR WAY TO WEALTH
KIPLINGER'S TAKE CHARGE OF YOUR CAREER
KIPLINGER'S SURE WAYS TO CUT YOUR TAXES
KIPLINGER'S MAKE YOUR MONEY GROW

KIPLINGER'S

BUYING & SELLING A

HOME

BY THE STAFF OF
KIPLINGER'S PERSONAL FINANCE MAGAZINE

KIPLINGER BOOKS, Washington, D.C.

**KIPLINGER
BOOKS**

Published by
The Kiplinger Washington Editors, Inc.
1729 H Street, N.W.
Washington, DC 20006

Library of Congress Cataloging-in-Publication Data

Kiplinger's buying & selling a home : the only guide you need for
  success with your principal residence, vacation home, investment
  property / by the staff of Changing times magazine. -- 3rd ed.
      p.   cm.
    Rev. ed. of: The Kiplinger/Changing times guide to buying and
  selling a home. c1987.
    ISBN 0-938721-12-7 : $10.95
    1. House buying. 2. House selling. 3. Home ownership. 4. Real
  estate business.   I. Changing times. II. Kiplinger/Changing times
  guide to buying and selling a home. III. Title: Kiplinger's buying
  and selling a home.
  HD1379.K52   1990
  643'.12--dc20   89-71681
                                                             CIP

This publication is intended to provide guidance in regard to the subject
matter covered. It is sold with the understanding that the author and
publisher are not herein engaged in rendering legal, accounting, tax or
other professional services. If such services are required, professional
assistance should be sought.

Third Edition. Third Printing. November 1991.

Book and cover designed by S. Laird Jenkins Corp.
Cover illustration by Jim McGinness

CONTENTS

Introduction by **Knight A. Kiplinger**
Editor-in-Chief, *Kiplinger's Personal Finance Magazine*

PART ONE
FOR BUYERS

PART TWO
FOR SELLERS

INTRODUCTION

◆

Housing markets are distinctly local and highly cyclical, so it is difficult to give guidance on home ownership that suits all regions and all moments in time. The revisions that this book has gone through in nine years illustrate the fickle nature of real estate counsel. With changing mortgage rates and economic conditions, preferences swung back and forth between adjustable mortgages and fixed-rate financing. When markets were slow, exotic new kinds of mortgages and seller-financing plans flourished, only to disappear when the selling climate improved.

At any particular time, market conditions vary greatly by region and kind of housing. In the mid-'80s, for example, housing values were in the doldrums in many parts of the Middle West and the Oil Patch of Texas, Oklahoma and Louisiana. But the coastal regions, from New England and the Mid-Atlantic to California and the Pacific Northwest, experienced jack-rabbit home appreciation through most of the decade. Then the tables were turned, when slow growth and then recession hit the once-hot regions. By 1990, prices were declining from unsustainable peaks in such cities as Boston, New York, Washington and Los Angeles, but values were rising in the agricultural Midwest and the industrial cities of the North Central states, where manufacturing was once again booming.

Meanwhile, some interesting demographic trends were beginning to be felt in housing markets. During the 1970s and '80s, America built amazing numbers of small homes and condos for the first-time home buyers of the Baby-Boom generation. But the generation that followed, born during the mid-60s through the early '70s, is much smaller. So when it's time for the first-time buyers to move up to larger homes, there will be less demand for the small townhouses and condos they are leaving behind. That means that prices will flatten for starter homes, and the "affordability" crisis will begin to ease for young homebuyers. At the same time, there will be great demand for trade-up homes, as the Baby Boomers enter their highest-earning years. This also augers well for the value of vacation homes and retirement properties later in the '90s.

When home prices softened during the recession of 1991, forecasts of long, deep declines in real estate values began to appear in the popular press. We see no basis for these projections. Granted, home prices on a national basis will probably not see the rapid appreciation of the 1970s and '80s, but that doesn't mean residential real estate will become a bad deal.

We believe home ownership is returning to its traditional role in a family's finances. It won't be a hot speculative investment, but it will continue to be a good inflation hedge (matching or slightly exceeding the rate of inflation), an excellent tax shelter (just about the only one left), and a handy forced-savings plan, requiring you to add to your equity each time you write a mortgage check. And in case you forgot, an owned home will also be your shelter, someplace you know you can stay, without worrying about rent hikes or termination of the lease.

Every chapter of *Kiplinger's Buying and Selling a Home* has been fully revised to reflect the various realities of today's markets, plus the effects of federal tax reform. While the book concentrates on single-family dwellings, it also covers what you need to know if your interest is in condominiums or cooperatives—or even mobile homes.

The book is divided into two sections: Part One, for buyers, and Part Two, for sellers. Whichever you are (and many people are both simultaneously), carefully read the part addressed to the other party. You'll gain insight into the concerns and strategies of all the major players in a transaction, and the knowledge will help you get a better deal for yourself.

Recognizing that the vast majority of real estate transactions are handled by brokers and agents who receive a commission on the sale, *Buying and Selling a Home* tells you the right way to select and deal with these professionals. It also describes how buyers can often benefit from using a "buyer's broker," who is clearly working for the buyer, not the seller. And for homeowners who have the time and marketing flair to try their hand at selling without an agent, we give realistic, step-by-step advice on how to do it.

But *Buying and Selling a Home* offers much more than a comprehensive guide for buying or selling your primary home. It includes chapters on buying a vacation home and investing in residential real estate, fully covering what to look for when considering these properties and explaining the tax consequences that come with ownership.

The book also recognizes that your home is most likely your major investment. In addition to assisting you in investing wisely, *Buying and Selling a Home* will help you safeguard your investment—and tells you how to use the equity you'll build up to relieve other financial concerns, from remodeling expenses to college tuition. Special solutions to problems senior citizens may face are also covered.

This edition of *Buying and Selling a Home* is the work of many talented people. Major updating was done by Priscilla Brandon, chief of research for *Kiplinger's Personal Finance Magazine*. Kevin McCormally, senior editor of the Magazine and author of *Kiplinger's Sure Ways to Cut Your Taxes*, provided new material on the tax angles of real estate. Dianne Olsufka assisted with the research and proofread the manuscript. David Harrison handled the editing, while Don Fragale and Millie Thompson held us to our printing and production schedules.

We hope that *Buying and Selling a Home* helps guide you through the murky and often turbulent waters of real estate deals in America today—and tomorrow. Real estate has long been a core subject of *Kiplinger's Personal Finance Magazine*, the first magazine of personal-finance guidance, so the subjects discussed here will be periodically updated there.

Don't hesitate to write us with your questions or comments. Your ideas will help us strengthen the book in future editions.

Knight A. Kiplinger
November 1991

PART ONE

FOR BUYERS

◆

CHAPTER 1

To Buy or Not to Buy

◆

HOMEOWNERSHIP has long been regarded as one of the key elements of the "American dream." America has one of the highest proportions of home-ownership in the world, with more than six out of every ten families living in owner-occupied housing.

The reasons for America's love affair with homeownership are many. Some are financial. Our tax code continues to subsidize heavily the ownership of homes, making it more attractive than renting for most people. Homeownership is also America's favorite forced-savings and investment plan, with an increasing share of the monthly mortgage payment going into the building of equity for future uses—another home, college expenses, retirement, etc. A home is, truly, the only investment you can live in, and over the past 40 years, it has been a generally well-performing investment, relative to alternative uses of money.

But much of the motivation behind homeownership is psychological. This country was founded on principles of individual destiny, personal control over one's life and surroundings, and freedom of individual expression. A home of one's own helps fulfill all of those promises, giving the owner freedom from rent hikes and the whim of the landlord, and the freedom to live life as he or she wishes. A home can provide a sense of security and pride. A home gives a feeling of stability and commitment, not to mention autonomy and privacy. It is often the first step in an owner's putting down roots in a community.

But like most freedoms, the benefits of homeownership also carry heavy responsibilities—financial obligations and duties of maintenance, recordkeeping, and planning.

THE INTANGIBLES

It's no wonder that psychologists rank buying a home high on the list of stress-producing events. Not only is it the biggest purchase most people make in a lifetime, but it also forces a wholesale examination of goals, commitments and lifestyle. It's an emotional as well as a financial investment.

People buy homes for lots of different reasons. Before you go into the market for a home, examine your motives, clarify your wants and needs, and focus your investigation.

With so much at stake, don't rush into the market without thoughtful preparation. If you join the ranks of buyers charging about searching for answers without knowing the right questions, you may, by luck, end up with a house you can live with. Then again, you may spend weeks, even months, looking at houses only to end up feeling thwarted and confused.

Before you take the plunge, address questions like these: What does being a homeowner mean to you? To your spouse? What do you really want in a home, and from a home? If you have children or plan to some day, how will your choice of home affect them? Your home determines where children will go to school and what facilities will be nearby for recreation, shopping and worship. What about proximity and convenience for friends? Its location or design can make it a favorite gathering place for your friends or extended family.

How will becoming a homeowner change you and the way you live? Who hasn't heard stories about the totally unhandy new buyer who ends up renovating his or her home from top to bottom; the successful business that had its beginning in a spare room or basement; or the irrepressible free spirit who is transformed into a model of financial responsibility by homeownership?

FINANCIAL BENEFITS

Treating a home solely as an investment probably is impossible. Financial calculations alone fall short of giving you the perspective you need for such a big decision. Still, a home is a major investment, and the financial aspects of homeownership should not be ignored.

Here are some key financial benefits of homeownership:

Budgetary Discipline

Accumulating the down payment on a home is often the goal that creates a family's first real savings program. Later on, paying the mortgage is a strong inducement to creating and sticking with a budget. Depending on your personality and level of discretionary income, this form of enforced savings (and consequent equity buildup) can be an important factor in boosting family net worth. Stripped to its essentials, equity is the difference between what you would get if you sold your home and any debt outstanding. Equity includes the down payment, all payments against the principal balance, and any appreciation in the market value of your home that occurs after you buy it.

The Power of Leverage

Buying a home offers you the opportunity to magnify the purchasing power of your money through what is called leverage—the use of borrowed money to purchase an asset that is likely to appreciate, magnifying your profit.

Normally, you buy property—whether it's a home or a commercial building—with some of your own funds plus a long-term mortgage. That use of borrowed money enables you to profit from price increases on property you haven't yet paid for.

The larger your loan as a proportion of the home's value, the greater your leverage and potential gain. Say you purchase a $100,000 single family house with no loan and sell it three years later for $125,000. The $25,000 gain represents a 25% return on your $100,000 outlay.

Suppose, on the other hand, that you had invested only $20,000 of your own money, while borrowing the other $80,000. When you sell (ignoring for the sake of simplicity the cost of the loan, tax angles, commissions and other costs) you have made $25,000 on your $20,000 investment, a spectacular 125% return on your investment over the three years of ownership.

Using maximum leverage—with a very small down payment and very large mortgage—isn't prudent or advantageous for everyone, but most first-time buyers will need all they can get just to open the door.

Appreciation

If your home is worth more now than when you bought it, that's appreciation. When you sell it you can use the profit as a springboard to a better home. Or you can tap the equity/appreciation build-up to pay college tuition, to buy a vacation hideaway, to take a long dreamed-of ocean cruise. For many people, the equity in their homes becomes a major source of retirement funds.

Tax Benefits

Homeowners benefit from the tax deductibility of mortgage interest and property taxes. When you sell, you can defer federal taxes on all the profits if within two years you buy another home of equal or greater value. When you reach 55, you can sell the home and keep up to $125,000 of profit completely free of tax.

THE RISKS AND HARD WORK OF HOMEOWNERSHIP

So far, it may sound like there's no way to lose. But homeownership is not for everyone. There are risks—as well as burdens.

Financial Risks

The value of your home is not guaranteed to go up, and it could go down. The leverage that is so alluring when real estate values are on the rise can act to magnify losses as well as gains. For example, suppose you invested $20,000 in a home valued at $100,000 in a booming economy. Then recession hits your community, you lose your job and you're forced to sell for $80,000; the $20,000 loss wipes out 100% of your investment, and you'll probably have to dig into your pocket to cover commissions and other expenses. Real estate is not a liquid asset. You can lose if you have to sell in a hurry, because of a divorce or job loss, for example.

You lose, too, if you invest in a home a sum of money that could have been invested elsewhere for a better return. If alternative investments—such as stocks or bonds—are rising in value faster than homes in your area, you might do better, in the short run, as a renter/investor rather than a homeowner.

Even if you buy a home, you may want to hold back some of your cash to invest in income-producing assets, rather than pour it all into your new home; this is especially relevant for the trade-up home buyer who has substantial cash from the sale of the previous home.

Homes cost money to maintain. You have to be prepared to pay for routine maintenance (usually with time and money) and for the inevitable replacement of big-ticket items. Figure on annual maintenance costs equivalent to 1% to 3% of the cost of your home, not counting major replacements such as the roof or furnace.

Reduced Mobility

Homeowners have less freedom of movement; it's not as easy to pack up and move for a change of scenery or a new job. And a hefty mortgage payment may make it hard to maintain any other savings and investment programs for retirement, vacations and other things.

Rent vs. Buy

In the short run, renting can make more financial sense than buying, in terms of how much shelter you can afford for a given price.

Rents tend to be an accurate reflection of the free-market pricing of housing simply as *shelter*. But the ownership cost of a house or condominium is a combination of both *shelter* value and *investment* expectation.

So at any given moment, you can usually rent an apartment or house for less than the monthly carrying costs that a buyer of that property would have to pay to carry it through the early years of ownership.

This explains why many young people can't afford to own the very condominium that they've been renting with no financial strain, or why a young family might be able to rent a much fancier, more spacious house than they would be able to buy.

That's the short-run picture, but the long-range view is different. Over time, rents tend to rise, but, if you have a fixed-rate mortgage, the basic cost of owning your own home—the monthly payment of principal and interest—stays the same. This relatively stable cost, combined with price appreciation, is what makes homeownership financially attractive in the long run.

Until the "long run" arrives, however, you may have to make some sacrifices to become a homeowner. You may have to put up with less space if you have to pay more to own a small home than to rent a larger one. To find a house you can afford, you might have to move to a location farther from your job and favorite haunts; that means extra traveling cost and possibly two cars for your household, where one used to suffice.

BUYING A HOUSE WITH OTHERS

The vast majority of houses are either solely owned by individuals or jointly owned by married couples.

But with a surge of unorthodox living arrangements in the 1970s came a new variety of ownership arrangements among unrelated individuals sharing the same principal residence or vacation home. Single people living as couples or in groups wanted the advantages of homeownership, too.

Many lenders are still cool to such arrangements, but some are not.

There are proper ways to go about buying property jointly with relatives or unrelated friends, the two most common being tenancy-in-common and partnership. A good real estate attorney can explain them to you.

Owning in a group can create problems. When a tenancy-in-common ownership share changes hands, the lender may declare the loan due. The only recourse, if you don't want to sell the property, is to refinance.

Setting up a general partnership to own the place can head off many of those problems by anticipating and dealing with them in the partnership agreement. Use your lawyer to draw up the agreement.

Make sure the partnership agreement addresses the following points:

♦ How ownership will be divided, which in turn determines who pays how much of the down payment, monthly payment, maintenance and repairs. The contract should also describe how any profits or losses from rent or sale of the place will be divided and how tax benefits will be distributed.

♦ How use of the house's space is to be divided.

♦ What constitutes a deciding vote and under what circumstances such a vote is considered necessary.

♦ Which owner will act as managing partner and thus be responsible for signing checks and paying routine expenses.

♦ How much advance notice a withdrawing partner must give and how the buyout price will be set.

A partnership may also protect the existing mortgage when a new owner enters the picture if the lender agrees that it is an interest in the partnership—not an interest in the property—that is being transferred.

Ideally, a general partnership should try to find a lender who is willing to limit each partner's liability on the loan to his or her respective percentage of ownership, even though such agreements are unusual. Otherwise, each partner is responsible for 100% of the loan, so a lender could single out any partner to sue for the money if there's a default, instead of going through complicated foreclosure proceedings. Regardless of this protection, you'll want to be confident that each member of the buying group is financially responsible, creditworthy and stable in his or her career.

The legal and financial techniques associated with ownership by unrelated individuals are just the beginning of your consideration of this issue.

Just as important, or even more so, is compatability of lifestyle and the prospects of a durable friendship among all involved. As for investment value, keep in mind that partnership interests in a commonly owned house are not highly liquid. To get full value for anyone's share, the group may have to sell the whole house.

There are a lot of obstacles to overcome in such an arrangement, but with careful planning and thoughtfulness among friends, it can work out well both socially and financially.

CHAPTER 2

ASSESSING YOUR
RESOURCES

◆

ONCE YOU have determined that you're serious about buying a home—and before you start looking at houses—gather the information you will need to present to lenders. Review your financial situation to determine what you can pay down and how large a load you can carry monthly.

When you've completed that task, visit with lenders to get your figures plugged into the available mortgage formulas to yield an affordable price range. This kind of preparation—called "prequalifying"—will give you a financial comfort zone within which to shop. You'll know what's easy, what's possible and what's out of the question.

FIGURE YOUR NET WORTH

If you don't have a net worth statement already, it's time to put one together. An inventory of your assets and liabilities will help you determine the maximum down payment you can make. If money you will need is tied up in such illiquid assets as your current home, land or collectibles, you must allow yourself plenty of time either to sell or borrow against them. Use the worksheet provided on the following page to calculate your net worth.

NET WORTH WORKSHEET

What You Own		What You Owe	
Cash:		**Current Bills:**	
Cash on hand	$	Rent	$
Checking accounts		Utilities	
Savings accounts		Charge accounts	
Money-market funds		Credit cards	
Life insurance cash value		Insurance premiums	
Money owed you		Alimony	
		Child support	
		Other bills	
Marketable Securities:			
Stocks	$		
Bonds		**Taxes:**	
Government securities		Federal	$
Mutual funds		State	
Other investments		Local	
Personal Property (Resale Value):		Taxes on investments	
Automobiles	$	Other	
Household furnishings			
Art, antiques, other collectibles			
Clothing, furs		**Mortgages:**	
Jewelry		Homes	$
Other possessions		Home equity	
		Other properties	
		Debts to Individuals:	
Real Estate (Appraised Value):			$
Homes	$		
Other properties			
Retirement Funds:			
Vested portion of company plan	$	**Loans:**	
Vested benefits		Auto	$
IRA/Keogh		Education	
Annuities (surrender value)		Other	
Other Assets:		**Total Liabilities**	$
Equity in businesses	$		
Partnership interests		What you own minus what you owe equals your net worth:	$
Total Assets:	$		

THE DOWN PAYMENT

Now use the worksheet below to find your maximum down payment, if you wanted to put all your liquid assets into the home purchase. Take your total *liquid* net worth (including the equity you'll get from the sale of your present home), and subtract from that figure 1) savings for emergencies, educational expenses or retirement; and 2) settlement and moving costs, and cash you'll need for improvements and decorating and furnishing your new home.

The bottom line will be the sum that you *could* put down on the new house, if you wish to use it all. The more cash you pay up front, the less you will have to pay month by month on the mortgage, and the lower your total interest costs will be over the term of the mortgage.

Conversely, the less you put down, the greater will be your leverage, tax deductions for mortgage interest, and available funds for other expenses, including decorating and furnishing. Also keep in mind that the money you hold back from your down payment, if invested wisely, might earn you more than the appreciation on your property will add to your equity.

WHAT YOU CAN PUT DOWN
Estimating your available cash for a down payment

Net worth (total assets minus liabilities): $ _____

Less funds reserved for college expenses, savings,
  retirement, emergency needs, etc.:   − _____

Less cash needed for costs related to the new home:
  Settlement expenses: − _____
  Sales expenses for current home: − _____
  Moving and relocating expenses: − _____
  Immediate improvements to new home: − _____
  Decorating, furnishing new home: − _____

                          Net Assets Available: $ _____
                   Plus gifts from parents, relatives: + _____
        Total Available Cash for Down Payment: $ _____

As you figure the amount of your liquid assets, remember that you don't have to put it all into the down payment. The minimum required will be determined by the type of loan, the lender and whether the mortgage will be sold in the secondary market.

Mortgage lenders, of course, prefer a big down payment to a minimal one. That tells the lender that the new homeowner has a major stake in the property and won't be tempted to default on the loan and walk away from the house. The larger the down payment the less risk of foreclosure and the less chance the lender will suffer any financial loss on the property.

In most cases you will need to pay at least 10% down on the purchase price of the property. If you plan to buy with a down payment of less than 20%, you will be expected to have a higher income relative to total long-term debt than someone putting down 20%.

If your calculations indicate that you can't put at least 10% down,

1) Consider buying a less expensive condo, or a house that needs fixing up.

2) Find out whether you are eligible for a VA-guaranteed or FHA-insured loan, with little or no down payment.

3) Consider an equity-sharing purchase with a relative who is willing to make the down payment (see Chapter 10).

4) Look into state and local programs for low- and moderate-income families and for first-time buyers. You may be able to get a lower-rate mortgage, with a small down payment requirement. Check what's available through any lender or real estate agent, or through your state or local housing agency. Contact the National Council of State Housing Agencies (444 N. Capitol St., N.W., Washington, D.C., 20001; 202-624-7710) for the number for your state's agency.

5) Try to get help from family or friends. As a general rule, you'll be expected to make at least a 5% cash down payment in addition to any funds received as a gift toward the purchase price of the home.

A relative or friend may be willing to make you a second-trust loan (at a competitive market rate, not subsidized) to close the gap between down payment and the first mortgage. But "simultaneous second trusts" are not allowed by many lenders, and even if acceptable, the lender will scrutinize your finances carefully to make sure you can afford to carry both mortgages.

Some lenders will regard this loan as a gift and require you and the lender to sign a form saying the money is a gift that need not be repaid; if you and the "giver" want to convert the gift to a loan later—after the purchase—that's up to you; there may be gift tax and estate considerations, so consult an attorney.

6) Look for property where the seller is willing to take back a second mortgage.

7) Use a balloon loan. This lets you make payments comparable to those for a much longer-term loan. When the note is due, you must make a lump-sum payment of the balance of the loan, typically within two to ten years. Balloon loans can bridge the gap for first-time buyers, but be sure to negotiate a term of at least seven years to give yourself time to sell the house or refinance the loan before the lump payment comes due.

8) Inquire from lenders about private mortgage insurance (PMI). For a full discussion of PMI, see Chapter 11.

HOW BIG A LOAN?

How much you can borrow will depend on your income and the size of your down payment. Job stability, credit references, payment histories and other indications of creditworthiness also are factors.

The old rule of thumb about qualifying for a loan up to twice family income is just that. Using that outdated guideline, $50,000 of income should translate to a $100,000 mortgage. Sound too simple? It is. A family with $50,000 of annual earnings, three children, $5,000 in savings and a new car loan just won't stack up the same way with lenders as a childless couple with the same income, no debts and a $30,000 stock portfolio.

You'll get closer to reality by applying some of the same tools lenders use to evaluate the creditworthiness of prospective buyers. One common method is to apply a number of ratios to gross monthly income. For example, if you are making a 10% down payment, you may be allowed to devote up to 28% of gross, pre-tax monthly income to housing expenses (including

HOW MUCH CAN YOU PAY MONTHLY?

Family income
 annual salaries (before deductions)   _____
 bonuses, commissions   _____
 interest, dividends   _____
 other   _____
 total annual income   _____
  monthly income (divide annual total by 12) _____
Family expenses other than housing costs
 food   _____
 clothing   _____
 debt payments   _____
 alimony or child-support payments   _____
 education   _____
 home furnishings   _____
 life, health, auto insurance   _____
 recreation   _____
 transportation   _____
 medical   _____
 charities, other contributions   _____
 other   _____
 amount you would like to save   _____
 total annual expenses   _____
  monthly expenses (divide annual total by 12) _____
Housing budget
 monthly income, from Section 1   _____
 monthly expenses, from Section 2   _____
 maximum amount available for housing
 (subtract expenses from income)   _____

mortgage, property taxes, insurance, condominium fees, utilities and maintenance). However, your combined housing expenses and installment debt obligations may not exceed 33%.

If your down payment works out to 20% of the sales price, lenders will be more generous. Monthly payments and other housing expenses still can't exceed 28% of gross monthly income, but total monthly debt payments can go as high as 36%.

To help you calculate the debt burden of hypothetical mortgages at various interest rates and terms, buy yourself a paperback book of mortgage amortization tables that will show the monthly principal and interest expense. If you have a personal computer, you can purchase software that will run amortization tables, and some real estate analysis programs will do much more. (One widely available book is *Interest Amortization Tables*, by Jack Estes, published by McGraw-Hill Paperbacks.) Then add in a monthly amount for your probable real estate taxes, homeowners insurance and utilities.

Loantech (P.O. Box 3635, Gaithersburg, MD 20878) sells pocket-sized mortgage loan slide charts for estimating maximum mortgage payments. It also sells, among other things, amortization schedules, a prequalifying service, and adjustable-rate mortgage analyses.

CLEAN UP YOUR CREDIT FILE

Any lender is going to scrutinize your monthly income and outgo at the time you apply for the loan. Debts and other obligations reduce the amount of cash you can spend on housing, so try to clear the decks as much as possible before applying for a mortgage loan. Pay off as many high-interest consumer loans as possible. If you are planning to buy a new car, boat, or major furniture (paying by either cash or credit), postpone the purchases until after you've bought your home.

On the other hand, a good credit record requires that you have used credit in the past. Some people who have always been cash-only buyers find themselves hampered by their own prudence when it comes time to buy a home. If you have been diligently saving up a down payment and haven't been borrowing for two or three years, it's a good idea to create a record of credit activity during the year in which you plan to buy. Stick to small-ticket items and make minimum payments promptly.

If you have a question about whether anything in your credit record might present a problem when seeking a loan, it would be wise to check on it before making your application. At best such problems cause delays. At worst, you can be turned down for a loan. A long delay after you have filled out a loan application could cause you to lose out on the interest rate commitment from a prospective lender.

Federal law gives you the right to know what's in your credit report. Get the names of the credit reporting agencies doing residential loan reviews in your area from the Yellow Pages or by writing to the Associated Credit Bureaus (P.O. Box 218300, Houston, TX 77218). Or ask real estate brokers and major lenders for the names of credit bureaus in your area. In most cases, you will need to write a letter including your full name, names of current and past spouses, your social security number and current and previous addressses going back five years. Expect to pay anywhere from $8 to $15.

If you discover an unfavorable report has been turned in by a creditor with whom you have disagreed, now is the time to seek a settlement. Depending on the problem, your record may still contain information on the case when you apply for a loan. A lender may view it more objectively if the file shows that the matter recently has been satisfactorily resolved. If your credit application is turned down, you are entitled to know why.

If you feel you have been tagged unfairly for nonpayment or slow payment, you should write a well-documented letter setting forth your understanding of the facts and file it with the credit bureau or bureaus in your area. If you aren't sure which bureaus have a file on you, find out from the problem creditor. Or, if the problem has been completely resolved, request in writing that the creditor inform all the reporting services to which it had sent information. This could take 30 to 90 days.

When you finally make a loan application, the lender will request a complete update on your file, and you may be charged up to $100 or so for this credit check. In most cases, the credit agency will be asked by the lender to reverify your employer, salary, address, etc. If your company ordinarily does not release income and other personal data on employees, you should instruct your personnel office in writing to cooperate with the credit checker who calls.

Typically, your credit file will contain information covering the preceding three years. No adverse credit information, except bankruptcy, can be kept on file for more than seven years. Lenders look for these red flags: late payments, overextension, liens, garnishments and, the biggest flag of all, bankruptcy.

PREQUALIFYING YOURSELF

Rules and formulas used to evaluate the creditworthiness of borrowers vary depending on the type of loan being sought. But whether you are seeking a conventional loan from a savings & loan or a government-backed VA or FHA loan from a mortgage company, the less you pay down, the more closely your finances will be examined. In the case of VA and FHA loans, the lender will want to know how many people you are supporting and their ages. Government rules require lenders to estimate your living costs, rather than take your word for it.

As you work through these worksheets and examine your budget, try to assess the impact homeownership will have on you and your family's spending patterns. Will you take fewer vacations? Will you spend less on clothing? Will the cost of commuting to work rise or fall?

Most importantly, how much will your tax bill go down—and your monthly take-home pay rise—once you begin taking big deductions for mortgage interest, which constitutes most of your monthly mortgage expense early in the term of the loan? Study the next chapter carefully to get a full appreciation of the range and variety of tax breaks you'll get from the purchase and ownership of your new home.

How much down, how much borrowed? In deciding how much cash to put down, remember that getting settled in a new home always costs more than people realize. You'll want to hold back some cash for furnishing, and add an extra cushion of cash if you're buying an older home that might surprise you with a plumbing or roofing expense.

Use this list of major home components, along with their probable life spans and their average cost of replacement, to get a handle on what you'll need to worry about and when.

Roof: wood shingles, 15 to 25 years, $2,000 to $3,000; asphalt shingles, 15 to 20 years, $1,500 to $2,200; cedar shakes, 20 to 40 years, $3,000 to $5,000.

Gutters/downspouts: 20 to 30 years, $600 to $900.

Exterior paint: two to five years, $2,000 to $5,000.

Heating systems: Hot-air furnace, 15 to 20 years, $1,500 to $1,800; hot-water boiler, 20 to 25 years, $2,000 to $2,500; water heater, seven to 12 years, $350 to $500.

Central air-conditioning: Compressor, six to ten years, $800 to $1,000; compressor/condenser, ten to 20 years, $1,500 to $2,000.

Major kitchen appliances: eight to 15 years, $500 to $1,000.

Should you borrow as much as you can? When inflation runs as high as or higher than mortgage interest rates, and you are paying back what you borrowed with dollars that are steadily losing their purchasing power, the answer is easy: "The bigger the mortgage the better." Many homeowners and speculators in single-family residences made a killing in the 1970s by putting down miniscule down payments and then trading up to larger (or more) houses as inflation made their equity grow enormously.

But is that still the best strategy? Current tax law stacks the deck in favor of the largest possible mortgage. Your original mortgage sets the cap for debt on which interest is deductible. (One exception lets you add to acquisition debt amounts you borrow—via refinancing or a second mortgage—for major home improvements. See Chapter 3.) If you make a large down payment but later change your mind, you can take out a home equity loan or refinance the house. But interest on home equity loan amounts over $100,000 isn't deductible, and neither is interest paid on refinance debt once it exceeds $100,000 of your original mortgage debt, plus improvements.

Small down payments and big mortgages give you the power of leverage (page 5) as well as available cash for other investments.

For most first-time buyers, there's no point in weighing the various trade-offs. Most will have to borrow to the hilt and scrape hard to come up with the minimum down payment. However, many so-called move-up buyers will come into a substantial sum of money when they sell their old homes. Their decision will be tougher: whether to invest the cash in the new home and take out a small mortgage, or invest the money and borrow a large amount.

Nationally, investment returns on average single-family homes recently have been modest compared with returns on such financial investments as stocks and bonds. Home values on average may continue to keep pace with inflation, and in some areas may do significantly better. But don't expect a repeat of the boom of the late 1970s.

You've got to assess the future of the economy in your home area and the demand for homes of the type, location and price range of the one you'll be buying. For example, within a given metropolitan area, some neighborhoods may appreciate very well, while others stagnate. Luxury-priced homes are expected to go up relatively more in value than starter houses in most places because of the decreasing number of younger people looking for a first home compared to a growing number of 35- to 45-year-olds trading up to bigger houses.

If you have unusually good job security, you may want to gamble on a bigger mortgage than someone in a precarious field of work. Job security will affect the kind of mortage you choose, too. If your job is safe in high-inflation or recessionary times and your earnings will likely keep pace with the cost of living, you'll be more comfortable with an adjustable mortgage than someone who lost ground in the last period of high inflation and high interest rates.

Remember that home equity—unlike financial assets such as bonds, CDs and dividend-paying stocks—pays no current income whatsoever, so you shouldn't pour everything you have into your home unless you have to. For example, if the stock market is moving upwards, your cash will be tied up in a home that is not paying you any income and which may be appreciating less rapidly than good-quality stocks. If you do put all your cash into your home and then need some money later, you can borrow against it, but you'll be paying at least 1.5% to 2% over the prime lending rate for a home-equity loan, and usually more for a fixed-rate second mortgage.

PREQUALIFYING WITH A LENDER

Now that you've got your financial affairs in order and checked out your credit record, the next step is a visit with a lender—mortgage company, savings & loan, bank or credit union—where you can translate all the data into hard facts about the types of mortgages suited to your particular needs and what your upper price limit will be.

A real estate agent also can prequalify you. Some agents will do a professional job—one that will give you the same information you would get from a lender. Just keep in mind, however, that the more costly the home you buy, the more an agent stands to earn in commission from the seller.

The prequalifying interview should be free to the potential borrower. And you are not obliged to use the lender who does the prequalifying interview. When you're ready to borrow, you'll need to talk with several competitive lenders, and you may make more than one loan application (even though each one will cost you some fees). Take all of your basic financial data to the prequalifying interview—the cash flow and balance sheets you've already prepared at home.

KINDS OF LOANS

You'll want to find out how much mortgage debt you can carry under the most commonly available mortgages.

"Conventional mortgages" are transactions between borrowers and institutions operating in the private sector of the economy. They are not insured or guaranteed by the government. Traditionally they featured set monthly payments, fixed interest rates, extended loan terms and full amortization.

Because the 30-year fixed-rate mortgage is still the benchmark against which other loans can be compared, find out what size conventional 30-year loan you can qualify for under the guidelines issued by secondary-market mortgage buyers like Fannie Mae (the Federal National Mortgage Association) or Freddie Mac (the Federal Home Loan Mortgage Corporation). Because these institutions buy only loans that meet their criteria, such mortgages are often referred to as "conforming" loans.

Get information on a conforming 30-year fixed-rate mortgage, a one- and three-year adjustable-rate mortgage, and perhaps a 15-year fixed-rate loan as well. Knowing what you can afford to buy with these four mortgages is a useful starting point.

If you are planning to get a VA-guaranteed or FHA-insured mortgage, you may be able to get a bigger loan. However, keep in mind that sellers in a hot market are usually not eager to do business with buyers using this type of financing. They may expect to have plenty of would-be buyers using conventional mortgages, so it's not uncommon for sellers to put the phrase "no FHA and no VA financing" right in the sales contract.

Due to the extra paperwork and appraisal delays these loans often entail, it may take longer to reach settlement, and some sellers won't put up with that. In addition, under VA financing, the buyer is permitted to pay no more than a 1% loan origination fee ("point"), so if the lender is asking for more discount points, the seller will have to pay. For these reasons, it's a good idea to see if you can manage a home purchase without resorting to a FHA or VA mortgage.

When interest rates are changing rapidly, home shopping can be frustrating. What you can afford may vary from one week to the next. In such a market you can ask the institution prequalifying you to provide a computer list of the various size mortgages for which you qualify at the widely varying interest rates. Another option would be to figure it out yourself with a paperback book of amortization tables or real estate analysis software for your personal computer.

GET YOUR EARNEST MONEY READY

Some people are short on liquid assets, but have substantial equity in their homes. This could pose a problem when they have to write a check for earnest money to submit to a seller along with their purchase contract. Earnest money shows the seller that you're a serious, qualified purchaser. (Of course, if the contract is not accepted or the deal later hits a snag through no fault of yours, you'll get the earnest money back, with interest if you specified in your offering contract that the money be held in an interest- bearing escrow account.)

If after assessing your resources you find that you'll be short on earnest money when it comes time to begin house hunting, consider getting a home-equity loan—a line of credit secured by the equity in your current house. (See Chapters 3 and 16 for details.) But don't succumb to the temptation to use your new equity credit line for unneeded things. As you prepare for the mortgage application process, you'll want to avoid adding to your current debt.

C H A P T E R 3

HOME SWEET TAX SHELTER

◆

YOUR HOME, probably the biggest investment of your life, is likely to be the best tax shelter you'll ever enjoy, too.

Uncle Sam is standing by to serve as a generous partner in your investment, ready to subsidize your mortgage payments while you're paying for your house and willing to turn a blind eye to profit you make when you sell it—so long as you buy another home that costs at least as much as the one you sell.

Given the favored status of homeownership in America, it is no surprise that the sacrosanct deductions for mortgage interest and local property taxes have survived the onslaught of tax reform. Homeowners have not only held their own at a time many tax breaks were being sacrificed in the name of lower overall tax rates, they have actually won a valuable new tax-saving right: the opportunity to use their homes for protection against the elimination of the deduction of consumer interest. (A small chink in the armor—that affects only taxpayers with incomes over $100,000—is discussed on page 26.)

There is no doubt that buying a home will cut your tax bill. But as veteran homeowners know, it will also complicate your tax life. If you don't itemize deductions now, you're almost sure to begin once you buy a home. After all, the mortgage-interest

24

portion of the first 12 monthly payments on a $100,000, 10%, 30-year mortgage is nearly $10,000. That's almost twice the standard deduction for married couples filing jointly. You'll also get to deduct whatever you have to pay for state and local property taxes.

And once you begin itemizing, other expenses that are of no value to non-itemizers—such as state income taxes, charitable contributions and, possibly medical bills—are transformed into tax-saving write-offs.

The mortgage-interest and property-tax deductions just scratch the surface of the tax benefits attached to owning a home. While becoming a homeowner doesn't demand that you memorize chapter and verse of the tax law, you do need a general awareness of the rules to take advantage of them.

This review is designed as a refresher for veteran homeowners in the process of moving, as well as a primer for first-time buyers. For a discussion of the tax implications of selling a home, see Chapter 17.

POWERFUL TAX DEDUCTIONS

The opportunity to trade nondeductible rent payments for mostly deductible mortgage payments is a powerful lure for homeownership.

Whether you are looking for your first home or planning to move up, when you do the number crunching necessary to determine how much house you can afford, you have to study two sets of books: one for your actual monthly outlays, the other for the true, after-tax cost.

In the early years of a home mortgage, nearly all of every monthly payment is interest. That's disappointing from one standpoint: it means you are paying off only a tiny bit of the loan principal. But it's great in terms of tax savings. Look again at the $100,000, 30-year, 10% mortgage cited above. The monthly payment would be $877.57, and the table on the next page shows the breakdown in various years between principal repayment and deductible interest.

In the first year, $9,974.96 of your monthly payments—fully 95%—would be deductible as mortgage interest. Even in the 15th year, 79% of your payments would be deductible. In fact,

YEAR	ANNUAL PAYMENTS	PRINCIPAL	INTEREST
1	$10,530.84	$ 555.88	$9,974.96
2	10,530.84	614.10	9,916.74
3	10,530.84	678.39	9,852.45
4	10,530.84	749.44	9,781.40
5	10,530.84	827.91	9,702.93
10	10,530.84	1,362.16	9,168.68
15	10,530.84	2,241.18	8,289.66
20	10,530.84	3,687.44	6,843.40
25	10,530.84	4,971.33	4,463.90
30	10,530.84	9,981.07	548.84

only in the unlikely event that you live in the house for 24 years would the scales tip so that less than half of the total paid during the year would be tax-deductible.

Just what the deductions are worth to you depends, of course, on your tax bracket. If you are in the 28% bracket, every $1,000 of deductible interest and taxes translates to a $280 subsidy from Uncle Sam. In our $100,000 mortgage example, assume that in addition to the $877.57 monthly mortgage payment you also pay $150 a month for local property taxes. During the first 12 months, you pay a total of $12,330.84—just over $1,000 a month.

But $11,774.96 is deductible. In the 28% bracket that generates tax savings of $3,296.99 and pulls the after-tax cost to $9,033.85, or about $750 a month. The tax savings built into the home-buying equation is why you can afford to make higher mortgage payments than your current rent payments without squeezing your budget. As disgruntled renters often complain, there is no similar tax subsidy for tenants. In this example, the after-tax cost of home payments of $1,000 a month are the equivalent of rent at $750 a month. Of course, owning the house could present you with repair bills a renter doesn't have to worry about, but on the other hand, as an owner you reap all the appreciation on the value of your home.

A Squeeze on Deductions

Starting in 1991, a new twist in the tax law can restrict the deduction of mortgage interest. This curb applies to taxpayers whose adjusted gross income (AGI) exceeds $100,000. (AGI is basically your income before deductions and exemptions are subtracted.) If you puncture that threshold, you lose deductions equal to 3% of the amount by which your AGI exceeds $100,000. If your AGI were $150,000, for example, you would lose $1,500 in deductions (3% of the $50,000 excess.)

Although this takeaway doesn't hit all deductions, mortgage interest and property taxes are among those threatened. But don't assume this diminishes the tax-saving power of a bigger mortgage or higher property tax bill. Since the law sets a floor for itemized deductions—only those that exceed the 3%-of-excess-AGI count—it takes away the first dollars of itemized deductions, not the last. Once deductions pass the floor, every extra dollar of deductible expenses has full tax-saving power.

Even if your AGI makes you vulnerable to the squeeze, you're likely to get to deduct 100% of any increases in mortgage interest and property taxes that go along with buying a more expensive home. Say, for example, that AGI of $150,000 costs you $1,500 of your $30,000 of itemized deductions, so you deduct just $28,500. If buying a new home hikes your interest and property tax expenses by $5,000, you'd get to add the full $5,000 to bring your itemized deductions up to $33,500. Only if your AGI rises would the amount of lost deductions increase.

Adjust Your Withholding

What good is the tax subsidy if you're worrying about coming up with the cash needed each month to make the mortgage payment? Fortunately, you don't have to wait until the following year when you file a tax return to cash in on the savings. As soon as you purchase your first home or buy a new house that carries higher deductible expenses, you can direct your employer to begin withholding less from your paychecks. If you are self-employed, it's likely you will be able to scale back your quarterly estimated tax payments beginning with the next one due. In either case, your cash flow can increase almost immediately to help cover the mortgage payments.

To reduce withholding, you must file a revised W-4 form with your employer. Get a copy of the form and its instructions from your personnel office or local IRS office. The form can be complicated, but basically, for each $2,150 of added itemized deductions, you earn one extra withholding allowance. And each allowance trims withholding from each paycheck, leaving you with more take-home pay to cover your mortgage.

Record Keeping

Buying a home may be your introduction to the endearing term "tax basis." That's the home's value for tax purposes. Keeping track of it is as demanding as it is important. The basis of your home is the figure you'll compare to the amount you get when you sell the place, which determines whether you have a taxable profit that piques the interest of the IRS.

Although the basis of a home begins simply—it's what it costs you to buy the house—it will change often from the time you buy to the time you sell. As discussed in Chapter 17, the basis of each home you own affects the basis of the next one you buy. You must keep track of all adjustments to the basis—for your entire homeowning career—to ensure you are not overtaxed.

This record-keeping chore begins with sorting out the tax consequences of the closing costs you pay at settlement. (Those fees are discussed in Chapter 13.) Although a few of these expenses may be deducted in the year of the purchase, most are considered part of the cost of acquiring the house and are therefore included in the basis.

First, consider the deductible closing expenses because they have the most immediate financial impact.

Closing Costs

Points you pay to get a mortgage. A "point" is a fee—1% of the loan amount—that the mortgage lender charges up front. Assuming the charge is for the use of the borrowed money—as it clearly is when the number of points charged affects the interest rate on the mortgage—rather than a fee to cover loan-processing costs, the point is considered prepaid interest. As long as the home you're buying will be your principal residence, these points are fully deductible in the year paid.

Assume, for example, that to get a 10%, $100,000 mortgage you have to pay the lender three points, or 3% of the loan amount. You can write off that $3,000 on the tax return for the year of the purchase. The IRS even provides a special line for the deduction on Schedule A, in addition to the space for deducting the interest paid on the mortgage. The deduction effectively serves as a rebate of part of the costs. In the 28% bracket, $3,000 in points translates into $840 in tax savings.

Keeping the special tax status of points in mind can come in handy when you're negotiating the purchase of a home. A buyer often suggests, for example, that the seller pay part of the buyer's points. From the seller's point of view, the effect of paying $1,000 in points is identical to accepting a $1,000 reduction in the price of the house.

Not so for the buyer. Knocking $1,000 off the sales price is worth *more* to the buyer than sloughing off $1,000 in points. Because the buyer can write off the points, the $1,000 out of pocket has an after-tax cost of just $720. In this example, cutting the price by $720 would give the buyer the same advantage as avoiding $1,000 in points. Uncle Sam could effectively be called on to help close the deal.

To lock in your deduction the year you buy, get a written statement from the lender listing the points separately from fees for specific administrative charges. It used to be recommended that you write a separate check to pay the points, but that's no longer necessary. As long as you put enough cash into the deal—including your downpayment—to equal the points charge, the IRS won't assume you borrowed the money to pay the points. In the past, if the points charge was added to the mortgage amount, the IRS could block the deduction.

The right to deduct points fully in the year paid applies only to points paid on a mortgage to buy or improve your principal residence. Points paid on a loan to buy a vacation home or rental property don't get this special treatment. Neither does the loan-processing fee charged on VA mortgages because it is assumed by the IRS to be for services rather than for the use of the borrowed funds. And special rules apply if you refinance your mortgage, as discussed on page 37.

When points are not fully deductible in the year paid, the expense is deducted ratably over the life of the loan. On a 30-year mortgage, for example, one-thirtieth of the points generally would be deducted each year. In the first year, though, an even smaller amount would be deductible, based on the month you bought the house. If the house is sold before the mortgage is paid off, the undeducted points are fully deductible in the year of the sale.

Prepaid interest and property-tax adjustments. If your settlement costs include reimbursing the seller for interest or taxes he or she paid in advance for a period you will actually own the house, you may deduct those amounts as though you paid the bills directly. Such adjustments ought to be spelled out on your settlement sheet.

If the seller made such payments and you do not reimburse him at settlement, the prepayments are considered to be built into the price you are paying for the house. In that case, you still write off the prepaid interest and taxes as itemized deductions on your return and reduce your basis the same amount.

Additional closing costs and acquisition expenses are generally not deductible unless you qualify to write them off as job-related moving expenses, as discussed later. Instead, many such out-of-pocket costs are added to the purchase price to hike your tax basis. Since additions to basis don't produce immediate tax savings, you might be tempted to dismiss them. That would be a costly mistake. Eventually, you'll need to have to know the adjusted basis of your home, and the higher you can prove it to be, the better. The higher the basis when you sell, the smaller any potential taxable profit you have to report to the IRS.

Maintaining detailed records from the beginning is the best way to assure accuracy. It's also a lot easier than trying to reconstruct the basis later on. As you begin the running tab on your adjusted basis, add the following to the purchase price:

- ◆ Appraisal and credit-report fees.
- ◆ Attorney and notary fees.
- ◆ Recording and title-examination fees.
- ◆ State and county transfer taxes.
- ◆ Property inspection fees.
- ◆ Title insurance premiums.
- ◆ Utility connection charges.
- ◆ Amounts owed by the seller that you agree to pay, such as part of the real estate agent's selling commission or back taxes.
- ◆ The cost of an option to purchase under a rent-with-

option-to-buy arrangement. It is also possible that part of the rent payments made prior to closing may be added to the basis if they were applied to the purchase price.

THE TAX SIDE OF OWNING

It's easy to take advantage of the basic tax benefits—the write-offs for mortgage interest and property taxes. If your mortgage is held by a financial institution, you will receive a statement early each year showing how much deductible interest you shelled out in the previous year. (The IRS gets a copy, too.) The statement will also show how much you can deduct for property taxes if you make those payments through your lender. Otherwise, copies of tax bills and your canceled checks provide the information you need to claim that deduction.

Your tax situation is more complicated if your mortgage is held by an individual or you are buying with the help of some sort of "creative financing." The specifics of your arrangement control what part of your payments qualify as tax deductions.

Assume, for example, that in addition to a first mortgage at a bank, the seller holds a $10,000 second mortgage that calls for monthly interest-only payments for three years and then a balloon payoff of the entire principal. All of your payments on the note during the three years would be deductible as interest.

With a shared-appreciation mortgage (SAM), the home buyer gets a lower-than-market-rate loan in exchange for promising to share with the lender the future appreciation in the value of the house. As far as the IRS is concerned, the part of the appreciation that winds up in the lender's pocket is interest, too, and is deductible when paid. That can result in a huge interest deduction in the year a SAM-financed home is sold.

Say, for example, that a $125,000 home is purchased with a SAM that entitles the lender to 40% of the appreciation. If the home is sold three years later for $165,000, the borrower owes the lender $16,000 (40% of the $40,000 profit). In the year that sum is paid, the taxpayer can deduct the full $16,000 as mortgage interest, in addition to the interest portion of any regular monthly payments made before the sale.

What about a "zero-interest" deal involving seller financing at the best of all interest rates: 0%? Even if you find such a deal, beware that the IRS does not believe such generosity exists. The law assumes financing costs are actually built into the price of the home, so the buyer's basis is reduced by subtracting the value of interest-free financing from the purchase price.

The law also requires the seller to report as interest income each year an amount that reflects what would have been charged if the note carried a reasonable rate of interest. And the buyer can deduct as interest paid the amount the seller must as interest, even though the buyer doesn't actually make those payments. If you consider a zero-interest deal, be sure the price you pay reflects the tax consequences.

Special rules also apply to graduated-payment mortgages and other financing plans. The more you stray from conventional financing, the more you need to consult with an attorney or accountant to discuss the tax twists and turns involved in your home-buying pursuits.

Local Assessments

In addition to real estate taxes, it is not unusual for local governments to assess homeowners for services or benefits provided during the year. Such bills need to go in your home file because, depending on what the charge is for, the cost may be either a deductible expense or an addition to your basis.

In general, assessments for benefits that tend to increase the value of your property—sidewalks, for example—should be added to the basis of your property. Special charges for repairs or maintenance of local benefits, such as sewers or roads, however, can be deducted as additional local taxes. Fees for specific services, such as garbage collection, are neither deductible nor additions to basis.

Improvements and Repairs

Monthly payments are just the beginning of the costs of owning a home. You can count on spending plenty of money over the years maintaining, repairing and improving your property. Here, too, Uncle Sam gets involved.

For tax purposes, work around the house is divided between projects considered *repairs* and those constituting capital *im-*

provements that enhance rather than just maintain the value of your home. The distinction is critical. While the cost of repairs and improvements are nondeductible personal expenses, improvement expenses add to your basis.

The idea here is that although you will use and enjoy the improvements, they also are likely to boost the amount a buyer will pay for the place. Because you can add 100% of the cost of improvements to your basis, every $100 of such expenses will cut $100 of the potentially taxable profit when you sell. An improvement is anything that adds value to your home, prolongs its life or adapts it to new uses. There is no laundry list of what the IRS considers an improvement. However, the box on the next page is a checklist of items and projects that can qualify.

Repairs, on the other hand, merely maintain the home's condition. Fixing a gutter or replacing a window pane are repairs rather than improvements. In some cases, though, the cost of projects that ordinarily fall in the repair category—such as painting a room—can be added to basis if the work is done as part of an extensive remodeling or restoration of your home. Also, some major repairs—such as extensive patching of a roof—may qualify as basis-boosting improvements.

Keep detailed records of any work done around the house, including receipts for items that might qualify as improvements. The pack-rat habit can pay off handsomely for homeowners. It's better to save papers you might not need than to toss out evidence that could save you money. In addition to receipts and canceled checks, keep notes to remind yourself exactly what was done, when and by whom.

When toting up the cost of improvements, be sure to include any incidental costs. If you pay to have your lot surveyed as part of installing a fence, for example, the cost of the survey can be added to your basis. Although you can count what you paid hired workers, you are not allowed to add anything for your own time and effort if you do the work yourself.

HOME-EQUITY LOANS

The latest tax advantage bestowed on homeownership comes in the guise of the home-equity loan. The ability to borrow against the equity in your home—the difference between its value and

BASIS-BOOSTING IMPROVEMENTS

◆ Addition or conversion of unfinished attic, basement or other space to living area.

◆ Air-conditioning: a central system or window units that will be sold with the house.

◆ Attic fan, furnace, furnace humidifier, heat pump, thermostat, hot-water heater, radiators and radiator covers.

◆ Bathroom: bathtub, jacuzzi, shower, shower enclosure, faucets, toilet, sauna, medicine cabinets, mirrors, towel racks.

◆ Built-in bookcases.

◆ Doorbell, burglar- and fire-alarm system, smoke detector, intercom and telephone outlets.

◆ Electrical: new or upgraded power lines, replacement of fuse box with circuit breakers, additional outlets or switches, floodlights.

◆ Fireplace, mantel, chimney, built-in fireplace screen.

◆ Insulation, weather stripping and caulking.

◆ Kitchen: refrigerator, freezer, dishwasher or stove sold with the house; cupboards, garbage disposal, countertops, exhaust fan.

◆ Landscaping: trees, shrubs, underground sprinkler systems.

◆ Outdoors: aluminum siding, skylight, deck, garage, garage-door opener, carport, shed, fences and gates, lamppost, walls, screen and storm doors, porch, new roof, gutters, termite-proofing, waterproofing, paving and resurfacing of a driveway or sidewalks, barbecue pit, birdbath, hot tub, swimming pool.

◆ Plumbing: new pipes, sump pump, septic system, solar-heating system.

◆ Rooftop TV antenna and wiring.

◆ Washer and dryer sold with the house.

◆ Windows: screens, storm windows, shutters, awnings, weather stripping.

the amount you owe on the mortgage—can protect you from the elimination of the deductibility of personal interest (on credit cards, car loans, student loans, and so on). This interest deduction was phased out between 1987 and 1990. At the same time, home mortgage interest retains tax-favored status.

The creation of different classes of interest—some deductible and some not—has also created problems. How do you distinguish one from another and, more importantly, how can the law discourage ever-ingenious taxpayers from rearranging their financial affairs to sidestep the intent of the law? If you use a second mortgage on a house to buy a car, for example, would the interest be deductible mortgage interest or nondeductible personal interest? Congress drew up a set of rules to answer such questions, but in doing so gave homeowners a new break.

Here's what you need to know to take advantage of the law as it now stands. Debt secured by your home—and a second home—can fall into two categories:

Acquisition debt. You can deduct all the interest you pay on up to $1 million of "acquisition debt." That's money you borrow to buy, build or substantially improve your principal residence or a second home. For the interest to be deductible, the loan must be secured by the house.

Although $1 million is an enormous amount of mortgage debt, the amount of debt on which you can deduct mortgage interest is likely to be far less. Your personal ceiling is set by the size of the original loan used to buy or build your first or second home, plus amounts borrowed for major improvements. As you pay off those loans, the amount of tax-favored acquisition debt declines. This can throw you a curve if you refinance the mortgage, as discussed later. (There is an exception to the general definition of acquisition debt. If your mortgage debt on October 13, 1987, exceeded the amount borrowed to buy, build or substantially improve your home, you can count that higher amount as acquisition indebtedness.)

Home-equity debt. Here's the end-run around the loss of deductibility of interest on personal loans. In addition to deducting interest on acquisition debt, you can fully deduct interest on up to $100,000 of "home-equity debt"—whether you tap your equity via refinancing, a second mortgage or a home-equity line of credit—as long as the loan is secured by your principal residence or second home.

Although the interest is deductible almost regardless of how the borrowed money is spent, there are a couple of exceptions. If the borrowed money is used to invest in tax-exempt bonds or single premium life insurance, the interest can't be deducted, no matter what kind of loan is involved. Also, if you are subject to the alternative minimum tax discussed in Chapter 15, interest on home-equity debt is not deductible, unless the mortgage was taken out before July 1, 1982, and secured by a home used by you or a family member. Interest on acquisition debt is deductible for purposes for the AMT.

Another restriction—unlikely to come into play because it's doubtful any lender will let you use your home as security for a loan for more than your house is worth—blocks the deduction of interest if the combination of home-equity debt and acquisition debt exceeds the fair market value of the house.

Refinancing. Restrictions also come into play if you refinance your home mortgage. The amount of the new loan qualifying as acquisition debt is limited to the debt outstanding on the old loan, plus any part of the new money used for major home improvements. This tale is best told with an illustration:

Assume that you bought a $150,000 home with $30,000 down and a $120,000 mortgage. The debt is now paid down to $90,000 and you decide to refinance for $150,000. What's the tax status of the new loan? Interest on $90,000—the remaining balance on the old loan— is sure to be deductible because that amount qualifies as acquisition indebtedness. The treatment of the other $60,000 depends on how the money is used.

Any part spent for major home improvements also earns the status of acquisition debt. Plunge $20,000 of the new loan into a swimming pool, for example, and your acquisition debt jumps from $90,000 to $110,000. Any part of the new loan that neither replaces the old mortgage nor pays for improvements—$40,000 in this example—is not acquisition debt.

That doesn't automatically mean you can't deduct the interest, however. Because the debt is secured by your home, the interest may be deducted as home-equity interest, subject to the $100,000 rule. If the extra funds are used in a business, the interest can be written off as a business expense. If you use the cash for an investment, the interest on that portion of the loan may be deductible as investment interest. If none of those options protects you, however, the interest is personal interest, the deduction for which is disappearing.

Although the rules are complicated, the opportunity is extraordinary. To the extent that you can exchange nondeductible personal borrowing with deductible home-equity borrowing, you can continue to have Uncle Sam help pay the interest on your debts. The dwindling deductibility of personal interest has made home-equity loans the debt of choice for millions of homeowners. These loans offer a line of credit—which you can usually tap by writing checks—secured by your home. In addition to preserving the deductibility of interest, these loans often carry lower interest rates than unsecured borrowing.

That makes a home-equity line of credit a powerful tool. Beyond considering this source for your future borrowing needs, you may want to tap a home-equity line to pay off higher-priced debt on credit cards, auto loans and personal notes. Trading $10,000 of 12% nondeductible debt for $10,000 of 9% deductible debt would slice the after-tax carrying costs from $1,200 to $648 a year for a taxpayer in the 28% bracket.

A note of caution is necessary. Because these loans must be secured by your home, if you find yourself unable to repay, your home is at stake. Don't let the siren song of deductible interest pull you into a deal if you don't fully understand the terms. If you consider a home-equity loan, shop carefully. The cost of setting up the line of credit varies widely and can be stiff. Interest rates and repayment schedules also differ substantially. For more information about these loans, see Chapter 16.

When you buy a home, the rules on acquisition indebtedness may encourage you to limit your down payment. Remember that the size of your tax-favored debt is based on your original mortgage—not the price of the house. The law can also encourage you to borrow to pay for a home improvement rather than pay cash. As long as the debt is secured by the home, the amount that pays for the improvement counts as acquisition debt. The tax subsidy of the interest cost could make borrowing cheaper than the amount you'd lose by pulling cash out of an investment to pay for the improvement.

It's important to keep reliable records of your borrowing to back up the deductions you claim. If you use a home-equity line, distinguish between borrowing that pays for major home improvements and loans used for other purposes. The amount that goes for improvements counts as acquisition debt, rather than eating away at your $100,000 home-equity allowance.

REFINANCING

If you decide to refinance your mortgage—either to reduce monthly payments via a lower interest rate or to tap the equity in a home with a larger first mortgage rather than adding a second trust or home-equity line—beware that points paid to get the new mortgage are not fully deductible in the year you pay them. Although that's the rule when you buy the house, refinancing points must be deducted over the life of the new mortgage, except to the extent that the funds are used for home improvements.

Here's an example: A homeowner with a $100,000 mortgage refinances at $120,000 and uses $20,000 to build a swimming pool. Assume that two points (2% of $120,000, or $2,400) were charged. Because one-sixth of the money went for a home improvement, one-sixth of the points, or $400, may be deducted in the year paid. The rest must be deducted evenly over the life of the loan. On a 30-year mortgage, that would mean one-thirtieth of the remaining $2,000, or $66.66, would be deducted each year, assuming the homeowner remembers to do so. If the house is sold and the mortgage paid off before the end of the term, any remaining portion of the points could be deducted as interest at that time. (If the refinancing is part of the original purchase of your home—say you refinance to pay off a bridge loan or a short-term balloon note—the points can be fully deducted in the year paid.)

Refinancing could deliver an extra deduction if the lender holding the original loan slaps you with a penalty for paying it off early. Such a penalty is considered interest and is fully deductible in the year you pay it.

But what if the lender is willing to cut the amount due to encourage you to pay off the mortgage early? That's not as unlikely as it may appear. In times of soaring interest rates, lenders sometimes offer sweet deals to get out of long-term loans at low, fixed interest rates. But if you're on the receiving end of such an offer, beware. The amount of such a discount is taxable income. Here's an example: You still owe $60,000 on a 7% mortgage and market rates have risen far above that level. To get that low-rate loan off its books, the lender offers to let you pay off the debt for $50,000. If you agree to the deal, the IRS will want a share of your windfall. The $10,000 discount is considered taxable income—costing you $2,800 in the 28% bracket. If you are offered such a deal, be sure to consider the tax consequences.

CHAPTER 4

DEFINING YOUR HOUSING NEEDS

◆

N OW THAT YOU know *how much* home you can afford, it's time to do some hard thinking about *what kind* of home you want and need. This chapter and the next two—dealing with location and kinds of housing—will help you narrow the choices.

Buying a piece of real estate is a science. Buying a home is an art. The science is getting the legal and financial parts right. The art is finding a property that you can be happy living in.

You can hire all the help you need with the technical side. The nontechnical part is another matter. Only you know what you like. If you don't decide what you like before wading into the market, someone out there will try to make up your mind for you.

Your best preparation for home buying is to be clear about your needs, your financial ability, your preferences and your prejudices. The central questions: What kind of home do you want, and where do you want it? If you are sure about those things, you will be immune to pressure tactics and hype.

At any given time in a metropolitan area of a million inhabitants, thousands of residential properties are for sale. With a little thought you could divide them into a dozen or more categories: homes falling within various price ranges, those within certain types of neighborhoods, new or resale homes, townhouses, homes within a particular school distict and so forth. Unfortunately you still would be left with several hundred potential homes in each category. Start with the general—your price range and approximate location—and then move to the specific: neighborhood, age and type of home, and kind of ownership (condominium or co-op).

Shopping only within your chosen location can scale down the range of properties to be inspected. Finally, examining only selected properties within your price range should bring the operation within manageable proportions.

Knowing your financial limits is a good beginning. However, you probably will find 10 or 15 entirely different sorts of homes within your price range. Decide now whether you want to be on the east or west side of town, whether you will accept a cookie-cutter housing development or will go to any length to avoid that, whether you can handle a "fixer-upper." Otherwise, you're in for an emotional tug of war when you find the living room you want in a house on the west side and the school district you want on the east side.

It can't be overstated: Focus on the location and general quality of the property. Don't go chasing an exact price or a particular feature, be it a deck, a high-efficiency furnace, or a finished basement. Price can be worked out in negotiation with the seller (given the right general ballpark), and a good-quality home in a good location can be tailored to your specific needs later.

There are two phases to a home-seeking strategy. In the first you are getting the feel for different areas and an idea about what is being offered at what price. From that you draw up a list of specifications. The second phase is the search to fill those specifications.

MAKE A LIST OF NEEDS AND WANTS

Most buyers are in search of something they cannot describe. They may be trying, often unknowingly, to replicate a childhood home, if it was a happy one. If it wasn't happy, whatever stands out about that home goes on the buyer's negative list. This doesn't mean that they are looking for the same red-brick

	MUSTS	WANTS (rank)		
		high	medium	low
Commuting time:				
less than one hour	____	____	____	____
less than half-hour	____	____	____	____
Setting				
suburban	____	____	____	____
urban	____	____	____	____
country	____	____	____	____
Particular neighborhood	____	____	____	____
Particular school district	____	____	____	____
Public transportation	____	____	____	____
Zoning laws (parking, pets, in-law suites, etc.)	____	____	____	____
Particular architectural style	____	____	____	____
1 story, 2 stories, split level	____	____	____	____
Yard	____	____	____	____
Number of bedrooms	____	____	____	____
Number of baths	____	____	____	____
Bath in master bedroom	____	____	____	____
Eat-in-kitchen	____	____	____	____
Separate dining room	____	____	____	____
Basement	____	____	____	____
Expandability	____	____	____	____
Fix-up house	____	____	____	____
Energy efficiency	____	____	____	____
Fireplace	____	____	____	____
Garage	____	____	____	____
Other:	____	____	____	____

house with privet hedge, but rather they seek a feeling, an ambience. It could be a feeling of spaciousness, warmth, airiness, the amount of daylight, the quality of the light, coziness, the abundance of nooks and crannies, a parklike backyard.

If you're looking for a home with the help of an experienced agent, he or she should be able to help you define your needs and wants. However if you are too vague, a really good agent may decide not to waste time on you and you could end up with someone who is more a hindrance than help. He or she may have endless patience, but no direction.

Start your want list by recalling houses you have liked and write down a description of each. Since you have already determined your price range, that combined with the want list below, will give you a sieve through which to sift the dozens of ads you will read in conducting your search. Keep in mind, though, that the final choice of a home almost always requires compromising.

MAKE A "DON'T WANT" LIST, TOO

Say you have a well-defined want list, you screen ads carefully, you carefully instruct every agent you work with, and you refuse to look at any property that doesn't have the requisite family room, master bath or whatever your firm requirements are. After weeks of looking, the seemingly perfect home shows up. It has every one of the items on your list.

First there is euphoria over finding all the desired features in one package. Then, to the bewilderment of the agent or the seller of this perfect home, you go silent. You may announce, "I need more time to think it over." That thinking-it-over time might take hours, days, possibly even a week. At last your final answer is no.

Why does the perfect home fail to win the only test that counts: whether, when it comes right down to crunch time, you are willing to plunk down a deposit? The reason may be that you failed to identify your "don't wants."

Finding a home with all the desired features is only half the challenge. The property must also be free from objectionable features.

Objections, which constitute your don't want list, are of two major types: personal prejudice and economic fear. And there's plenty of overlap between the two.

To avoid getting into a situation where you have to veto a house that has everything you say you want, do some systematic soul searching.

Go back through your past again, and this time think of all the homes you have not liked, whether you lived in them or merely visited them. Include the ones occupied by friends, acquaintances, family—all the houses and apartments that for one reason or another made a negative impression on you.

If they gave you a "I wouldn't want to live here" feeling, now is the time to identify the causes. Make a written list of the things you didn't like.

Identify your personal objections, whatever they are: windowless inside kitchens, small bathrooms, northern exposures, frame construction, casement windows, dormers, fake brick siding, floor plan, scary neighborhood, too little daylight, house incongruous with its surroundings, too far out, too close to the road, too much of a child-rearing neighborhood, proximity to a commercial zone, deadend street, heavy traffic, street with no trees, street with overgrown trees, whatever.

Also consider things that other buyers might object to. Heavy traffic on the street might not bother you, but it's legitimate to be concerned that it might make resale tougher.

Other buyers might also balk at buying your house if it's overimproved. A home may have great entertaining space, a swimming pool and extensive landscaping—all features that are normally attractive to upscale buyers. But if the house is the only upgraded home in an area of ordinary homes, it will not be attractive to the typical high-income buyer. That makes it an interesting white elephant, and it could be a terrific bargain if you can negotiate the price down to reflect the home's wrong location. Such bargains can be deceptive though: sweet on the buying end and sour on the selling end.

After you have your list of things you don't want in a home, assign them weights. Decide which objections are negotiable and which aren't. You might, for example, give in for a house with a western garden when you really wanted a southern one, but you would not give in on a heavily trafficked street.

If you are buying a home with a spouse or a partner, compare your don't-want lists. Frequently, the person with the strongest objections is the silent partner of the team. The more vocal one may take the lead in putting together the "want" list, but when it comes down to crunch time, it is often the silent one who produces a veto, often for an objection not voiced previously or not even thought about until then.

Besides harming the home-hunting process, these out-of-the-blue vetoes can put terrific strains on a relationship. Agents, mortgage loan officers and escrow agents never cease to be amazed at how a couple may know all about each other's tastes in food, vacations, cars, clothes and entertainment and not be aware of strongly held prejudices and opinions about what makes a permanent place to live a home. Since rental apartment living is so often a matter of expediency or convenience, it doesn't offer an adequate test.

Objections are much more elusive than demands because they don't get thought about or talked about as much. But if you know yours, as well as their relative importance, you will be ahead in the home-hunting game.

CHAPTER 5

Choosing a Neighborhood

◆

YOU'VE PROBABLY heard the old cliché that the three major determinants of housing value are 1) location, 2) location, and 3) location. Like many cliches, it's basically true.

When an agent rushes into the office with news of a hot new listing, the first question colleagues ask is not "How much?" or "How big?" but "Where is it?"

No single factor affects the value of a home as much as location. If you can't afford what you want *where* you want it, sacrifice something inside the house rather than sacrifice the location. You can add a second bathroom or install hardwood floors to bring a house up to your standards, but you can't improve the neighborhood singlehandedly. Better to take a house that needs work in a good neighborhood than to take one at the same price (or even a bit lower) that's all dolled up but in a marginal location.

Price doesn't guarantee a fine location either. Just because a builder puts a $175,000 house on a particular site doesn't mean the market will justify that price. Some builders, in an effort to fatten their profit, can't resist gambling on a cheap piece of land, often to their later regret.

Obviously, everyone can't live behind the country club overlooking the seventh fairway—nor would many buyers want to. A good location, like many other features of a home, is relative. Confirmed city dwellers won't be put off by a restaurant or corner deli on the block. But suburbanites might find the same low-key establishments intrusive.

WHAT IS "LOCATION" ANYHOW?

Depending on the market, "location" can be a city, a town or a county. Location also is a neighborhood. It may be a home on a particular plot of land. Consider all three in choosing your home. Pick a town or community with a character and style that match your own. Then, scout out the town's best neighborhood—within your price range. Finally, zero in on the best home on the best lot within that neighborhood.

Much of the value of a home rests in its surrounding economic and social environment—its neighborhood. In general, the more defined a neighborhood, the more likely that homes located there will maintain their value. You are looking for more than just a cluster of homogeneous properties. A few blocks of carefully tended homes otherwise surrounded by blight isn't a viable neighborhood. Typically, it takes at least a dozen blocks, marked off by recognizable boundaries, for a neighborhood to sustain its character. The boundary might be a park, a highway, a campus, a river, a county line, a string of stores—anything that interrupts the pattern. One highly visible boundary gives residents a sense of belonging within it. Several make the neighborhood identification even stronger.

In the 1970s and 1980s, city planners, developers and financiers redesigned single-family lot subdivisions and replaced them with larger-scale planned unit developments, or PUDs. PUDs trade off mixed-use, higher-density plans for community designs that incorporate bands of open space separating neighborhoods and retail and commercial users. Schools, religious centers and shopping centers are located within each community. The "new towns" of Columbia, MD, and Reston, VA, are large-scale models of the PUD concept.

Small towns and villages are the inspiration for one of the newest types of planned development—the village design. The idea is to integrate residential, retail, office and civic use of the land in a way that enhances a sense of community. Each development has a mixed-use town or village core that includes a major civic space and large open public areas. There is a mix of residential designs—often on the same street—and roads and parks are laid out to encourage walking. Montgomery Village, N.J., Seaside Village in Tallahassee, Fla., Mashpee Coomons in Cape Cod, MA, and Blount Springs in Birmingham, AL, are examples of these communities.

In addition to being located in the right neighborhood, a home must not clash with its surroundings. A poor fit imposes a harsh penalty on any home's value. Pick any $1,000,000 home in the poshest neighborhood of your city. Mentally move it to the worst slum you can imagine and guess what it would be worth.

Next pick a setting in between—say a nice middle-class community. If you have an appraiser's eye for value, you will recognize that bringing that $1,000,000 mansion from the slums where it is unsalable to a midway location won't restore even half its value. What's true for a transplanted mansion is just as true for a $250,000 house in a $70,000 neighborhood. Be especially wary of the overimproved house in a neighborhood of lesser houses; even if you love it, it may be hard to find others who feel just as you do when the time comes to sell.

Some homes command premium prices because of the special cachet of their neighborhoods. Even the plainest, smallest homes on Beacon Hill in Boston, Nob Hill in San Francisco, Beverly Hills in Los Angeles, and Georgetown in Washington, D.C., command high prices on a per-square-foot basis. Professional appraisers call such premiums "caprice value."

In any city, some neighborhoods enjoy inflated values because the "right" people live there. By comparison, other neighborhoods with strong schools or other highly desirable features may be undervalued because they aren't "in." A buyer who is indifferent to fashion can find good values in neighborhoods that offer desirable amenities and services—and end up with a lot more house for the money.

Deliberately choosing to pay caprice value can be a perfectly sound investment, if social prestige is very important to you. If you want to buy a home with a socially desirable address, make sure the high price is in line with the market. Get a professional appraisal. Properties in prestige areas sometimes attract speculators who hope to make exhorbitant profits off unwary buyers, especially wealthy newcomers from out of town. And not all residents of such neighborhoods are above doing a little "fishing" for gullible buyers.

CHECK IT OUT

If you're looking for a new home in an area where you already live, you'll have a good sense of the strengths and weaknesses of various parts of town, and you can do your neighborhood scouting on your own, without an agent.

But if you're coming from out of town, you'll need help, especially if you're relocating on short notice. Try to find acquaintances or friends of friends in the area you're moving to, and get their opinions of neighborhoods. If you're being relocated to a branch office of your current employer, talk to your new colleagues and secure the services (at your employer's cost) of a relocation firm that works with real estate agents in your new area. Long-distance house-hunting is very difficult, and it can be smoothed by the services of professionals. Try to schedule several lengthy house-hunting trips, allowing enough time to drive around the whole area and get a feel for neighborhoods.

Don't overlook the obvious. Make sure you choose a place you'll enjoy living in six months after moving in. If you like it, others will in the future when you're ready to sell.

The look and feel of a community as you walk and drive around its neighborhoods can't be quantified, but it's important. Trees, shrubs, cul-de-sacs, curved streets and landscaping around small retail stores are good signs. But unless you already live there, you need to probe deeper.

Read up on the local politics and history. It will offer clues to the future. The chamber of commerce, the town hall and the local library are other good sources for background. They also may have information on population and income trends. County and city governments also can provide critical tax information and zoning regulations.

Start your research by getting a detailed map. It should

indicate schools, fire departments, parks, lakes and shopping areas. Ask the local real estate board or title company for prices of homes in the desired neighborhoods and jot them down to give you a base for comparison shopping. Use the map to familiarize yourself with the area, and to get a general feel for the proximity of individual homes to schools, stores and the like, once you begin househunting.

If time permits, attend a community meeting. A political fundraiser, a PTA meeting, a zoning hearing or church or synagogue service will enable you to meet some of the residents.

Visit the schools! Schools affect the taxes you pay on your property. And good schools increase property values for parents and non-parents alike. Even if you aren't a parent, don't neglect to inquire about the quality of neighborhood schools. What schools are nearby? How many elementary schools are operating? What is the average class size in grades 1 through 6? How do most children get to school? How do students in the town or county rate on standardized tests? What enrichment courses are offered? Where do graduating high school seniors go to college? Parents may want to meet the neighborhood school principal.

Shop the stores. Is parking adequate during hours of peak demand? Can you buy aspirin and sodas nearby, or will you have to hop in the car to meet unexpected family requests? Note the kind of stores and the quality of the merchandise. Merchants have to be responsive to subtle changes in the socioeconomic level of their patrons. They buy what they perceive their customers want. For example, the mix of staples to "luxury" items in a supermarket might tell you something about whether it's a neighborhood you'd feel comfortable in.

Do at least one rush-hour practice commute. Make it on a weekday at the time you normally would be en route. Use the public transportation system. How often do buses and subways run during morning and evening rush-hours? What is the weekend and off-peak schedule? If you are depending on buses or trains to get to work, or for other commuting, try to determine whether there are proposals to reroute or drop the line you would be using.

Consider your travel patterns. Figure what roads you might travel to deliver children to day-care centers or school. Will it be convenient to stop after work to pick up groceries, or will buying bread and milk entail a lengthy side trip? Does the surrounding community offer recreation and entertainment that suits your interests, or will you find yourself facing frequent lengthy drives for a movie, concert, or athletic contest?

WEIGH THE NEGATIVES

A town or neighborhood can decline, or take off toward renewal before home sales figures reflect it. Before you take a fancy to a home, rule out locations where negative factors outweigh positives.

Crime. Pass up casual conversations here and go to the police precinct station for records of robberies, break-ins, vandalism, assaults and drug-related problems. Is crime increasing, decreasing or staying about the same? Parents with young children will want to know how safe their children will be going to and from school and playing in the neighborhood.

Traffic. Heavy traffic is a major drawback in any residential area. It generates noise and pollution. Of course, being on a busy street is less a problem for highrise condominium dwellers than for families in detached one- and two-story homes. Even so, a unit on the quiet side of the building certainly is more desirable than one where you can hear the steady roar of automobiles.

Visual pollution. Look for public utility substations and transformers, radio or television broadcasting towers, gas stations, auto dealerships, salvage yards, overnight parking for commercial auto fleets, bus stops, ball fields where night games are played.

Smells and sounds. Does the commuting pattern create air pollution or smog in the area? What about food-processing or chemical plants? Even something as delightful in small doses as the smell of bread wafting from a bakery is a nuisance when you never can escape it.

Visit the area during the day and at night, and on weekdays as well as weekends. Does it lie in the flight pattern for airplanes? Is it too close to a bus stop, fire station or school?

Overcrowding. Are roads, parks, stores, and pools too crowded? Are there too many cars parked on streets and in driveways? Is there any sign that homes are being used as rooming houses or broken into multiple housekeeping units?

Full-blown blight is easy to spot. What you need to be alert to are the earliest signs of neglect or decay. A neighborhood that appears slightly down-at-the-heels may not reveal any other signs of decline . . . yet. Perhaps nothing is broken, littered or really shabby. You still should try to find out why the level of maintenance has slipped. Is the ratio of owners to renters shifting? Are such municipal services as sidewalk and road repairs being postponed or reduced?

EXAMINE THE LOT

Give some thought to whether you will enjoy living on a lot before you fall in love with the house on it. Do you spend a lot of time outdoors? How much privacy do you want? Will you maintain the grounds yourself, or will you hire someone for such routine chores as mowing the lawn and trimming hedges? Do you want to be involved with landscaping, or would you prefer an established yard with mature trees and shrubs?

Once you find a home you like, give the land it sits on more than a perfunctory once-over. Step back and notice the overall pattern of blocks and streets in a neighborhood. Most subdivisions are laid out in lots and blocks. A section of land is blocked off and divided into lots. Use a map to determine the physical layout of a community that has piqued your interest. Common street patterns are: gridiron, curvilinear, loop, and Radburn Plan. (See illustrations on next page.) In addition, many developments use what is called a cluster plan.

Gridiron. Lots generally are rectangular, and homes face the street. In neighborhoods where lots are large, traffic is limited and back alleys are safe, the pattern works best. But such a layout can be monotonous, and the design doesn't provide for open spaces and recreational areas.

Curvilinear. When done well, this system is an improvement over the gridiron. Traffic patterns are improved by meshing major roads with secondary streets and cul-de-sacs. Small parks often are placed at intersections.

COMMON STREET PATTERNS

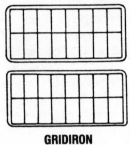

GRIDIRON

CURVILINEAR

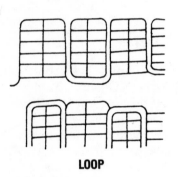

LOOP

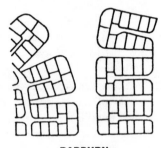

RADBURN

CLUSTER PLAN

Loop streets. This pattern reduces the traffic on residential streets while still providing good access to the main highway. Compared to the gridiron system, fewer lots face busy roads, and there is more open space.

Radburn Plan. Named after Radburn, N.J., where the plan originated, it clusters units into large cul-de-sac blocks. There is open space between each cluster, and pedestrians are well separated from auto traffic.

Cluster. This plan groups homes around cul-de-sacs. Street patterns are more varied, and there can be a dramatic increase in the amount of land available for recreation and other community uses.

Each system has its pluses and minuses. An older neighborhood may not have an ideal layout or the best traffic flow, but those drawbacks may be more than offset by its proximity to downtown offices, theaters and restaurants. Similarly, a new development offers a quiet cul-de-sac for bike riding and roller skating but requires a long commute to work. Which of these features are more important to you?

Finally, don't overlook the physical dimensions and composition of the lot itself. Shape, size, slope, and soil composition should be noted.

Shape. Look for a basically rectangular or square lot with adequate road frontage and enough land behind the house. Lots with unusual shapes can make it harder to sell your home.

Size. A lot that falls pretty much within the average for the neighborhood probably is the best bet. Bigger isn't necessarily better. Many couples don't have time for large-scale groundskeeping, and help is expensive and hard to find. Acreage that can't be subdivided can keep a property on the market.

Slope. The contour of a lot determines not only what already was built on it but what could be added after you move in. A home built on a steep hillside may preclude the addition of two extra bedrooms that might be needed later by a growing family.

Drainage. Slope and the ability of the soil to absorb water combine to determine where and how fast water drains from it. Low areas that hold water can mean trouble inside and outside the house. Muddy spots are a nuisance, particularly just outside the back door. They may be only a symptom, however, for the real problem inside. A wet basement goes beyond the nuisance level. Drying it out permanently will likely be expensive. It may even be impossible.

Get a feel for a house's drainage problems by checking whether the building is on a rise or in a low spot, and simply asking yourself where rain is going to go after it falls on the roof. You want an obvious slope away from your foundation on all sides. If you are worried about what you see, go back for a look during and just after a hard rain. Also check local flood information—often available through mortgage lenders. You must get federal flood insurance through a commercial insurance agent if you live in a flood-prone area.

Soil composition. Look for a good layer of topsoil that will support a healthy lawn and border plantings. Is there an established vegetable or flower garden? An inexpensive soil analysis can provide you with answers about soil quality. Some lots are scraped bare in construction and extensive preparation may be needed for a top-notch garden. Soil composition also affects settling of a house. Unstable soil conditions can make settling a never-ending process, leading to cracked walls and other eyesores or even damaging foundations and other structural components in the home. Contaminated soil can raise health anxieties or even cause illness.

CHAPTER 6

MANY KINDS OF HOMES

◆

THE POPULATION size, land, climate, history, and even ethnic heritage of a region determine the kinds of homes in its local housing inventory. By targeting a particular locale and price range, you've already made some decisions about the kind of housing you'll select.

If you've chosen a particular school district in a small county, for example, your choice may not include condominium townhouses or cooperative apartments. You may have to find the single-family detached dwelling that best suits your needs.

If you've been thinking about a mobile or manufactured home, local zoning law will dictate where you live, limiting your choices. A large metropolitan area should offer a good mix of all kinds of homes. But in many expensive locales, the middle-budget homebuyer has to choose between a small condominium close in or a slightly larger detached home at a lengthy commute.

Here's a run-down on the major kinds of housing, with their pros and cons:

SINGLE-FAMILY DETACHED HOUSES

The single-family detached house is the essence of homeownership, with all its joys and headaches. You have four walls to call your own, and often a yard or garden, too. These offer privacy, but they also present a burden of upkeep (painting, planting, mowing, snow removal, etc.) that would be less or non-existent in a condominium townhouse or apartment.

◆ The big choice in detached housing is the older home or something new.

THE NEW HOUSE

Advantages:

Predictable cost and low maintenance. Assuming competent design and craftsmanship in the new house (which is not always a good assumption today), the major mechanical systems—plumbing, wiring, heating and air-conditioning systems—as well as structural members should hold up for a long time after purchase. You can expect a minimum of repair and fix-up headaches, so the monthly mortgage payment and utilities should be the entire cost of maintaining the property into the near future.

Modernity. New homes may have the latest in floor plan designs, kitchen and bathroom layouts, as well as adequate storage and closet space.

Cheaper to furnish. Decorating costs can be reduced because many new homes come with wall-to-wall carpeting and window treatments, as well as more installed appliances and fixtures.

Energy efficiency. A new house should be well insulated and should come outfitted with storm windows. It should be less expensive to heat and cool than a comparably sized older home.

Recreational features. Community swimming pools, craft workshops and fully equipped gymnasiums often are found in large, new developments. Some even have tennis courts and bridle paths for residents' use.

Disadvantages:

Location. Communities tend to grow from the center out, so new developments usually are located on the fringes of suburbia. That means a long commute to downtown, both for work and for personal outings at museums, restaurants and theaters.

Uneven quality. Shoddy construction always is a concern when buying a new home, because many structural flaws take time to show themselves. They may be the result of a marginal builder looking for ways to cut costs, but they can surface in houses built by large well-known firms, too.

The raw look. In all but the most carefully planned and expensive projects, developers tend to skimp on trees, foundation plantings and lawns. New developments can look downright barren. And, if you're one of the first ones to move in, substantial sections may still have to be built, graded and paved, so buyers should expect to encounter noise, dust, mud and a good deal of general nuisance.

Look-alikes. Brick chimney, stone chimney; white shutters, brown shutters; garage on the left, garage on the right—those may be your only choices among the houses in a new development. While some people might like the consistency such look-alikes give to the character of a development, others detest it, preferring instead to own a house with at least a few unique characteristics.

THE OLDER HOUSE

Advantages:

Location. An older home often is situated near work, schools, downtown shopping and public transportation.

Size. Many older houses have large rooms with high ceilings, or lots of rooms that can be remodeled to suit your needs. You often get a lot more square feet (and often cubic feet) for your money in an older home.

Individuality. If you want a house with character, and perhaps even a history of its own, consider an old home. Middle-aged houses often reflect the love and care that have been lavished on them through such owner-added touches as crown moldings, carved fireplace mantels and built-in bookcases.

Better construction. This is often, but not necessarily, true of older homes. It's something you have to check out case by case. If you respect the quality of slate roofs, copper gutters and chimney flashing, hardwood floors, and plaster walls, you're more likely to find them in an older house than in a new house in the same price range.

Lower property taxes. Property taxes on an older home may be less than on a comparable new home. Then again, they could be more, but be less likely to rise as rapidly as they might in a new community or development where streets, sewers, schools and public utilities have yet to be built.

Ambience. Mature trees and lawns and a variety of architectural styles, as well as a range of color and texture of materials, present a more varied environment.

Disadvantages:

Functional inferiority. Unless an older house has been modernized, its floor plan and traffic flow may not suit modern living as well as that of a new home.

Unpredictable expenses. If the older house needs renovating, you can get estimates of the cost before you make a purchase offer, but don't be surprised if the eventual work ends up costing significantly more. In addition, it is difficult to predict exactly when such items as a roof, furnace or hot water heater will need replacing.

Remodeling costs. If you plan to update the kitchen or modernize a bathroom, you will have to finance the job with a home improvement loan, a home equity loan or a second mortgage. All of these typically carry a higher interest rate than on a first mortgage.

Sometimes, however, if you submit detailed plans and contractor bids for improvements that you intend to do immediately after settlement, your first-mortgage lender will give you enough to cover both purchase and renovations with one loan. A more common financing deal involves temporary construction financing until the renovation is finished, when a permanent mortgage will be placed after a fresh appraisal.

For both of these arrangements, the lender will require blueprints and cost estimates in advance, so buyers of houses needing renovation should get moving on design plans as soon as the purchase contract is accepted.

CONDOMINIUM OWNERSHIP

The term *condominium* refers to a legal form of ownership, not a particular type of property. Under such a plan, the owners of individual dwelling units in a housing development also own undivided proportional interests in such common facilities as the grounds, hallways, elevators and recreation areas.

Just about any kind of development you can think of comes in condominium form: converted older apartment houses, townhouse complexes, elegant old mansions divided into luxury apartments, commercial lofts and office buildings in busy downtown areas, apartments fitted into former schools and farm silos, and virtually self-contained villages of free-standing houses, complete with tennis courts, golf courses, pools and community houses.

Condominiums give owners virtually the same financial advantages as single-family houses. The federal income tax breaks are identical: Mortgage interest and property taxes on your home are deductible. You may be able to defer part or all of any profit made on the sale by buying another home. And when you are 55 or older, you may be able to exercise a once-in-a-lifetime right to exclude from income as much as $125,000 of gain on the sale or exchange of the condo unit.

When the housing market goes into a tailspin, condo prices are usually the first to suffer and the last to recover. That certainly was the case in the late 1970s and early 1980s. Overbuilding in places like Denver and Dallas-Fort Worth gave condos a bad reputation. Around the Orlando and Tampa Bay area of Florida, many run-of-the-mill condos linger on the market, and units offered at $50,000 ten years ago go for $40,000 today.

But that's only part of the picture. Since 1986, condos in general have been appreciating faster than single-family detached homes. Well-designed luxury and semi-luxury condos in Miami and Ft. Lauderdale, Atlanta and San Diego are being snapped up. Higher-density living is becoming more acceptable—and in some cases, the first choice—as leisure time shrinks and commuting distances from affordable, single-family developments become longer and more onerous. And often it is the price spread between condos and detached homes—

typically 10% to 20%—that makes home ownership possible for many first-time buyers.

Condos typically offer a trade-off: less cost for less space. Instead of having your own backyard, you may share one with 200 or so other residents. In place of your own full basement or attic for storage, you get a storage bin in the basement. You may have to share coin-operated washers and dryers. And you can't keep a bike and workbench in your parking space.

On the other hand, less space is precisely what many buyers are looking for. They want the enjoyment of an indoor swimming pool an elevator ride away, or having ready access to a tennis partner on Saturday mornings. They don't want to rake leaves and mow the lawn.

While cost may be your first priority, a condo's facilities and the lifestyle it requires—especially interaction with other owners—should not be ranked too far behind. You may buy for one reason and end up disliking what you've bought for another reason. Your neighbors may be noisy, or otherwise objectionable. You will be subject to rules adopted by other owners. Certain activities and hobbies may be restricted or banned. Pets may be forbidden. Whether it's a garden apartment, townhouse or high rise, a condominium locks you into community living.

Questions to Ask

Before you shop, learn as much about condominium ownership as possible. Line up a good lawyer who understands condos. And start making a list of questions to ask.

What's the area like? You want your unit to be a good investment, as well as a good place to live.

Generally, look for residential areas with good quality apartment buildings and homes in the middle- to upper-price range. Assess convenience to public transportation, stores, schools, hospitals and parks.

Find out if units have been appreciating. Compare recent selling prices with original purchase prices. How much of that appreciation occurred in the months or year after the development sold out? How much is occurring now? Information on sales is available from county land transfer records.

Try to visualize the neighborhood in five, ten or 15 years.

What are the zoning rules covering nearby unbuilt areas? Could the view be obstructed by a future high rise? Could a highway be constructed nearby?

Is it financially sound? What debts does the condo association owe, and to whom? Are there adequate funds held in reserve to handle routine maintenance, as well as replacement of expensive items, such as boilers and roofs? Has the association tended to rely on special assessments for emergency needs?

Will you fit in? Do you desire compatability with other tenants, in terms of lifestyle, occupations, age, or any other characteristic? How are problems resolved? Will you be expected to vote on every little detail—like what color to paint the halls—or will routine decisions be made by the elected board?

What's the vacancy rate in the region? An oversupply of condo units in an area can depress prices generally. Too many vacant units in a particular building not only can depress prices, it can, among other things, reduce the funds available to the condo association for maintenance and repairs and increase the pressure on the developer or current owners to rent rather than sell.

How many units are rented? Some units usually are rented out by investors; others by owners who have moved away temporarily. In resort areas, most of the units in a project may be on rental during the vacation season, but that's a special case. A high proportion of renters is undesirable, so much so that the FHA won't insure condo loans in projects with less than an 80% owner-occupancy rate. Renters, it's charged, are less concerned than owner-occupants with preserving the building and grounds, and investors are less likely than homeowners to upgrade and renovate their units.

Is there a heavy sales turnover? You expect turnover in a resort project. But heavy turnover in a year-round residential community can create an uncomfortable feeling of impermanence; increase the wear-and-tear on elevators, hallways and other common elements; weaken security controls; and discourage compliance with rules.

Who owns the common facilities? Developers sometimes hang on to such facilities—laundry room, the parking areas, the pool and other recreational facilities—for the income from rental fees. Avoid a project in which important amenities are not owned by the condominium owners. Otherwise, you become a captive user, exposed to uncontrollable fee increases and inconveniences.

Are the facilities adequate? Inspect the pool, tennis courts, parking area and other facilities at times of peak usage. A pool that's big enough for a 200-unit building occupied mainly by working couples and singles could prove an overcrowded mess with the same number of apartments filled largely by families with small children. Free parking may be limited or unavailable. You may have to pay to use a party room or gym.

What are the restrictions? There are sure to be some, so read the declaration or master deed, the bylaws and house rules before you sign a contract. Ironically, you may find it best not to buy if the condo does not impose enough controls.

Are you adequately insured? Does the condominium board have enough liability insurance? There have been suits brought by both condo owners and visitors against condo associations, especially involving violent crime on the premises. Find out if you as an owner would be personally liable in such a suit, and if so, does the association carry insurance that would cover you? Are reserve funds invested by the board or is their management delegated to an outsider? How would you be protected in case of theft or mishandling of funds? Are the funds in an insured account? If not, what would happen if investment losses occurred? Ask to see evidence of liability insurance, property insurance and fidelity bond.

Where to Find the Answers

Answers to many of these questions can be found in the following documents, which you should examine before you buy:

◆ *Master deed*. Also called an enabling declaration, a plan of condominium ownership or declaration of conditions, covenants and restrictions, the master deed is the most important document. When recorded, it legally establishes the project as a condominium. It also, among other things, authorizes residents to form an operating association and describes individual units and commonly owned areas.

◆ *Bylaws*. These spell out the association's authority and

responsibilites, authorize the making of a budget and the collection of various charges, and prescribe parliamentary procedures. They may empower the association to hire professional managers or contain other special provisions. The bylaws may also set forth insurance requirements and authorize the imposition of liens against the property of owners who fail to pay monthly charges, although these provisions sometimes may be included in the condo's master deed.

◆ *House rules*. They state what owners can and can't do. Any restrictions on pets, children, decorations, use of facilities and such will be found here. The rules may be incorporated in the bylaws or set apart in a separate document.

◆ *Sales contract or purchase agreement*. It's basically similar to other real estate contracts, but there are differences. In signing, you may acknowledge receipt of the other documents. Check whether there is a cooling off period during which you can back out of the contract. Will you be able to get out of the deal if you can't get financing? There should be written assurances, if necessary, that the project will be completed as promised, and you should have the right to make an inspection prior to settlement. Your deposit should be placed in an escrow account.

◆ *Other papers*. No less important, these could include a copy of the operating budget, a schedule of current and proposed assessments, a financial statement on the owners' association, any leases or contracts, a plan or drawing of the project and your unit and an engineer's report if one was done. One of the financial documents should show how much money has been reserved for unforeseen or emergency outlays. Some states require developers to give each potential buyer a prospectus that details the important facts about the offering.

The board should include in monthly condo fees a realistic contribution to reserves for large repairs and replacements. Otherwise you may be confronted with repeated emergency assessments at times that may be inconvenient to your budget.

Ask the board treasurer for copies of recent budget reports and obtain an engineer's summary of the physical condition of the building, including projections for major repairs.

Find out what assessments have been made during the past five years in addition to the regular condo fee. While some associations deliberately choose to operate with minimal reserves, relying on special assessments as needed, good management is generally associated with a healthy reserve to make special assessments unnecessary.

Study and Ask Questions

You and your lawyer should take the time to evaluate all this material before you decide to buy, no matter how onerous the job appears. If you live in a state that does not require the delivery of documents before you sign a contract, insist on your right to obtain and examine them.

If you've never lived in a condo, you may be astonished by the power held by the board of directors. It can put a lien on your unit if you don't pay your monthly fee or you are late coming up with the money for a special assessment. It may have the license to spend tens of thousands of dollars on a repair or improvement without prior approval of the other owners.

The board is elected by the condo owners and serves as a miniature government. Even if it turns the day-to-day operating details over to a resident manager or outside management company, the board retains the ultimate authority for running the project.

Request information on the background of each board member, and plan to attend at least one board meeting. If you are serious about condo ownership, you should plan to participate in a certain amount of organizational activity in order to protect your interests.

Getting Financing

You may be asked to make a larger down payment on a condo than on a comparable single family property. But, otherwise, getting a mortgage for a condo is no different than getting a loan on a single family house.

Lenders in some areas may be reluctant to give you a loan if you plan to put down less than 10%, and FHA-insured mortgages are not available to prospective owners of condo projects less than a year old. In recent years, high foreclosure rates on condominiums purchased with very low down payments and on units in smaller buildings have caused many lenders to reexamine their lending requirements in such cases.

COOPERATIVE APARTMENTS

The "stockholder in 202-F" may sound like someone with a seat on a securities exchange, but if you live in a cooperative apartment, that's how you might describe your neighbor.

Unlike condominium ownership, which gives you title to a particular unit and an undivided interest in common areas, purchasing a co-op entitles you to a share in a corporation. Owning stock or a membership certificate in the corporation in turn grants you the right to live in a particular apartment. You become a tenant-stockholder of the corporation, and, in most states, your collateral is considered personal property rather than real property. Typically, the corporation owns the co-op property, is responsible for management and property taxes and finances the project with a "blanket" mortgage.

Tenant-stockholders are allowed to deduct their proportional share of real estate taxes and mortgage interest for federal tax purposes, providing that at least 80% of the cooperative's income comes from the shareholders, and no more than 20% comes from parking fees, interest on reserve funds and the like.

Because a new co-op owner is a fellow shareholder in the whole building, current co-op tenants tend to be very choosey about new owners. It is common for a co-op governing board to require prospective owners to appear before them for an interview and to submit personal references in addition to statements of financial resources. Most co-op boards zealously protect the lifestyle of their buildings, and prospective owners are sometimes rejected because the board believes they would be too noisy, reclusive or sloppy, or might throw large boisterous parties. However, co-op boards are prohibited by federal law and many state statutes from rejecting or discouraging a prospective buyer on the basis of that person's race, gender, creed or national origin.

Co-ops have been operating in the U.S. since the end of the 19th century, but for years they took a back seat to condominiums as the preferred method of apartment ownership. Now co-ops are making a comeback in Boston, Chicago, New York and Washington, D.C., thanks in part to local caps on condominium conversions. But most important impetus behind the recent rise in popularity is the availability of financing.

Financing a Co-op

In the past, it was nearly impossible to get a loan to buy a co-op. Few banks offered them, mainly because there was no secondary market for them. Prospective co-op owners simply paid cash or took out personal loans with high interest rates. This tended to make co-op ownership more suitable for upper-income people, with the exception of some co-ops sponsored by state housing agencies.

Then, in 1984, the Federal National Mortgage Association began buying co-op "share loans." These Fannie Mae loans are secured by the stock and occupancy rights of co-op ownership, with terms similar to those of mortgage loans. They are still not as easy to get as mortgages, however, and they are slightly more expensive, with interest rates about 0.25 percentage points higher. Closing costs on this kind of loan are generally less than with a regular mortgage.

Many banks, savings and loans and mortgage companies offer share loans. If you are having difficulty locating a lender in your area, contact the Share Loan Service Corporation (1630 Connecticut Avenue, N.W., Washington, D.C. 20009). This organization is backed by the National Cooperative Bank, a national bank specializing in cooperative lending. Their address is 139 S. High St., Hillsboro, OH 45133. Once a cooperative meets the standards set by the National Cooperative Bank or Fannie Mae and becomes a participating shareholder of Share Loan Corporation, share loans are available to individuals wishing to buy a co-op unit or to refinance.

Lenders who want to sell share loans they originate into the secondary market usually must make sure a project meets Fannie Mae's minimum underwriting and legal standards. Among the requirements are structural soundness, restricted commercial use, fiscally responsible operating budget and appropriate management.

Share loan and cooperative documents of projects meeting Fannie Mae's legal requirements must include various legal safeguards to protect the interests of the tenant-stockholders, the corporation and the lender.

The following are common cooperative documents you will need to study before you buy:

♦ *Articles of Incorporation.* A cooperative is incorporated under state law and the corporation's purpose, powers and obligations are described in the Articles of Incorporation.

♦ *Bylaws.* These spell out the duties and responsibilities of shareholders, officers and directors.

♦ *Stock, Shares or Membership Certificate.* Shares or membership certificates are your proof of ownership in the corporation.

♦ *Proprietary Lease or Occupancy Agreement.* The lease sets up the terms and conditions by which you occupy your co-op unit. In it, you are obligated to pay your pro rata share of the corporation's expenses, including real estate taxes, operating costs and debt. Rules on using your unit, subleasing and maintenance also are found in the agreement.

♦ *Recognition Agreement.* A share loan lender and the cooperative corporation enter into this agreement in order to document the lender's rights and the corporation's responsibilities and obligations to the lender. A corporation may enter into recognition agreements with more than one lender.

♦ *Security agreement.* In this document, the share loan borrower assigns the proprietary lease (or occupany agreement) and pledges his or her stock, shares or membership certificate to the lender in return for a loan.

The Right Questions to Ask

Is it financially sound? Is there adequate income to meet expenses? Income comes from three primary sources: the tenant/stockholders, commercial use—for example, rental income from parking, and from interest or dividends earned on reserve funds. Expenses include debt repayment, real estate and income taxes, building maintenance and operations and reserve fund pay-ins for replacements and capital improvements.

A cooperative financed with an FHA-insured blanket mortgage is required to have reserve funds that meet the agency's criteria. In addition to collecting money for taxes and debt, adequate sums must be set aside to replace structural elements and major components, such as heating, cooling, plumbing and electrical systems. In addition, a general operating reserve must be established for other contingencies and for resale problems. These reserves are established under the cooperative's regulatory agreements and documents should be available to prospective owners.

Fannie Mae's project approval standards give lenders the tools they need to evaluate cooperative projects. Typically, they require, among other things, that each project have an adequate cash flow and that monthly assessments be structured to handle operating expenses and to build sufficient reserves.

Age and condition of the building? The answer to that question sets the stage for what kind of financial experience you will have once you become a tenant- stockholder. Is there an engineering report on the condition of the project? If you discover that the galvanized plumbing in the building is nearing the end of its anticipated 40-year life span, you know it will have to be replaced, not repaired. How does the board of directors plan to pay for the job? From the reserve fund? With a special assessment? By refinancing the mortgage?

How will you fit in? How old is the average shareowner? What is the financial status and philosophy of the majority? A building full of up-and- coming professionals in their early forties may have a very different money management philosophy than one filled with retired or soon-to-be retired people. Likewise, if you can afford to buy into a particular cooperative only by living in the smallest unit, you may be at odds with affluent neighbors who insist on a uniformed doorman— regardless of the cost.

Composition of the board and its financial philosophy? Is there a fair amount of consensus among board members on how to conduct the corporation's affairs? Do their views on important issues reflect those of other tenant-stockholders? Do they jibe with yours?

Are you prepared to participate in cooperative living? Many of the problems of condo and cooperative living are similar. How willing are you to be involved in meetings and group efforts?

How many units are rented? A possible concern for would-be tenant-stockholders in new cooperatives is a 1986 change in the tax law that permits shares held by partnerships, trusts, estates and corporations to count toward the 80% of income that by law must derive from tenant- stockholders. In the past such stockholders were required to weigh in on the 20% side of the ratio. Find out what the bylaws permit. Conceivably, a majority of a cooperative's units could be occupied by tenants or "nominees" of partnerships, trusts, estates and corporations rather than by shareowners who have joined together as "cooperative homeowners." If a building is dominated by tenants rather than owners, it changes the nature of cooperative living. It also may have tax and resale consequences for individual tenant-stockholders.

Existing co-ops are not affected by the 1986 change unless they alter their articles of incorporation and bylaws to permit investors to become stockholders.

May you sublet your apartment? Some cooperatives forbid it. Others allow it, but may impose a one-time sublet fee or impose an additional monthly maintenance surcharge.

For More Information

For more information about cooperatives and co-op financing, write to the National Association of Housing Cooperatives, 1614 King St., Alexandria, VA 22314, and to the National Cooperative Business Assocation, 1401 New York Ave., N.W., Suite 1100, Washington, D.C. 20005. And take a look at the following books:

◆ *A Member's Guide to Cooperative Living*, by Multi-Family Housing Services, Inc. (available from NAHC at the above address).

◆ *A Consumer Guide to Financing a Cooperative Using Share Loan Financing*, free from the Share Loan Service Corp. (1630 Connecticut Ave., N.W., Washington, D.C. 20009).

MOBILE HOMES

Despite their name, most mobile homes aren't in the least mobile. Nine out of ten stay on their original sites. This fact, plus changes in design and construction methods over the years, means that as you shop you may hear the term "manufactured home" used interchangeably with the more familiar term "mobile home." Built in factories and assembled in the plant or on site, manufactured homes make ownership possible for many families and individuals who might otherwise be priced out of the market. On a per-square-foot basis, manufactured homes cost about half as much to build as site-built homes.

Before you buy such a home, you must decide whether you will place it on land you own or on land you rent or lease. The decision you make is important because if you later regret your choice of a homesite, you may find the only practical solution is to sell.

The majority of buyers put their manufactured homes on land they own. It's best to select a lot before you buy the home. While some of the zoning restrictions that kept mobile homes out of residential neighborhoods have been eased, many have not. Nevertheless, there are well-designed, attractive subdivisions to choose from, and you may be able to buy land in a ready-made community, complete with swimming pool, recreation center and nearby school and shopping. A good subdivision developer should help you select a lot that will suit the home you have in mind.

If you plan to rent the land on which your home will be situated, you must be prepared to have certain of your activities controlled by park management on the one hand and by a group of your neighbors on the other. If you move into an established community, you will rent a small piece of property and have your house installed on it at your own expense. A written lease may or may not be involved. There generally are rules and regulations, but they may not be given to you in writing. In most cases you will rent your space month to month or on a yearly lease.

In a new development, on the other hand, the management may also be the mobile home dealer, and you can get into the park only by buying a home from the dealer. This arrangement is not entirely sinister. It allows management to enforce strict standards for the homes that go into its park. When you select a lot, you get to pick a home from the listing of models approved by the management. You will be shown complete catalog and price information, and in some developments the management will encourage you to go to the factory to custom design your model.

New developments and those still under construction are often promoted on the basis of such amenities as swimming pools, shuffleboard courts, recreation halls that don't yet exist. If you move into such a park, you may discover—to your dismay—that the landlord lets the amenities wait while funds and space are devoted to developing more sites for homes. To add insult to injury, you may be asked for an entrance fee of several hundred dollars, although some states have outlawed such fees.

Keep in mind that if you lease a site rather than buy it, you will be in a particularly vulnerable situation. You will own a valuable piece of property located on someone else's land. In a dispute with the landowner you may have no recourse but to sell your home or move it. It is very costly to move a single-section home even a short distance. Including necessary dismantling and reassembly, you can pay thousands of dollars to move a luxury multisection home less than 50 miles. Because of the expense and the damage that can result from vibration and road shock, you probably will decide to sell, possibly at a loss, and be faced with the prospect of buying another home elsewhere.

Selecting a Site

Whether you intend to buy or rent a homesite, visit several developments. Stay a few days if you can, to sample the neighborhood and meet the residents. Familiarize yourself with each community's rules and regulations. In condominium developments, for example, residents own part of the common facilities as well as their own units and lots. Try to determine how much turnover there is and how the majority of residents view their community. Is your lifestyle compatible with that of your potential neighbors?

Check on security, fire protection and trash collection. Remember that the complexion of a rental park can change much more rapidly than a community of landowners. As a tenant there may be little you can do if a park is sold, or if the management becomes lax.

Study the purchase contract or lease, bylaws and the rules and regulations, and all other pertinent documents. Do not commit yourself to a lot or a home until you've had time to consult with an attorney. Don't sign anything you don't understand.

Cost and Quality

You might pay around $18,600 for a single-section unit; $36,600 for a multi-section. Those were average prices for new single- and multi-section units in the late 1980s. The purchase price usually includes some furniture, major appliances, draperies, carpeting, and delivery from the manufacturer to a homesite.

"Single section" or "single-wide" mobile units may give you up to 1,000 square feet of living space. You can join two or more single-sections together. The most luxurious multi-section models—featuring wood siding, pitched roofs, cathedral ceilings, fireplaces, bay windows, drywall interiors, and the like—can be hard to distinguish from their conventional site-built counterparts.

Questions of quality. Manufactured homes are not subject to local building codes. Units built after June 14, 1976, are covered by the National Mobile Home Construction and Safety Standards Act and must display a permanent label saying that the manufacturer has conformed with the standards.

The standards do not apply to units made before then, nor to multifamily mobiles or special units for the handicapped. The Department of Housing and Urban Development (HUD) has overall responsibility for enforcement, but inspections are conducted by approved state or private agencies.

Judging quality yourself can be difficult, because the innards of a mobile home are hidden from view. Nevertheless, a careful inspection can be revealing. Signs of good construction include a floor that is level and firm; windows and doors that open and close smoothly; walls that do not give excessively when pushed; a firm ceiling; a chassis with two parallel steel I-beams ten to twelve inches high that are reinforced over the axle area; and three axles if the unit is 60 feet long or more.

Look for a 2-by-4-inch aluminum label—located at the taillight end of each section—indicating that it conforms with HUD standards, and a data plate near the main electrical panel or in some other visible location. The plate gives the name and address of the manufacturer, serial number, model and date of manufacture, as well as other information about appliances, the design approval agency, and the wind and snow loads for which the unit is designed. You should also get a booklet giving specifics about the unit.

Single-section mobile homes are more prone to wind damage from hurricanes, tornadoes and severe thunderstorms than site-built homes. Multi-section units, though, are quite stable when they are properly tied or attached to a permanent foundation. A significant number of structural problems have been traced to improper installation of units on their sites, which HUD does not regulate.

Financing the purchase. You may be able to finance your home with a conventional mortgage if the unit is permanently set up on land you own or on land you will finance along with the unit. Manufactured houses also are eligible for a number of government-backed loan programs. But most homes still are financed like motor vehicles with personal property, or chattel, loans, and mobile home dealers and park and subdivision developers still arrange most financing. Interest rates are higher and payback periods shorter, as a rule, than for mortgages on site-built homes.

Interest on debt you take on to buy or renovate a manufactured home (or home and land together) is fully deductible for federal tax purposes, so long as it is secured by the house and you use it as your principal residence or second home.

When you find a unit you like and know how much you want to borrow, ask as many lenders as possible about rates and terms. A few phone calls just might save you a lot of dollars.

Mobile home loans are subject to the federal truth-in-lending law, which means you must be informed in writing of the finance cost expressed as an annual percentage rate (APR). If you're quoted an unusually low figure, it's probably an "add-on" or "discount" rate, neither of which reflects the true cost. Always insist on being told the APR, and make sure it is the figure in the contract. With add-on loans the interest is added to the amount borrowed before payments begin. If an interest rebate formula called the rule of 78s is used on prepayment or refinancing, you could actually owe more than you borrowed even after making payments for several years.

Two FHA programs are available for financing mobile homes. FHA Title I insures loans of up to $40,500 for terms of up to 20 years if the home meets HUD standards. FHA Title II covers homes on permanent foundations sold with the land as real estate. Such loans are insured up to $54,000 with a maximum 20-year term for single section homes and a maximum 25-year term for multi-sections.

The VA guarantee for mobiles is $20,000 or 40% of the loan, whichever is smaller, for up to 23 years. A 5% down payment will be required.

Warranties

Once you've bought your unit, you may get warranties from the retailer, the transporter, the installer and the appliance manufacturer as well. Make notes on what each warranty covers and doesn't cover. How long does each warranty last? Who will actually do any work necessary under the warranty? And where will it be done?

For More Information

See the following two information sources:
◆ The latest edition of the *Manufactured Housing Industry Directory of Financing Services and Other Housing Related Organizations* (Meetings + Plus, P.O. Box 1981, Palm Springs, CA 92263). It gives you, among other things:

1. Names, addresses and phone numbers of the lending institutions providing manufactured home/land financing;

2. Names, addresses and phone numbers of major lenders offering VA and/or FHA financing;

3. Names, addresses and phone numbers of housing and finance agencies in the federal government;

4. Information about manufactured housing appraisal services;

5. Names and locations of the various state and national manufactured housing trade associations.

◆ *How to Buy a Manufactured Home*, by the Manufactured Housing Institute, in cooperation with the Federal Trade Commission's Office of Consumer & Business Education; single copy, 50 cents (Consumer Information Center, Department 429V, Pueblo, CO 81009). Includes information on warranties and other consumer protections; home selection and placement; site preparation, transportation and installation; and home inspection.

CHAPTER 7

HOUSE HUNTING STRATEGIES

◆

IF YOU'VE GONE through the steps outlined in previous chapters—assessing your resources, prequalifying for a mortgage, deciding on your needs and wants—you're ready for some serious house hunting.

To be successful, your house hunting strategy must adapt to the mood and economic realities facing buyers and sellers in your targeted location and price range. The "hot" or "cold" condition of the market at the time you begin looking will determine how you approach the task—with or without the help of a real estate agent; with intensity or at a leisurely pace; relying on classified ads and open houses, or using the grapevine to give you a jump on other buyers when a desirable house first comes on the market.

The biggest determinant of the housing market, of course, is the national, regional and local economy. But within every kind of economy, there are also recurring seasonal differences in market strength. If possible, shop when other homebuyers are not out in force.

Across the country, many properties come on the market in April and May, and homebuyers swarm into the market. Sellers generally don't feel pressured to cut a deal right away. Some will feel differently by June, and more will be downright eager to sell by the time the July/August summer doldrums descend.

Fall usually brings a brisker pace, so September, October and November are generally good months for both buying and selling. From Thanksgiving on through the winter, holiday activities and cold weather generally combine to slow activity. Buyers will find sellers more interested in dealing, but offsetting this is the smaller number of houses on the market in mid-winter.

Naturally, the seasonal ebb and flow of market activity varies from one part of the country to another. You may live in a winter ski area or in a beach resort town where investors and second-home buyers dominate the market. Each region will have its own seasonal pattern. A seven-year seasonal analysis of prices and sales activity in Texas, for example, showed that July, August and September were the best months for selling a home in that state; by contrast, the first quarter—January, February and March—is usually a buyer's market in Texas. Learn the local pattern and, if possible, exploit it to your advantage.

You might be able to swing a good deal by finding a corporate seller trying to unload the home of a transferred employee. Companies want to avoid the cost of carrying unsold houses. When sales are slow, most will reduce listing prices, often below appraised values. How to find those bargains? Ask local real estate brokers. Major corporate relocation management firms use their own relocation brokerage networks. Since corporate homes are often vacant, chances of working a deal are that much better if you can close quickly.

THE BUYER'S MARKET

In a buyer's market, there are many houses for sale relative to the number of serious lookers. Houses will sit on the market for some time, and sellers are often willing to cut their asking price and even assist the buyer with cut-rate financing by taking back a second trust.

As a qualified buyer, you have time on your side. You can be more deliberate, and you can bargain harder. You can ask the seller for an appraisal of the house before you submit an offer, and even ask the seller to pay all or part of the cost. You can take your own time to check comparable sale prices in the neighborhood. You can load your offering contract with contingency clauses that protect only you—inspection, financing at a specified interest rate, seller's help with mortgage points, even the condition that you be able to sell your current home before closing on this purchase. In a hot market, the seller wouldn't touch so one-sided a contract, but in a slow market, the seller may have to swallow it.

In a buyer's market, the diligent house hunter can do reasonably well without the aid of a real estate agent. Although you won't have access, without an agent, to new listings in the local multiple listing service computer (the real estate trade's clearinghouse of properties for sale), you won't miss much; most houses will remain on the market long enough to be advertised in the newspaper and shown at a weekend open house.

THE SELLER'S MARKET

A seller's market is the situation when prices are firm or rising and every new listing is snapped up fast, even those that seem at first to be over-priced. In a truly hot market, good houses are often sold before they're advertised or even punched into the MLS computer; several contracts are submitted on the same property; and buyers vie with each other by offering more than the asking price. In a hot market, there will be more sale-by-owner properties, too.

If this is the kind of market you're working in as a buyer, you had better be ready—financially and emotionally—to move fast when you spot something that meets your needs.

The seller won't give much attention to timid or unprepared buyers, or buyers who load their offering contract with lots of protective contingencies. The would-be buyer who must have the contract reviewed by a not-yet-selected attorney, and the buyer with insufficient earnest money who wants the seller to take a personal note for a few days, probably won't get serious consideration from owners of desirable properties.

In a seller's market, select in advance the attorney and home inspector who will be needed as soon as you decide to submit a contract. If you don't know a good real estate attorney, get names from friends, lenders, title company and real estate agents. If you are buying a condo, co-op or farm, find a lawyer who specializes in that type of transaction.

You will save precious time if you and your attorney are familiar with the contract to be used. Have contingencies you definitely plan to insert drawn up by your attorney in advance, but remember that a "clean" contract—one not littered with lots of escape clauses for the buyer—will be treated with more respect by the seller.

Financial Readiness

As you begin a serious house hunt in a hot market, be prepared to write a check for the earnest money, which usually accompanies your contract offer as evidence of serious intentions, good faith, and ability to close the deal. Arrange for cash tied up in certificates of deposit (CDs) or in stocks and bonds to be moved to your checking account. If you own a home now, consider putting a home-equity line of credit on it well before you begin looking for your next home. (See the discussion of home-equity loans in Chapters 3 and 16.)

In a hot market, one of the things that might set your offer above other bids will be your ability to go to settlement fast (if that's what the seller wants). Several companies now offer speedy mortgage commitments, cutting your time from application to approval from weeks to days or even minutes.

If you already own a home, be prepared to settle on the new house before you've closed the sale of your current one. If the money you're putting down on the new house is tied up in the current one, talk to your banker about ways to bridge the gap between selling and buying with a short-term advance. The solution may be a bridge loan. Also known as a swing, equity-advance or gap loan, a bridge loan amounts to a short-term advance against the equity in your present property.

The Search for Houses

In a hot seller's market, you must use every tool at your disposal to spot good new listings as soon as the seller decides to sell—or even before.

It is not enough just to watch the newspapers every day for advertisements of houses just put on the market. It is especially not enough to wait for weekend open houses. Many fine offerings will be sold by word of mouth, without ever being advertised in the paper or being registered with a multiple listing service.

Some of these unpublicized sales will be "by owner," with no agent involved. Some will be transactions started and completed within one real estate firm, where one agent's new listing is sold to a buyer assisted by another agent in the same office.

For the reasons above, it is necessary in a hot market for the house hunter to use the scouting services of at least one aggressive, experienced agent who knows the targeted neighborhoods. In some cases, it is useful to have several agents in different firms helping you simultaneously. (But keep in mind that when agents are competing to sell you a home they are under tremendous pressure to get you to buy fast. Helping you find the best property may take second priority.) In addition, you should use your own energy and ingenuity in combination with the help of an agent.

For example, ask all your friends who live in or near your ideal neighborhood to let you know if they hear anything that suggests a house might be coming on the market soon. It could be news of an executive's relocation, a split marriage, a retirement move, or the recent death of an elderly person living alone. As ghoulish as it sounds, some house hunters watch the obituary pages and look up the address of the deceased to see where he or she lived; after a suitable period of time, they write or phone an heir listed in the obituary and inquire respectfully if the house will be for sale.

Many smart house hunters will approach the owners of houses they admire, even if the house is not for sale. They do this by driving through the target neighborhood and jotting down the addresses of houses they like the look of, then using a criss-cross directory (available at many public libraries) or public land records at the courthouse to determine the owner's name and phone number. A note or phone call sometimes yields the information that the owner is, indeed, contemplating sale. Sometimes the owner has never thought of selling, but is surprised to hear what his house might be worth; suddenly, you've got an interested seller.

If you're looking at houses with a particular agent, the agent can make this "cold" contact for you and work with both interested parties to make a deal, earning a commission in the process. If you're going it alone, you'll want to encourage the owner not to call an agent until you've had a chance to tour the house, get an appraisal, and make an offer. Point out that a private transaction, without the seller paying a 6% commission, could net him or her substantially more than through a conventional realty listing. Of course, the savings of that commission could be split in some proportion between the seller and buyer, benefitting you both.

Perhaps the seller will be reluctant to sell to you without first finding out how much an agent could get for the house. Here's your strategy for dealing with that: Ask the seller to add a clause to the agent's listing contract specifying that the seller may sell the house to you directly (you must be named in the listing contract) without payment of a commission. The seller should be happy to go along with this, because he has nothing to lose and the possible gain of all or part of the commission.

If you are initiating a negotiation with an unprepared seller, for the seller's protection and your own, suggest that a professional appraisal be done, with the cost shared by you and the seller.

SHOPPING WITH A REAL ESTATE AGENT

Some people like to look for houses on their own, unaccompanied by a real estate agent. Other people wouldn't think of venturing into the housing market without the help of an agent scouting out new listings, accompanying them on tours of open houses, and offering advice.

Most houses for sale are listed with realty agents, so the house hunter who calls to inquire about an advertised house or who visits an open house on Sunday is going to encounter agents at every turn. If you identify yourself by name—for example, by signing the registry book at an open house—you'll soon start getting calls from agents offering to help you find your dream house. At this point, it's "choose or be chosen." If you are interested in being helped, take the initiative and do the selecting, by contacting agents with proven reputations in the neighborhoods and price range in which you're looking. If you are not interested, be firm and avoid entanglements until you're ready.

Keep in mind that the house hunter who is looking on his own, without an agent's help, is at a considerable disadvantage. Unless very knowledgable about the market in a given area, this house hunter will miss the agent's deep knowledge. More significantly, this looker will have no access to the MLS computer listings of houses for sale. That might be alright in a slow market, but in any kind of active market, the solo house hunter will simply miss a lot of good houses that sell quickly.

Most real estate agents are compensated from the commission sellers pay on the sale price, so why does an agent who doesn't have the listing want to help you find and buy a home? Because the sales commission is split between the seller's listing broker (and the broker's agent) and the broker (and broker's agent) who brings in the buyer. Real estate agents make money from finding both houses to sell and people to buy them, so a well-qualified, serious house hunter represents a paycheck to the agent—but only if the sale goes through. There will usually be no compensation for all the hours of accompanying a buyer through houses unless that agent submits the buyer's successful contract.

If an agent takes you to a house and tours it with you the first time you see it, you should submit your contract offer through that agent. Even if you don't, that agent may be entitled to a share of the sales commission from the seller in the event that you buy the house.

If an agent merely mentions to you that a given house is for sale, but you first tour the house by yourself or with another agent, the first agent will probably not have any claim on part of the commission. That's why agents are often coy about giving house hunters the address of a listing when they first call. Instead, they'll offer to pick you up and drive you to the house for an appointment to tour it. The agent who tells you about a new listing doesn't want to risk that you'll cross the threshold with another agent, costing the first agent a piece of the sale.

Remember that unless you hire your own agent (a so-called "buyer's broker"; see page 85), an agent works for a seller and is paid by a seller. This is true even when an agent spends hours and hours working with you, the buyer. It is true even if "your" agent has never met the owners of the home you ultimately buy. (Most states and the District of Columbia now require agents working for sellers to disclose to buyers they work with the legal and financial arrangements they make with the sellers.) When an agent works with a buyer, they are both gambling. The agent gambles that in return for his time you will be loyal and buy a home through him. You gamble that your loyalty will reward you with service and produce a suitable property.

So why would a buyer consider using several agents to help in the house hunt? Perhaps because the house you're looking for is very special in some way, and you don't want to risk missing the few possible listings. The best reason for using several agents is to extend your reach in a hot market. When houses move very quickly, the buyer needs more eyes and ears and scouting energy than one agent can supply. Some good listings will be sold within one firm, with the seller's commission being shared by the listing agent and a colleague in the firm who brought in the buyer. The listing won't ever show up in the MLS computer, so if you don't have a relationship already with an agent at that firm, you wouldn't hear about the house in time to see it or bid on it.

In short, you want to be the first person to hear about every good new listing on the market, so you must encourage agents at different firms to compete for your patronage. Tell each agent that you'll reward hustle by accompanying him or her immediately to see the new listing—providing that agent is the first one to call and tell you about it.

You'll be loyal to that agent for all dealings relating to that particular house, but the next day you might go see another house with a different agent who happened to be the first to call you about it.

Pretty soon, you'll start getting calls from several agents within minutes or hours of each other, each trying to be the first to tell you that something good has just shown up in the MLS computer, or even better, that a new listing has just come into the firm and won't go into the computer for 24 hours—a typical period after which the firm is obligated to enter the new listing for other agents to see. (Some privacy-minded sellers specifically ask their agent to keep the listing unadvertised and strictly "in house" for a while, with no notice to the MLS computer.)

HOW TO PICK AN AGENT

There are only two functions in the real estate business. They are broker and agent (or sales associate.) A broker is licensed by the state to conduct a real estate business and to negotiate transactions for a fee. An agent is a broker's representative and is usually an independent contractor rather than an employee. He or she is permitted to sell real estate under the supervision of a licensed broker. Both brokers and their representatives are properly called agents because they act as agents for their clients.

Contrary to public impression, not all brokers and agents are Realtors. A Realtor (capital "R"—it's a trade name) and a Realtor Associate (who works for a Realtor) are members of the National Association of Realtors, a trade and lobby organization.

If location, location, location are the watchwords for picking a property, experience, experience, experience are the watchwords for picking an agent.

Most buyers, however, don't pick an agent; they acquire one at an open house, or by responding by telephone to an ad. Many select an agent who is a friend, relative or neighbor. You could be lucky; such an agent may turn out to be skilled, experienced and resourceful. On the other hand, you could end up with an amateur.

There is a better way to acquire an agent:

Obtain the names of brokers and agents active in the area where you want to buy. The classified ads are a good place to start. Brokers with agents that list and sell homes in a particular neighborhood will advertise regularly. Ask friends, associates, lenders and attorneys for recommendations. And by all means, consider using a buyer's broker, who will be paid with a fee from you, not from the sales commission. (See the full discussion that begins on the next page.)

Check the broker's reputation in the community. In the case of an agent, find out who the broker is, then check out the firm. Inquire about complaints or problems at the local real estate board and the state real estate commission. Survey some of your prospective neighbors.

Call the most promising brokers. Ask them to put you in touch with one or two of their most experienced agents. Tell each broker what kind of buyer you are and what kind of property you want. For example, a novice buyer may need an agent who is especially intuitive and patient, while a much-transferred corporate executive needs one who lists exclusive homes and has sophisticated negotiating skills.

Interview the agents. Find out what each knows about the community. Ask how many years he or she has been selling real estate and for whom. Determine what kind of service you can expect.

After your screening, select one or more agents to work with, and be candid with them about what degree of service you're expecting, and whether you'll be looking at houses with them alone or with other agents, too. Give them good guidance on how much variation from your ideal specifications—size, price, location, etc.—you'll tolerate. Do you want them to narrowly screen new listings or tell you about everything that is remotely similar to your target house?

USING A BUYER'S BROKER

When the market is brisk, it may be hard to find an agent to give you a lot of special counsel and hand-holding. This is because most agents are working primarily for the seller, not the buyer. This fiduciary relationship between seller and agent sometimes causes buyers to wonder whether they can trust the agent— even an agent who is ostensibly helping them find a house to buy. How can an agent who is going to be paid by the seller, and whose pay will be based on how *high* the sale price is, negotiate in the buyer's best interest?

This concern is the reason that savvy buyers study the art of real estate negotiation, so they can rely on themselves, not the agent. And it's the reason that smart buyers always retain an impartial attorney to review the contract and settlement papers. This concern about conflict of interest in residential real estate sales—or dual agency, as it is called—is also the reason that buyer's brokers came into existence.

The only way you can command an agent's undivided loyalties during a house hunt and price negotiation is by entering into a "single agency" relationship with an agent. It then becomes your responsibility, not the seller's, to pay that agent's fee. This fee should be set in advance and ideally should not be tied to the selling price of the house.

Peter Miller and Douglas Bregman in their manual *Buyer's Brokerage: A Practical Guide for Real Estate Buyers, Brokers and Investors* (Tremont Press, P.O. Box 2307, Silver Spring, MD 20902) list six advantages that they believe buyers have when they are represented by their own agent:

1) A broker employed and paid by a purchaser is obligated to get the best possible price and terms for the buyer. This means that a broker can openly suggest a smaller deposit, better financing terms, the use of a contract form more favorable to the purchaser and an offering price far below the listing figure created by the seller.

2) Because the fee for a buyer's broker is not tied to the selling price of a property, a major source of conflict between the buyer and broker is eliminated.

3) Buyer's brokers can assist with the purchase of properties outside the brokerage system, such as homes offered for sale by self-sellers.

4) Buyer's brokerage gives purchasers access to the same skills, training and services that have been monopolized by sellers in the past.

5) With buyer's brokerage there is a clarity of relationships since one broker openly represents the purchaser and another can represent the seller. The problem of confused representation, where a single broker appears to somehow be concerned with the conflicting interests of both buyer and seller, is eliminated.

6) Buyer's brokerage gives purchasers more control over real estate marketing costs and, ultimately, over acquisition costs as well.

But things are not always so neat and clean in the real world. Many buyer-brokers engage in so-called fee splitting. Under this arrangement, your agent will be paid out of the commission put up by the seller. Since compensation is once again tied to the sale price of the home, this payment method raises conflict-of-interest issues that should be hashed out and addressed directly in any contract you sign.

Before you enter into a buyer's brokerage contract, check the reputation and experience of the firm and agent. Set up a meeting with the broker to discuss your needs. In most situations you should not expect to pay for this initial consultation. A buyer- broker may require a non-refundable fee as a condition of starting work; the fee will vary with the difficulty of the search and with the overall compensation plan.

Buyers may ask their lenders to fold the buyer- broker fee into the mortgage loan; most lenders agree to this, but lenders making VA loans are not permitted to do so.

The Agreement Contract

The compensation plan you agree on is spelled out in the brokerage contract, your equivalent of the seller's listing agreement. It should address the following points:

◆ Will you pay the agent an hourly rate, a set fee, or a percentage of the purchase price?

◆ Will there be an incentive commission for getting a price lower than the asking price—say, 10% of the savings? (But remember, the lowest price is not necessarily synonymous with the best overall deal for the buyer.)

◆ Will you pay an initial retainer and will it be applied against the total fee due?

◆ Is there a minimum fee? Is there a cap on total cost? This is specially important if you are paying by the hour.

◆ How will conflicts of interest be handled?

◆ What will happen should you buy a property shortly after the brokerage agreement ends? Will the broker get a commission? If so, under what conditions?

◆ Exactly what kinds of services and advice will the broker provide?

◆ How will disagreements be handled? For example, both parties could agree to submit to binding arbitration, using a neutral third party.

Who Pays Whom

When you buy a house with a buyer's broker, the seller's agent should be willing to cut the 6% sales commission. If the total cost of two separate fees—one paid by you to your buyer's broker and one paid by the seller to the listing broker—is held to an amount equivalent to the 6% commission the seller expects to pay anyway, your agent should have no difficulty persuading a seller to accept your offer.

Here's an example: Say the owner lists her property for $104,000 and agrees to pay a 6% commission. If the house sells for $100,000, and commission is $6,000, the seller will get $94,000. In a conventional transaction, the $6,000 commission would be divided between the listing broker and the cooperating or selling broker, with each getting 3%.

Now suppose the owner receives an offer from a buyer represented by his own agent. The owner is told that the purchaser will pay his own agent and she accepts an offer of $97,000 for her home. Result: the seller still nets $94,000—after paying $3,000 to the listing broker. The listing broker goes along with the deal because he gets the 3% commission he was likely to earn anyway. The buyer pays $97,000 plus $3,000 to his agent, for a total of $100,000.

In another alternative the buyer offers a higher price to the seller—say, $100,000—and the contract stipulates that the seller will pay both the buyer's agent and his own listing agent, netting perhaps the same $94,000 (6% split between the two brokers) or less, if the listing agent won't accept the split.

Finding a Buyer's Broker

Ask for the names of buyer brokers at your local Board of Realtors and large real estate firms in your area. And professors of real estate at local colleges and universities may be able to recommend some.

The Buyer's Broker Registry, part of a larger directory entitled *Who's Who in Creative Real Estate, Inc.,* lists about 400 buyer brokers. The directory gives advice, too, on buyer brokerage and how to employ a broker.

All brokers listed in this directory submitted a completed buyer's brokerage transaction to the company for its review and completed a qualifying course on buyer brokerage. In addition, all listed brokers agree to work for, and be paid by, only one party in a real estate transaction, and abide by other professional real estate practices.

Copies of the directory are available for $25 from the *Buyer's Broker Registry*, P.O. Box 23275, Ventura, CA 93002. You can get the names of three registered buyer brokers in your state or region by sending $5.00 to that address, along with a cover letter mentioning this Kiplinger book; additional names are available for $1.00 each. *Who's Who in Creative Real Estate* also publishes a booklet, *What Is Single Agency?* (available for $15), which discusses in detail the concept of single agency.

DECODING THE CLASSIFIED ADS

Whatever kind of market you're hunting in, whether with or without an agent's help, you should get acquainted with the classified real estate ads.

They can help you survey a community when you are starting your search with no fixed ideas of where you want to live. A few weeks of discriminating reading can give you an indication of price ranges and neighborhood character. They can also acquaint you with brokerage firms that concentrate their efforts in a particular area and, sometimes, an individual agent who sells a particular kind of house. Most particularly, the ads uncover homes being sold by owners and builders, and each weekend they reveal a dazzling array of open houses.

If you're looking for a home in an area far away, subscribe to the local newspapers there and get a detailed map of the vicinity, showing neighborhood names. The two together will begin to give you an arms-length feel for the real estate market there, even before you make your first visit.

The classified section is especially useful in a slow market, even more so if you are conducting your search on your own, without access to a multiple listing service. For example, you can keep current on new offerings and price reductions, as well as probable sales. If you know how long a property has been advertised, what its starting price was, and how many real estate firms have offered it, you have a leg up when you're negotiating an offer. Start a notebook in which you paste in ads that you clip from the paper each day or each weekend.

A successful ad tries to entice you to a property. It tells you only about features that might attract you. It withholds details that might discourage you. Before you start calling agents to inquire about an advertised property, make a standard checklist with your wants and don't-wants listed on a grid. Have it handy when you call, and cut through the smoke screen of the ad with a few key questions at the onset. That way, you'll avoid a long conversation with the agent about how you can buy the property with seller financing, and then realize, after you have hung up, that you don't know how many bedrooms it has, whether it has a garage or when you could move in.

After a while, you get the hang of real-estatese, all those cryptic abbreviations, like "2b, 1ba, lctm, owc, q.pos." You'll decode it as: two bedrooms, one bath, low cash to mortgage, owner will carry mortgage, quick possession.

You'll also get acquainted with all the clever euphemisms that agents use in their ads. "Handyman's special" and "lots of potential" often mean the house is falling in. "Just awaits your loving touch" means a total redecorating is needed. "Charming dollhouse" means the rooms are tiny. "Convenient to everything" can signal a busy corner near the bus route. "Low upkeep" might mean it has no yard at all. And so on, limited only by the agent's gift for prose.

Don't overlook new developments and apartment condominium conversions. You won't be pointed to these properties by most agents, unless they specialize in condos or the builder has promised to compensate agents for bringing buyers in.

Condo and cooperative ads will usually be listed in the same classified section as detached houses, but under their own listings. The new-house market tends to be advertised apart from the classifieds, in large display ads in the newspaper's special real estate section, often on Saturdays.

HANDLING THE "SALE BY OWNER"

And don't overlook the "sale by owner" ads in the classifieds. They can sometimes result in a sticky, awkward negotiation, but if you're knowledgeable about the market and have the advice of a good attorney, a deal can be made—with or without an agent's help.

If you're looking at houses on your own, you and the seller can deal face to face or through an attorney.

Things get complicated if you've been looking at houses with an agent and you feel indebted to the agent for all the effort and advice you've received in the quest. You have a couple of choices:

1) You can abandon your agent and deal directly with the seller, with no compensation to the agent. After all, the agent knew all along that he or she would get paid only if you bought a house that you first saw with the agent; that's the risk of the business.

2) You could deal directly with the seller but pay the agent some modest fee for the time and trouble that was expended on you. Keep in mind, however, that you're not under any obligation to do so.

3) You could try to persuade the seller to accept your agent and pay the agent a 3% commission (or any other commission you can all agree on). The agent would provide service to the seller, helping with the negotiation, mortgage arrangements, and getting both parties to settlement without a hitch. The agent will end up getting the same commission (some part of the 3%, shared with the broker's firm) that he or she would have earned from a regular listing.

Why would a seller agree to this? Well, the seller has listed the house himself, performing the duties of advertising it, preparing fact sheets, and holding open houses. For that he has avoided paying someone a full 6% commission. Perhaps he would settle on paying "your" agent 3%, getting some service for the price and avoiding alienating you as a buyer, since you want to stay with your agent and work it out amicably.

This is why many "sale by owner" sellers put the phrase "brokers welcome at 3%" in their ads. They don't want to pay a full 6% commission, but at the same time they don't want agents to boycott their property, refusing to bring clients to see it.

If the seller balks and you really want to be loyal to the agent who's helped you, you could refuse to come see the seller's house without an understanding to protect the agent. In a slow market, that might convince the seller to relent, but if he has other buyers waiting in the wings, you might be hurting your own chances of getting the house.

TOURING THE HOUSE

If you have the luxury of deliberation, you'll want to make several visits to a house you're considering making an offer on. In a brisk market, however, it's not uncommon for a buyer to make an offer after only one brief visit to a house. Either way, try to get the maximum benefit out of every minute you're in the house. Consider yourself a reporter and detective, there to gather as much information as possible about the house and the sellers.

You probably know your wants and don't-wants list well enough that you won't need to take a check list with you, but by all means take a note pad and tape measure. At most open houses you'll find an information sheet about the house. The most complete sheets have such things as square footage of lot and house, the most recent property taxes, average monthly utility bills, and the age of appliances and major mechanical systems, as well as the basics of number of rooms, etc.

If, at first glance, this looks like a house you'll want to pursue, sketch out floor plans on your first visit; they'll help you envision the house hours or days later. You'll want a professional inspection made if you put a contract in, but you can make some tentative judgments on your own. Take a close look at the furnace, electrical box (fuses or circuit breakers?) and appliances; do they appear to be in good shape, or very tired? How about the roof, gutters and exterior finish? Does the house have storm windows, or will you have to add them at your own cost? If the floor plan doesn't fit the way you live, how easily can rooms be rearranged or new ones added on?

Some buyers who are looking primarily at older houses know in advance that they'll probably have to do substantial remodeling or expanding. As a matter of fact, some buyers would rather buy a slightly shabby but basically sound house and remodel it to their own tastes than pay a premium for a recently completed remodeling that doesn't suit them. These buyers have an architect and/or contractor standing by to accompany them through a house on the second visit, after a preliminary look proves promising. The judgment of these professionals on the ease and probable cost of renovation will play a role in how much the buyer offers for the house.

ASK QUESTIONS AND MORE QUESTIONS

You should try to find out as much as possible about the sellers, starting with the first visit to a house that you're seriously interested in. Everything you learn will make you a better informed, and therefore more capable, negotiator should you decide to make an offer.

Conversely, don't give away strategic information to the seller or the seller's agent or broker. You are put at a disadvantage, for example, if the seller discovers you have sold your current home and are anxious to find a replacement. The same is true if you have a soon-to-expire lease, or are shopping from out of town.

It's hard for buyers not to be forthcoming in a pleasant conversation with the seller or seller's agent, but if you can resist showing your hand, you'll be way ahead. Put on your best poker face and give noncommittal answers.

Some buyers would rather remain anonymous right up until the presenting of their offer. If that suits your style, then don't give your name to agents at open houses and don't sign their visitor register. And ask the agent who is helping you look to refrain from identifying you to sellers until an offer is submitted.

Here are some things you'll want to know about sellers:

♦ Are they truly "motivated," as the agents say, or are they just trying to find out what the market will pay for their house?

♦ Has the seller purchased another house, with a deadline for settling on it?

♦ Why are they selling . . . a job transfer, retirement, need for more (or less) space, divorce, financial setback, health problem, children off at college, death of spouse, or maybe some dissatisfaction with the house or neighborhood?

♦ How long have they lived here? (You can learn this, and also how much they paid for the house, from public land records.)

♦ When does the seller wish to settle, and do they wish to remain in the house after settlement, in a "lease back" from the new owner?

♦ Will the seller consider assisting you in the purchase, by taking back a second trust?

The degree of motivation will determine how the seller prices the house in the first place, and how receptive to price cutting the seller proves to be later on.

You need to ask questions like these, whether the house is being shown by the seller himself or by an agent. If you have hired an agent to represent you, he or she should learn as much as possible about the seller before you present an offer.

Keep in mind that the seller, and especially the seller's agent, will often be coy or less than candid, because everything told to you will make you a better informed, and therefore tougher, adversary in the negotiation that follows.

However, sellers and their agents are required by law to warn buyers of defects in a property that would not be apparent during a routine inspection by the buyer. A seller must reveal a known structural deficiency or building code violation. And some states have gone much further. In California, for example, a seller must provide a prospective buyer with a disclosure statement indicating, among other things, known defects or malfunctions in walls, ceilings, floors, insulation, windows, foundations, electrical and plumbing systems and other structural components.

An agent can't know everything about a particular property, of course. But honest ones will tell you about problems they're aware of, and agents can be held accountable for giving buyers wrong information on something they should make it their business to know about.

If you can, talk with the seller's neighbors in a non-threatening way that doesn't seem to be invading the seller's privacy. For example, you might ask whether any houses have been sold in the neighborhood recently. Then, try to steer the conversation toward information about the sellers, as well as details of selling prices, type of buyers, and how much houses had appreciated since the last sale.

If you haven't already cased the neighborhood, now is the time—before making an offer—for serious study of the condition of the area and the recent sale prices of comparable houses.

IF YOU ENCOUNTER DISCRIMINATION

It is not uncommon for members of racial and ethnic minority groups to encounter overt or subtle discrimination when they go looking for a home to buy.

It can take many forms. A real estate agent may try to steer a black family away from an all-white neighborhood, telling them they "wouldn't feel comfortable there." Or a seller may tell the listing agent not to bring any Hispanic families to see the house, or the seller will not seriously consider a bona fide contract from such a buyer. Or an agent will tell a Jewish home buyer that a house is already sold, when in fact it's still available.

All of these kinds of discrimination are illegal. The federal Fair Housing Law (Title VIII of the Civil Rights Act of 1968, as amended by the Housing and Community Development Act of 1974) has broad prohibitions against discrimination in the rental, sale and financing of housing.

In its application to single-family real estate, the law is most sweeping when a professional real estate broker/agent is involved. But the law exempts from its coverage private individuals who own no more than three single-family dwellings, providing that: 1) a broker is not involved in the sale or rental; 2) there is no discriminatory advertising; and 3) the owner has not sold more than one house (in which he or she was not the most recent resident) during any two-year period. As you can see, many sale-by-owner situations may be exempted from the provision of the federal Fair Housing Law.

But real estate professionals—who handle the bulk of the nation's housing transactions—are covered by strict sanctions against discrimination. Agents and mortgage lenders may not:

1) Refuse to sell, rent, deal or negotiate with a person because of his or her race, color, religion, sex or national origin.

2) Deny that housing is available for inspection, sale or rent when it really is available.

3) Persuade owners to sell or rent their homes by telling them that minority groups are moving into the neighborhood—a practice called "blockbusting."

4) Set different terms or conditions for mortgage financing based on race, creed, religion, sex or national origin.

If you believe you are being discriminated against by a real estate agent or seller using an agent, you should immediately confront the person and demand an explanation. If the expla-

nation is not satisfactory and your suspicions persist, write a
letter about the agent to the agent's employer-broker and send
a similar letter to the local Board of Realtors, if the broker is a
member. See if there is a fair-housing commission in the city,
county or state where you are house hunting, and tell it of the
situation in writing.

Also make a complaint to the Housing Discrimination Division, U.S. Department of Housing and Urban Development
(HUD) (451 7th St., S.W., Washington, D.C. 20410-5500), giving
all the details. HUD may intervene directly or refer the matter to
a state or local agency that administers a law comparable to the
federal statute. The state or local agency is required to begin
proceedings within 30 days and proceed with "reasonable
promptness." Complaints can also be taken directly to a U.S.
District Court or state or local court within 180 days of the
alleged discriminatory act.

CHAPTER 8

DETERMINE YOUR PRICE

◆

YOU KNOW WHAT you can afford to pay. Now decide what you are willing to pay for this particular home. There are several ways to go about this. Some methods are more realistic in slow markets when you have plenty of time to decide, but all require you to gather certain information.

Get an analysis of comparable properties from your assisting agent. There should be several properties on the list. Obviously, no two can be exactly alike, but be sure that those being represented as comparable are similar enough to the property you intend to bid on to be useful in setting an offering price. Look at the date of sale for each case on the list. Under normal market conditions, it should be no more than six months old. Note the location. A similar property in a different neighborhood may not really be comparable at all. The same house on a prime lot in the same block may be worth more because of its location. Examine the physical features of each property. Comparables should be roughly the same age and condition. The size of the lot, the number of rooms and baths, and total square feet of living space should be close.

Finally, the terms and conditions of sale should be scrutinized. A property sold with seller financing does not compare directly with one sold using standard financing. For example, if the seller took back a second mortgage at a below-market interest rate, that's the equivalent of a reduction of the sale price, so you should discount the price of the house when you use it for comparison.

GETTING AN APPRAISAL

If you already know the neighborhood, if you've obtained good comparables, and if you have an adequate sense of the seller's motivations, you may be prepared to make an offer without additional advice. But, if you're not certain—and if time permits, which is not the case in a hot seller's market—consider paying for an appraisal to determine the value of the property.

An appraisal may cost you a few hundred dollars, but weigh that expense against the consequences of paying thousands too much for a home. If your purchase offer turns out to be a lot higher than the appraised value, the mortgage lender may reject your application or at least reduce the amount of the loan. In addition, if price appreciation doesn't make up the difference between what you pay and what the property is actually worth, it comes out of your pocket when you sell.

You may be from out of town and under pressure to find a home quickly. The property may have a big addition that's unusual for the neighborhood, or it may have been on the market too long. In fact, any circumstance that makes a property or a sale unusual calls for a professional evaluation. You can hire a disinterested real estate broker to give you advice on how much to pay, or you can pay an independent professional appraiser for a report.

If you decide on an appraiser, pick one who specializes in residential appraisals. Check on work experience, education and training. Ask several prominent local mortgage lenders for recommendations from their list of appraisers they hire often. (The appraiser organizations listed in the appendix may be able to supply you with lists of their members in your area.)

You will be required to pay for a lender's appraisal before your mortgage is approved, but if the appraiser you hire before making your offer is on the lender's approved list, you may not have to pay for a second appraisal later.

Appraisals are not infallible, even those commissioned by the mortgage lenders. Appraisers can be inexperienced or incompetent. They can be subtly pressured to fudge the numbers so that the appraised value is the same as the full contract price being offered. Lenders anxious to make loans have rewarded appraisers with repeat business when they overvalued. Appraisal departments may find it difficult to resist pressures exerted by the loan production departments of their own institutions.

Whatever the current appraising standards of lenders, the problem for buyers remains. Unless you hire your own appraiser before you submit an offer, your offer may be higher than it needs to be.

If you get your own appraisal and the lender insists on another one by an appraiser of its own choosing, request a copy of the second one, too. You've paid for it, and unless there's some wording to the contrary, you're entitled to have it.

Appraisals vary in complexity. Before you hire an appraiser, tell him or her exactly what purpose the appraisal is to serve, and ask about the fee; both should appear on the final report. One appraisal report commonly used by lenders is written on a standard FNMA form. Depending on where you live, such an appraisal may cost from $175 to $350. It should show how the appraiser arrived at the value and include a list of limiting conditions, pictures of the house and street, a map locating the site and, possibly, a floor plan.

A full narrative report, which may run well over 100 pages, typically would be required as court testimony, or to settle an estate. But it is much more expensive, and it rarely would be needed for routine home purchases.

You cannot use an FNMA report for a VA or FHA purchase, or a VA or FHA appraisal for a conventional loan. A seller who is amenable to VA or FHA financing already may have obtained a conditional commitment, or a certificate of reasonable value, from the VA or FHA, whose appraisals are interchangeable.

ESTABLISH YOUR PRIORITIES

Price always is important, but it may not be the primary factor. Rank the elements of a deal according to your own wants and needs: price, financing, date of possession, extras. Put your priorities down on paper. They will be an important mental tool to employ in evaluating any counter-offer you receive from the seller. Also consider how you might accommodate the seller—at the right price.

◆ For example, if the seller must remain in the house for a period after settlement, what would make that worthwhile to you? Do you need financing help from the seller? Would obtaining a price reduction of several hundred dollars assuage your sense of loss at not having the bedroom curtains included? You probably won't get everything you want, so try to decide in advance what you might be willing to give up in order to complete the purchase, or what you might take in exchange for a feature both you and the seller really want to keep.

NEED SELLER FINANCING?

If your down payment and first mortgage are not enough to swing the deal, you'll probably need seller financing; whether or not the seller is interested in helping you will depend mostly on the condition of the housing market.

Seller financing was common in the late 1970s and early '80s, when market mortgage rates were very high and sellers had to help buyers if they wanted to make any deals at all. But as rates dropped in the mid-'80s, seller financing evaporated.

Because seller-assisted financing ties the buyer and seller together long past the purchase transaction, the seller has a strong interest in the buyer's financial resources, job stability and personal life. As such a buyer, be prepared to supply the seller with considerable detail about your financial affairs; as your prospective creditor, he's entitled to know.

Your need for seller financing will greatly reduce your negotiating strength on the purchase price of the house. The seller will expect a sale price high enough to make up for the below-market interest rate and stretched-out payment. On the other hand, you the buyer will likely be paying back the seller's loan with increasingly devalued dollars.

So if you're looking for seller help with the purchase, don't hold out for a great deal on the sale price, too—unless there are so few qualified buyers in the marketplace that the seller is desperate.

If you think you'll need seller financing, turn to the discussion of the various kinds of "creative financing" in Chapter 10. Bone up on the details before you make an offer.

HIRE YOUR OWN REPRESENTATIVE

This is a good time to get expert help, if you haven't already done so. A buyer's broker or a real estate lawyer you pay will represent your interests, deciphering the contract form, suggesting contingency clauses, and negotiating with the seller or seller's agent.

Get names of experienced lawyers from friends, associates, bankers, title insurance officers and the local bar association. When interviewing, ask for an advance estimate of the fee. Find out what kind of role attorneys typically play in sales for your particular area. What is the charge for reviewing a contract? For being present at settlement? Let the attorney know what you are expecting. Do you want assistance in drawing up a contract? During negotiations? At settlement?

HONE YOUR NEGOTIATING SKILLS

Buyers often are seriously handicapped by their lack of negotiating experience. Many don't realize they may bargain on every element of the deal, and agents don't always tell them. Keep in mind that, as a buyer, you initiate the bargaining, by making an offer to the seller.

Keep a log of the negotiating process. Make note of repairs and replacements that are needed or soon will be. Write down the negative features of the property.

Remember that good negotiating has more to do with knowing exactly what you want from a deal than it does with playing the role of tough bargainer.

If you're going to be doing your own negotiating, here are two current books that address the art of negotiation from the perspective of the homebuyer:

Successful Real Estate Negotiation, by Peter G. Miller and Douglas M. Bregman (Harper & Row).

Home Buyers: Lambs to the Slaughter?, by Sloan Bashinsky (Simon and Schuster).

THE OPENING BID

Whether you should make your highest bid right away or send up a trial balloon in the form of a lower offer depends on how fair you think the asking price is, and how brisk the market is—particularly the market for the property you want.

Many asking prices have a good bit of padding built into the price, to see if someone will take the bait. Don't feel you have to offer the full asking price, or even something close to it, just because that's what the owner is seeking. Offer what you think the house is worth—both in broad market terms and to you in particular—based on your study of comparables or the appraisal. If the owner is offended by a low bid, so be it. You'll find out in their counter-offer or lack of any response when the time limit expires. Conversely, a house may occasionally be priced below market value, because of owner ignorance or a desire to sell fast. If you're the first to spot this bargain, offering the full asking price is fine; but you may find yourself bidding against someone else who offers more than asking price.

Should you decide to try for a lower figure first, don't let the seller's agent know that you are willing to go up. If, during the contract presentation, the seller should ask the agent directly whether you might go higher, the agent would be obliged to answer yes; the same goes for any agent who is not employed by you. Buyers working with the sellers' agent or subagents should keep this reality in mind. "Your" agent is going to get paid only if you buy this house and he or she splits the commission with the seller's agent. "Your" agent wants to get the deal closed, and "your" agent owes primary allegiance to the seller. This person can't represent your interests in the negotiations, so you shouldn't tell him or her what your top price will be or any other major detail of your strategy.

BIDDING ON A SALE-BY-OWNER HOUSE

Theoretically, a given house should cost less if bought directly from the owner, rather than through an agent. And if the deal is structured right, the seller will do fine, too. What the seller wants is the most net proceeds from the sale, so a lower offer that is not reduced by a 6% sales commission should net as much or more for the seller than a higher offer from which the commission is subtracted.

Many sellers will try for a few weeks to sell the house themselves, before listing it with a broker at a slightly higher price. Even after a listing contract is signed by the seller, it may permit the seller to sell the house directly—with no sales commission to the agent—provided the seller finds the buyer himself, with no help from the agent. In either case, you may save by getting the house for a lower price than it will eventually be listed for.

How much lower? Well, it could be a full 6% lower, which presumes that all the savings of the commission will go into the buyer's pocket. More typically, the owner will want to share in that commission savings, perhaps splitting the 6% evenly with the buyer.

PUT IT IN WRITING

Do all your negotiating in writing. Don't telegraph your strategy verbally, and don't make any verbal offers.

A purchase offer in writing can become a binding agreement for both you and the seller. Whether it is called a contract-to-purchase, an offer, binder, or earnest money agreement, and even if it spells out only the terms of the sale, you can be held to that offer once it is signed by the seller.

The first contract you submit should be comprehensive; everything of any importance should be written into it. If accepted by the seller, it may be too late to add anything.

Not suprisingly, purchase contracts used by real estate agents often are written to meet the needs of sellers, not buyers. They may lack even the most customary contingency clauses for the buyer's protection, such as a home inspection, review of contract by an attorney, and requirement that the offer be accepted within two or three days or be void. A preprinted form is a good starting point, but you should amend or modify it in any way that meets your objectives. (If contingencies are typed onto the back of the preprinted form, they should be initialed by the buyer before the contract is submitted to the seller.) Feel free to have your own attorney draw up a contract or make the contract contingent on his review.

A real estate contract-to-purchase generally is assumed to be all-inclusive. It should include the sales price, down payment, legal description of the property and any items being sold with the home; the way title is to be conveyed; the fees to be paid and who will pay them; the amount of deposit; the conditions under which the seller and buyer can void the contract; the settlement date; how financing will be arranged; and so on.

Everything in real estate is subject to negotiation. That means the way you choose to negotiate, the contract form and everything that goes into it.

A well-written contract protects both the buyer and seller. In it, the buyer promises to pay the seller the purchase price only after the seller has shown that he can convey a good title. The seller, in turn, agrees to deliver the deed when the buyer pays for the property.

A SMART-BUYER'S CONTRACT

A purchase contract should make clear every aspect of the transaction. Each clause that makes the whole contract agreement subject to or contingent on its fulfillment is commonly called a "contingency."

Here are some of the major elements and contingencies to be considered for insertion in the contract:

Earnest money deposit. With the exception of court-ordered sales, no law requires buyers to make a deposit of a particular size, or any deposit at all. As a practical matter, however, a seller will look to the deposit as an indication of your earnest intentions. If your offer is accepted, and then you fail to follow though on your commitments, the seller may be entitled to keep the money. The amount of deposit varies with local custom. In some areas, it may run as much as 5% or 10% of the sales price. A seller might refuse to consider an offer that is not coupled with a reasonable deposit. Conversely, a large earnest money check can help swing a deal in your favor.

Most real estate agents expect an earnest money check when they present a contract. You will be asked to make it out to the firm's name or to the managing broker. Add the words "trustee" or "fiduciary agent" after the name on the check as further protection. Never make out a deposit check to a seller.

Find out whether the broker routinely deposits earnest money in a trust account, or with a neutral third party, such as a title company, escrow service or attorney acting as an escrow agent. If not, insert that requirement in your contract. Are you putting up an unusually large earnest money payment? Then stipulate that your money be held in an interest-bearing account and that interest earned will be credited to your side of the ledger at settlement. Your contract should contain a clause requiring all money to be handled in escrow. Private individuals are not answerable to any regulatory authority on how they handle funds while a deal is pending. If it goes sour, you might have to sue to get your money back.

Don't allow your deposit money to be tied up too long. Unless you have plenty of cash, you will need that money to make a commitment to another property if something goes wrong with this deal.

The check shouldn't be deposited until the contract has been accepted; write this clause into the contract. (On the other hand, if the seller has any qualms about your creditworthiness, you can urge him to have the check deposited as proof that it's good.)

If your offer is accepted by the seller, but the purchase falls through later, through no fault of yours, you should get your money back; a clause in your contract should obligate the seller and his agent to return the earnest money within a specified number of days after the contract collapses.

Settlement agent. It's usually the buyer's privilege to select the attorney or title company who will perform the settlement services; write the name into the offer contract. Select a skilled neutral party, to ensure that all the contract's requirements are lived up to before any money is disbursed or the title is passed. If you don't have a particular person in mind at the time you submit your contract, specify that the settlement agent will be selected by the buyer.

Deed and title condition. The buyer's offer should state what kind of deed and the condition of title he or she is willing to accept from the seller. The contract also should make it clear what actions the seller must take to deliver a good title by settlement, and what recourse you have should that not occur.

(Chapter 12 discusses getting a good title at length.)

Prorating. This is a method of equitably dividing continuing expenses, such as mortgage interest, property taxes and insurance, between buyer and seller. Suppose that in January the owner pays the annual premium for a homeowner's insurance policy. The owner then sells the property and goes to settlement midway through the year. What happens to the insurance coverage paid for but not used? In many cases, the new buyer "buys" the remaining coverage period from the owner by arrangement with the insurance company, and payment is made at settlement.

Settlement date and possession. The date of settlement and the date when you will be entitled to take physical possession of your home are stated in the contract.

The settlement date usually correlates with the length of time required for a title search and mortgage approval—typically 45 days to two months. In a busy market, such as during the refinancing boom of 1986, mortgage lenders get backed up, so if the climate is hot, allow yourself enough time. This is especially important if you are planning to sell your current house and need to take that equity to the settlement table on the next purchase. If the settlement is too soon, you'll have to seek an extension from the seller or get a bridge loan. If you're a first-time buyer without a house to sell, and the seller wants a fast settlement, you can oblige and make your offer a little more attractive than that of another buyer who needs a long delay before settlement.

Possession usually occurs immediately after settlement. When a buyer needs to move in before settlement, or a seller needs to remain after settlement, the preferred procedure is to arrange for a separate rental agreement between the parties. Such agreements can have unexpected legal and tax consequences, so the documents involved should be prepared by an attorney and carefully examined before being accepted. Rent can be set at any agreed-upon level; it's often set at a no-profit "wash" level, with the renter paying exactly the total monthly carrying costs on the house—principal, interest, taxes, utilities, and insurance.

Loan conditions. Unless you can swing the purchase without a mortgage, your offer should be contingent on getting a written loan commitment within a specified time, and at terms agreeable to you. State the maximum interest rate and number of discount points you are willing to pay. That way, should you fail to obtain the desired financing, you will be released from the contract, and your deposit will be returned. Once accepted, this clause temporarily takes the property off the market and enables you to shop for a mortgage.

If you went through a prequalifying process, you'll know what size loan and interest rate you will be eligible for, so use those figures on this section of the contract. Don't put down unrealistic numbers—a below-market interest rate or bigger loan than you'll be able to manage; these will raise suspicions and make your offer unattractive compared with others.

Discount points, appraisal fee and other items must be paid in order to get a loan. Your contract should state how these charges are to be apportioned between buyer and seller.

Just because an agent tells you it's customary for buyers to pay all points (one point equals 1% of the mortgage), this doesn't mean you must do so in this case. In many areas it is common for the seller to help the buyer with financing by agreeing to pay a point or so. Because this is equivalent to reducing the sales price, you may get an anxious seller in a slow market to pay more than one point.

Finally, if you're proposing that the seller help you with financing, this is where the terms and interest rate must be spelled out.

Sale of current residence. In a slow market, individuals trading up to more expensive homes may be nervous about committing themselves to the next purchase without assurance that they will be able to sell their current house. To lessen their risk, they add a clause in the purchase contract enabling them to back out of the deal if they don't get a viable contract on their current home within a specified period of time. Sellers are justifiably leery of this kind of contingency, and a contract containing it will be far less desirable than others.

Response time limit. Your contract should require the seller to accept the offer *in writing* (not verbally) within a certain time— such as 48 hours—or the offer will be void. How long depends on market activity in general and likely buyer interest in that home in particular. Failure to state a time limit invites having your contract "shopped." That means that the seller or agent may use your offer to stimulate slower-moving buyers to top your offer.

You are free to withdraw and cancel an offer at any time before the seller has accepted it and you have received "notice" of that acceptance in accordance with the terms set out in the contract.

The phrase "time is of the essence" should be included to emphasize the time limit on the offer and the closing date. This does not prevent you or the seller from obtaining a mutually-agreed-upon extension, but it precludes it from being available unilaterally on demand.

Home inspection. This contingency clause gives you the right to have the property inspected, and to withdraw your offer if the inspection report isn't satisfactory for any reason. The clause may also contain language that will let you negotiate price adjustments to pay for any necessary repairs. (See Chapter 9 for more information on home inspections.) Normally, you will not be granted a lot of time, because sellers and brokers regard this as a gaping loophole. Buyers with second thoughts may use the report to get out of a deal, so don't be surprised if your seller insists that the inspection be done within a week by a recognized professional. The seller also may request a copy of the report, and that request should be granted.

The critical portion of a typical inspection clause reads: "This contract is contingent on a property inspection report which, in the sole judgment of the purchaser, is deemed satisfactory." You can see that a contingency clause with that kind of wording leaves a loophole as big as the house itself.

If necessary, offset the negative impact of this clause with a larger earnest money deposit, or some other bargaining chip that will impress the seller with your interest in the property.

Most real estate contracts allow the seller to determine the period in which the inspection must be completed. Normally this is no fewer than three and no more than ten days from the date of the contract. If you have not already lined up an inspector or are uncertain about how to find one who is reliable and competent, try to negotiate with the seller for as much time as possible.

Radon test. You may want to include a clause requiring that the property be tested for radon by a company approved by the state's radiation-control or radiological-health office. (See Chapter 18 for information about what the seller might provide.)

Termite inspection. Many contracts require the seller to order and pay for a termite inspection. Look for or insert language that will permit you to void the deal or negotiate with the seller for extermination and repairs should termites, or damage, be found.

What goes with the house. There could be a clause specifying that certain curtains or special-sized rugs or furnishings be included in the deal. It's customary for the seller to leave all major appliances and all built-in things that would normally be construed as part of the property, such as lighting devices, wall-to-wall carpet, built-in bookcases, and outside landscaping. But custom varies from area to area, so you'd better be specific. The more things spelled out in the offering contract, the fewer the later misunderstandings.

Condition of house at settlement. Specify that everything in the house will be in demonstrable working order at the time of settlement, as verified during a walk-through of the premises a day or so before settlement. This includes mechanical systems like heat, plumbing, kitchen appliances, etc. Note that this is not a guarantee that these things will continue working after you buy the house—just that they are functioning properly at the moment you take title.

If there are exceptions, insert them in the contract. Indicate which appliances, if any, are being conveyed "as is," with no guarantee made as to working order. It may be impossible to test the air conditioning during the winter, so allow for a test to be done as soon as temperature permits.

As for cleanliness, specify that the house will be empty of all stored objects and debris (including things in the attic, basement and garage) and will be handed over in "broom-clean" condition.

Other conditions. The list could go on, but every condition runs the risk of making your offer more complicated and less appealing than someone else's cleaner contract.

PRESENTATION AND COUNTER-OFFER

At this point, your offer—signed and all clauses initialed—is presented to the seller, either by you, your attorney, the seller's agent, or the agent who has been assisting you.

You may bolster the appeal of your offer by providing evidence of your creditworthiness. Just as important as the terms of the contract—perhaps more so—is your ability to get a loan and get to settlement. The seller will be asked to take his property off the market while you arrange financing, so the seller's confidence in the your financial strength will play a big role in whether the seller accepts your contract or a rival bid.

The financial statement doesn't have to have a lot of detail, but it should include information about employment, current homeownership, etc. If you have prequalified for a mortgage sufficient to swing this deal, point that out, along with the name of the prequalifying firm. This information can be verified by the seller or the agent.

If the seller accepts everything in the contract, initials all clauses and signs the contract within the acceptance date specified, the offer becomes binding on both parties, subject to removal of contingencies such as inspection, financing, etc. Rejection of even the smallest provision of the offer is a rejection of the entire thing. If, however, the seller wishes to negotiate, a counter-offer is made.

The counter-offer typically takes one of three forms: a fresh purchase contract is made out that is identical to the buyer's offer except for the seller's changes; a counter-offer is written on the back of the original, or on a separate sheet of paper, accepting the buyer's terms with certain changes as stated; or the seller marks out on the original offer the unacceptable items and notes the proposed substitution above or below, initialing each change. A time limit to accept is noted, and the counter-offer is then dated and signed by the seller.

This is delivered to the buyer. If it is acceptable it is signed and dated, and the contract is complete. If not you can allow the counter-offer to expire or you can make a second offer. Have a new contract written out. Marking over and initialing extensively on a document can lead to confusion and mistakes.

Sometimes, negotiating goes on for days: offer, counter-offer,

offer, counter-offer. More commonly, an agreement is reached on the second or third offer.

If the seller has other contract offers besides yours, he will try to play one against the other, often with verbal messages. Sometimes a seller or seller's agent will not formally counter a contract in writing, but will merely tell the prospective buyer that the offer is "too low," promising acceptance if it is raised. Do not respond to such verbal signals; the seller has made no commitment to you, and you have no assurance that you'll get the house *even if* you raise your bid. The seller could change his mind again and keep trying to jack up your bid.

Instead, remind the seller that you have a formal offer on the table and you would appreciate a written counter-proposal, stating whatever higher price or other changes would make your offer acceptable. If the seller responds to your offer in writing, you're still in the ballgame. You can accept the seller's counter offer and nail down the deal; or counter again; or let the response time lapse. Your strategy should be to keep the seller involved with you alone until your negotiaton has run its course. Remember that the seller can give a counter-offer to only one buyer at a time. To do otherwise is to run the risk that both parties will accept.

How much you bend will depend on how much you want this particular house, which is a function of whether you have to buy quickly, the state of the market, and how unusual this house is. If you have the luxury of time, and houses similar to this one come on the market with some frequency, don't despair if negotiations break down.

Stick to your main objectives, whether price or some other point. If this house gets away, you may have a shot at a similar one later; it's not unheard-of for a house hunter to put in unsuccessful contracts on two or three houses before finally buying. You may even have another chance to buy the first house later on—possibly at a lower price than you originally offered; by the time the seller wises up to his overpricing, the other interested buyers may have bought other houses, leaving you as the only bidder.

If your offer is accepted by the seller, or if you accept the seller's counter offer, the agreement becomes a binding contract. Be aware that should you change your mind after your contract offer is accepted and signed by the seller, you could legally lose your deposit and even be liable for damages for failure to live up to your contract.

Likewise, if the seller simply backs out, you can sue for damages or try to enforce the contract terms. This sometimes happens, especially in a hot market, when a much better offer comes along after the seller has accepted yours.

If the seller dies before settlement, the contract should be binding on the late seller's estate, which must proceed with the sale of the house to you, but you may need an attorney's help to assert your claim and keep the process on track.

BRIDGE LOANS: BUY NOW, SELL LATER

If your contract is contingent on getting a bridge loan, don't delay arranging one. While loan approval can come as quickly as a week after you apply, the closing may take another two weeks. And the process could drag on longer if the lender insists on appraising your present home.

Many lenders consider bridge loans risky propositions because of the uncertainty of whether the old house will sell, the time it might take to sell, and whether you will be able to get a price high enough to cover the bridge loan repayment.

It's much easier to get a bridge loan if your current house is already under contract and you're well along in the application process for permanent mortgage financing on your new home. In this case, you need the bridge loan just to make your original settlement date, if there is a processing delay in the mortgage application.

A bridge loan, also called swing, equity-advance or gap loan, is often structured as a balloon note, with the principal and interest due at the end of the term (six months is typical) or when your old home sells, whichever comes first. Some lenders require monthly or quarterly payments on interest.

The interest rate is often one to two percentage points above the prime rate at the time the loan is closed. Another pricing plan bases the interest on a rate somewhat higher than the prevailing rate charged for regular mortgages. Closing costs usually range from 0.5% to 1.5% of the amount borrowed, depending on whether the lender requires a title search, title insurance, credit report or appraisal.

The three most likely sources of these loans are commercial banks, savings and loan associations, and relocation companies that are hired by firms transferring employees.

Often banks aren't keen about lending this money to any but their preferred customers. If you don't fit that description, your real estate agent may be able to turn up a lender.

If you're moving out of the area, your best hope lies with a bank at your current location. Lenders prefer to do business locally—where they have some knowledge of the real estate market.

You may be able to work out a more attractive bridge loan if you're being transferred by your company. Many companies reimburse employees for the interest paid on bridge loans. A large number act as lenders themselves or contract with a relocation company to do so.

CHAPTER 9

HAVE THE HOME INSPECTED

◆

$\mathbf{Y}$OU'VE MADE an offer, haggled over the contract, and a deal has been struck. Now is the time to let a home inspector give you an objective look at the current condition and potential problems of the house or apartment you're buying.

Remember that a purchase agreement with an inspection contingency clause allows you to void the deal based on the findings of the inspector, and if something very alarming turns up—such as serious structural defects—you may want to forget this property completely. Or you may decide to void the first agreement and submit a revised contract with a lower price reflecting the cost of correcting the problems—or one which offers the same price on the condition that the seller will make repairs at his expense.

In a brisk seller's market, the seller might not want to accept your new lower offer or agree to make the repairs your inspection deems necessary, even if he acknowledges that the house has problems. Why? Because he may have recently received a much better offer than yours, and he's delighted that you have voided the first agreement. Even if he eventually has to correct the problems as a condition of sale, he'll still come out ahead selling to the second bidder.

FINDING A GOOD INSPECTOR

Ask friends, your attorney, real estate agents and lenders for recommendations. Home inspection services may be listed in the Yellow Pages under "Building Inspection Services," "Engineers (Inspection or Foundation)" or "Real Estate Inspectors." By any name, the professional you want is one who knows old homes and new, inside and out, who makes a living poking into cellars and attics and crawl spaces looking for structural and equipment flaws, and who then gives clients detailed written reports that take much of the gamble out of home buying.

For more information about the inspection process, look for these books:

◆ *Buy Smart! The Complete Home Buyer's Guide to Residential Evaluation*, by R. Edward Brown (McGraw-Hill); a do-it- yourself manual and workbook.

◆ *The Complete Book of Home Inspection*, by Norman Becker (McGraw-Hill).

◆ *Inspection of a Single Family Dwelling*, by Sol Sherman (American Association of Certified Appraisers, Inc., Cincinnati, OH).

Satisfy yourself that the inspector you're hiring is professionally independent, not beholden to the real estate agent and not primarily interested in promoting a particular repair or remodeling business. Home inspectors' experience in the building field usually comes from a background in contracting, architecture or engineering.

Inspectors who are members of the American Society of Home Inspectors (ASHI), have agreed to abide by a written code of ethics and by prescribed standards of practice designed to protect prospective buyers. You can get names of ASHI members doing business in your area by writing to ASHI at 3299 K St., N.W., Washington, D.C. 20007.

There are also several state associations, among them:

◆ California Real Estate Inspection Association, 1100 N St., Suite 5D, Sacramento, CA 95814;

◆ Florida Association of Building Inspectors, P.O. Box 149202, Orlando, FL 32814;

◆ Texas Association of Real Estate Inspectors, Inc., P.O. Box 50153, Austin, TX 78763.

THE COST

Fees for inspecting homes generally vary according to contract price and geographical area, and sometimes with age, size and construction of the house. Assuming the home you are interested in is a fairly typical residential property, you might expect to pay anywhere from $150 to $300. Inspections in large metropolitan areas with more-expensive homes, such as New York and San Francisco, may cost more.

An inspector may charge one fee for all homes under $150,000, for example, and bill for inspecting those over that amount on a sliding scale according to price. ASHI members may provide a radon inspection, on request, for an additional fee of $75 to $100. Inspecting very new or very old homes may take more time, which is in turn reflected in the charge. And inspections on Sundays, holidays and after-hours also are likely to command premiums, as may those that require long-distance travel.

THE INSPECTION

A thorough home inspection normally takes three hours or more. Most inspectors encourage buyers to accompany them. Arrange to do so and come prepared to ask questions and to get dirty. If the house has a crawl space, get down with the inspector and see whether routine maintenance chores in that space will be within your capacity.

Let the inspector know whether or not you are handy with a pipe wrench or know something about carpentry so you can get an on-the-spot estimate of repair costs. Provide information about family size and habits. A water heater that is adequate for four people may be inadequate for your foursome if everyone showers in the morning and then again after soccer and jogging in the evening. (A formula used by one inspector when calculating demands on a water heater counts a teenage girl with short hair as one person, a teenage girl with long hair as a person and a half, and a teenage boy as two.)

THE REPORT

What you are really after is a written report covering the

structure from basement to roof. The report should include an assessment of the quality and condition of all the following parts of the house or property:

♦ Grading, drainage, landscaping, fences, paved areas, retaining walls, recreational facilities, garage;

♦ Exterior walls (possibly including insulation), doors, windows (including storm and screen), porches and decks, steps;

♦ Roofing materials and construction, vents, hatches, skylights, gutters, downspouts, chimneys;

♦ Crawl space or basement—construction, structural stability, settlement, water penetration, termite or rot damage;

♦ Attic—access, ventilation, insulation, signs of leakage, fire safety;

♦ Electrical system, including capacity, grounding, fuses or circuit breakers, wires, outlets and switches, safety of all parts of the system;

♦ Plumbing system—pipes, drainage faucets, water heater, laundry appliances, sink traps, water pressure;

♦ Heating and cooling systems—type, capacity and condition, distribution of sources of heat and cooling, controls, humidifiers, fire safety;

♦ Kitchen and bathrooms—fixtures and appliances, plumbing, ventilation, tile, flooring.

If the property has special features you want inspected—such as a swimming pool, tennis court, well or septic system—you may need to hire a specialist. If you are having the home inspected in the depths of winter, some testing may have to be postponed until a thaw; look to the wording of your contract to ascertain what obligation the seller will have at that time.

An inspector may use checklist-type worksheets covering the structure from basement to roof, adding brief remarks as necessary, or he may present a write-up of the overall condition of the property, along with suggested repairs and improvements.

The report should indicate current problems as well as those that may be impending. For example, the original wiring in homes built before World War II is usually not up to handling today's major electrical appliances. The inspector will make a note of such a shortcoming and give you some idea of what is involved in bringing it up to standard.

Whatever the reporting system used, the report itself should give you a realistic idea of what you have offered to buy. This gives you something to study in detail. It also gives you bargaining leverage.

NEW HOMES, CONDOS AND CO-OPS

If you're buying in a development before the house is finished, hire an inspector to visit the model and then inspect the house while it's being built to make sure that the contractor is duplicating the specifications of the model. You'll pay extra for trips to the construction site, but the cost could be a bargain if it saves you from taking possession of a home that is destined to give you headaches.

Many states and local jurisdictions have held that a builder or developer selling a new house must honor an "implied" warranty on the basic components and systems of the house. But if the problem is a major one and high cost is involved, don't expect the builder to make good on such an unwritten warranty without a fight. A comprehensive inspection report, signed by a qualified professional inspector, should constitute good evidence of the way things were before you moved in. (See also the HOW program offered by member builders, discussed on the next page.)

Apartment-type condominiums and co-ops require careful going over by inspectors knowledgeable and experienced about the special problems and considerations inherent in this type of ownership. For one, that means assessing the condition of a large-scale heating plant, common roofs, plumbing, halls, stairs, elevators and pools.

The typical inspection of a single apartment unit would leave the prospective owner with little or no information about the condition of the building as a whole. Remember, once you become a co-owner of this building, you will have to pay your share of the cost of a new roof, electrical system, furnace, etc.

When a building is converted to condominium use, the developer-seller must provide tenants (as prospective owners of units) with an engineering report on the condition of the building. Make sure you get a copy and have an inspector go over it before buying a unit. In addition, a tenant association or condo owners' association may commission its own engineering report; get a copy of that, too.

If an earlier report said that major work was required or advisable, find out if the work has been performed already or if it still lies ahead—at your expense; and find out if the work was paid for out of a reserve fund or by special assessment.

If you feel you need additional study of the building's condition, consider hiring the same engineering or inspection firm that did the earlier study, on an hourly basis. The re-inspection might take two or three hours and cost $100 to $200 per hour—a lot of money, but not so much when weighed against your share of the cost of major repairs to a large building.

BACK TO THE SELLER?

When a seller hears that a qualified inspector has found that the roof needs repair or that the hot water heater has already outlived its normal lifespan, he may agree to make repairs or replacements. If not, perhaps you can knock down the price to cover the cost of having the work done yourself.

What if something catastrophic is discovered? Perhaps the floors are heaving or the foundation is settling, causing cracks in the interior walls. At this point price may no longer be the object, and you may want out. If the deal is contingent upon a satisfactory inspection, and the contingency is written into the offer to buy the house, you'll be legally off the hook.

HOW TO AVOID THE NEW-HOME BLUES

If you live in a state that does not have strong warranty laws, and two or three years after buying a brand-new home, you face major expenditures caused by a faulty foundation or fireplace that's separating from its supporting wall, you may find that your dream house has turned into a nightmare.

Add to your woes the possibility of a lengthy, expensive court battle and you'll see the appeal of buying a home protected by the Home Owners Warranty Corporation or one of it's compet-itors. Home Owners Warranty Corporation (HOW) is an inde-pendent company owned by its member-builders.

HOW provides ten years of protection against major construction defects. If one of its 12,500 member-builders refuses to fix such a mistake, insurance covers the repairs. A built-in dispute-settling process determines the outcome when buyer and builder can't agree, and since 1974, when the program began, some 45,000 buyer-builder disagreements have been resolved out of court.

What It Costs, What It Covers

HOW policies can't be purchased on the open market but must be obtained through an active HOW member-builder. A builder pays a one-time premium averaging $1.80 per thousand of a home's selling price. Thus, a builder would pay about $180 for warranty coverage on a $100,000 home.

During the first year, HOW builders warrant their new homes against defects in workmanship and materials, major structural defects and flaws in the electrical, plumbing, heating, cooling, ventilating and mechanical systems.

During the second year, builders continue to warrant against major structural defects (such as a load-bearing wall), and against electrical, plumbing, heating, cooling, ventilating and mechanical systems breakdowns, but no longer cover defects in materials and workmanship.

If, during the first two years, a builder defaults on the terms of the warranty or goes out of business, claims are paid through the insurance portion of the warranty.

In the remaining eight years of protection, each HOW builder carries insurance against major structural defects. HOW covers the cost of all authorized repairs after the owner pays the first $250. This $250 deductible applies to each claim.

Another important feature of HOW protection is that it stays with the home for a full ten years regardless of how often ownership may change—a factor that may enhance resale value.

Hashing Out Disputes

When a buyer and a builder reach a stalemate over warranted items, either may request HOW to appoint an impartial third party to mediate, at no cost to the buyer. Referees for such disputes have no affiliation with either HOW or the construction industry and are trained by the independent National Academy of Conciliators.

If a mutually acceptable solution cannot be reached, the neutral party decides on the issue, based on the warranty documents. The builder is bound by the decision once it is accepted be the homeowner. A still unmollified owner, however, is free to reject the arbitrated settlement and go to court. The builder has the right to appeal, but ultimately must comply with the decision or be subject to expulsion from HOW ranks.

Most homeowners—some 82%—come away from the program's mediation process accepting the mediation results. Accepting a decision and being satisfied aren't necessarily the same thing, however. According to the National Academy of Conciliators, which provides mediators for the majority of HOW disputes, one source of dissatisfaction comes from not fully understanding what the warranty covers. Owners have the documents but they don't spend sufficient time reading them.

Another problem is that HOW has no authority to get tough on delinquent builders, except by expelling them from the program. An expelled builder is still free to go on constructing homes unless local or state regulatory bodies decide to take action.

HOW is the first and largest home warranty provider and its builders operate in every state except Alaska. Still, a HOW builder is not always easy to find. You can get a list of members by writing to HOW, Box 1214, Malvern, PA 19355, or by calling 800-225-5469.

Home Buyers Warranty, HOW's largest competitor, enrolls some 10,000 builders around the country. You can obtain a list of their members by writing to Public Affairs, HBW, 3774 La Vista Rd., Tucker, GA 30084.

PICK THE RIGHT MORTGAGE FOR YOU

◆

ONCE THE contract has been signed and the inspection contingency has been removed—usually within a week of signing—start shopping for financing as soon as possible (unless you're the rare buyer who doesn't need a mortgage). You must get loan approval in time to go to settlement with your mortgage money, and processing backlogs can force a delay of settlement or the necessity of a bridge loan.

Shopping around for the best mortgage can yield dramatic dividends, both in the short run (in "points" paid or saved) and especially in the long run. A difference of one-half percent in the annual percentage rate on a 30-year mortgage can mean thousands of dollars saved or spent needlessly. Paying 9.25% instead of 9.75% on a 30-year, fixed-rate $90,000 loan will save the prudent buyer about $33 each month. That may not seem so dramatic, but, over 30 years, it amounts to almost $12,000, not counting potential earnings if the monthly savings were invested over the years.

If you went through the prequalifying process before your house hunt, you have a head start on the mortgage hunt, in terms of having all your documents in order and knowing that you'll probably qualify for a certain size and kind of mortgage. If you prequalified with a given lender, you can continue to deal with that firm, but by no means should you stop there.

The message of this chapter is simple: *shop for a loan, not a lender.* Mortgage lending is a mechanical, impersonal process, and it's highly competitive. You should hunt for the best loan—interest rate, points, processing costs, and in the case of adjustable mortgages, the most favorable adjustment features; you shouldn't pay much attention to what firm lends you the money, the kind of financial institution it is, whether you have a prior relationship with the lender, or even what city or state it's in. You can often deal as easily with an out-of-town lender as one in your community. The odds are your loan will be sold on the secondary market once or several times over the term of the loan, and the firm that services the loan—that is, collects the payments and holds your taxes and homeowners insurance in escrow—may change, too.

The next chapter explains how to shop for a mortgage—which lenders make mortgage loans and how to use a mortgage reporting or finding service. But before you go into the market, try to decide what kind of loan suits your particular needs best; that's what this chapter is all about.

Learn the pros and cons of fixed-rate and adjustable borrowing. Get acquainted with the jargon of the mortgage business. A check list of the major characteristics of your ideal loan will enable you to do a lot of your shopping by phone. Then you can ask lenders the right questions and intelligently compare the many confusing offers that they'll put forward.

THE BASICS

In essence, there are two ways that mortgage lenders charge you for the use of their money: through the interest charges you'll pay each month over the life of the loan, and in "points," a one-time sum of money (one "point" equaling 1% of the loan amount) that you'll pay up front.

Compare interest rates by asking for the true annual percentage rate (APR) of the loans you're considering. There are many ways to state interest rates, but APR, which includes the cost of points and other fees such as mortgage insurance, is the standard form. Lenders are required by law to give you this figure.

Points are prepaid interest charges that raise the effective yield to the lender without raising the interest rate on the note. Points discount the value of the loan to you. If you pay $1,800 (two points) in order to borrow $90,000, you really have borrowed only $88,200. But you will have to pay back the full $90,000 face value of the loan, plus interest.

The payment of points to the lender is a standard part of the mortgage business, and they are factored into any calculation of annual percentage rates on mortgages. As a general rule, the payment of one point is equivalent to an additional ⅛th of one percent on the interest rate of the mortgage, over a 30-year loan. So the APR of a 10%, 30-year, fixed-rate mortgage with no points is equivalent to the APR of a 9% loan with eight points.

In reality, you'll never find a lender charging eight points, since that amount of prepaid interest would scare off all but a few affluent borrowers who know they'll own their homes for many years. In fact, most homeowners sell or refinance their homes long before their mortgages are repaid fully, so they wouldn't want to prepay that much interest. Consequently, the point differential between a 10% loan and a 9% one is more likely to be about three points.

Points on the buyer's loan are often shared between the buyer and the seller, with the seller paying something to help swing the deal. The sharing of points, like everything else in a purchase contract, is open to negotiation. In addition to points, many lenders charge an "origination fee, often calculated at 1% of the loan amount. Don't confuse the origination fee with the separate loan application fees you'll pay to cover the paperwork and approval of your mortgage. Application fees are not tax deductible, but an origination fee, which is a charge for the use of borrowed money, clearly is.

In some cases, the origination fee is labeled a "prepaid point," because it's a prepayment of one of the discount points to be charged at settlement or closing. If, for example, a mortgage calls for a buyer to pay three points (3% of the loan amount) at settlement, a credit will be given for the 1% origination fee the buyer paid when he applied for the loan, and only the remaining 2% will be collected at settlement. For a discussion of the tax implications, see Chapter 3.

FIXED OR ADJUSTABLE RATE?

After all the exotic mortgages are laid aside, the big choice for most homebuyers comes down to a fixed- or adjustable-rate mortgage.

The standard fixed-rate, fully amortizing mortgage—with the same principal and interest payment each month over the life of the loan—came into existence during the Great Depression and fueled the enormous expansion of affordable home ownership in the three decades that followed the end of World War II. Its beauty was—and still is—the peace of mind that homeowners get from predictable monthly payments. While taxes, utilities and other costs of homeownership may rise, the principal and interest payment remains the same. But if interest rates fall, the holder of a fixed-rate mortgage must refinance at a lower rate to get any benefit.

Lenders who made loans at fixed rates took a beating on the value of those loans when inflation and interest rates soared in the late 1970s. If they kept the loans, they had to settle for repayment in ever-devalued dollars. If they tried to sell the loans, they had to discount the value to reflect current and rising interest rates.

The increasing reluctance of lenders to make fixed mortgage loans in a climate of rising interest rates led to the creation of adjustable-rate mortgages (ARMs), under which the rate rises and falls with current interest rates charged throughout the economy. With an ARM, the borrower, not the lender, is assuming the risk of rising rates. But the borrower will benefit from declines in rates, too.

At one point in the early-1980s, when fixed-rate loans carried high interest rates, more than two-thirds of all new mortgages were adjustable-rate loans. As inflation and nominal interest rates declined in the mid-1980s, homeowners with high fixed-rate mortgages rushed to refinance; so did lots of homeowners with ARMs, because, although their payments were getting smaller, they wanted to lock in low fixed rates, rather than take a chance on a resurgence of inflation.

But as fixed-rate loans dropped into single-digit territory, the adjustable lost its appeal. By the spring of 1986, ARMs accounted for less than one-quarter of all new mortgages. (Unlike back in the 1970s, however, fixed-rate mortgage lenders are no longer shouldering the risk of rising interest rates all by themselves. They're passing the risk on to the investment community, by reselling their mortgages in the secondary market.)

So, what's best for buyers today? Conventional wisdom would have buyers lock in low interest rates with a fixed-rate loan when it looks like interest rates will be heading up over the next few years. If it's thought that rates will go down or stay about the same, an adjustable-rate mortgage should be considered.

For some buyers, especially those who can't count on rising income in a time of high inflation, a fixed-rate mortgage is safer. For others, a one- or three-year adjustable mortgage with rate caps is worth careful consideration. ARMs are especially attractive if you intend to own your home for less than five years and the current spread beween fixed-rate mortgages and the starting rate on the ARM is two percentage points or more.

Don't accept an ARM without annual and lifetime caps on interest rates; typical caps today are no more than a two-percentage-point hike in interest rate from one year to the next and no more than a five- or six-point increase over the starting rate at any time during the term of the loan.

FIXED-RATE LOANS

Fixed-rate loans offer an interest rate that does not vary during the life of the loan. In a traditional fixed-rate mortgage, the monthly principal and interest payment remains fixed, but the proportion of each payment allocated to principal and interest changes. In the early years, payments go primarily to interest, but as time goes by an increasing amount is used to pay down the balance. So over the life of the loan, interest payments (and tax deductions) dwindle, and equity buildup accelerates.

Long-Term Mortgages

The most customary mortgages are for 20, 25 or 30 years.

Advantages: Certainty is the big plus. You know exactly how much you will be paying for interest over the term of the loan. The monthly payment of interest and principal is fixed, and in the early years consists primarily of tax-deductible interest.

WHAT WILL PAYMENTS BE ON A FIXED-RATE LOAN?

This table allows you to calculate your monthly mortgage payment for each $1,000 of mortgage amount at common interest rates over four mortgage terms of varying length, from 15 years to 30 years. Only principal and interest are included; insurance and property taxes would be additional expenses. To calculate your monthly payment for a new mortgage, multiply the amount in the appropriate column by the number of thousands of dollars involved. Example: For a 30-year loan of $90,000 at 8%, multiply 90 by $7.34. The monthly payment of principal and interest would equal $660.60.

Interest Rate	15 Years	20 Years	25 Years	30 Years
6 %	$ 8.44	$ 7.17	$ 6.45	$ 6.00
6¼	8.58	7.31	6.60	6.16
6½	8.72	7.46	6.76	6.33
6¾	8.85	7.61	6.91	6.49
7	8.99	7.76	7.07	6.66
7¼	9.13	7.91	7.23	6.83
7½	9.28	8.06	7.39	7.00
7¾	9.42	8.21	7.56	7.17
8	9.56	8.37	7.72	7.34
8¼	9.71	8.53	7.89	7.52
8½	9.85	8.68	8.06	7.69
8¾	10.00	8.84	8.23	7.87
9	10.15	9.00	8.40	8.05
9¼	10.30	9.16	8.57	8.23
9½	10.45	9.33	8.74	8.41
9¾	10.60	9.49	8.92	8.60
10	10.75	9.66	9.09	8.78
10¼	10.90	9.82	9.27	8.97
10½	11.06	9.99	9.45	9.15
10¾	11.21	10.16	9.63	9.34
11	11.37	10.33	9.81	9.53
11¼	11.53	10.50	9.99	9.72
11½	11.69	10.67	10.17	9.91
11¾	11.85	10.84	10.35	10.10
12	12.01	11.02	10.54	10.29
12¼	12.17	11.19	10.72	10.48

Interest Rate	15 Years	20 Years	25 Years	30 Years
12½%	$12.33	11.37	10.91	10.68
12¾	12.49	11.54	11.10	10.87
13	12.66	11.72	11.28	11.07
13¼	12.82	11.90	11.47	11.26
13½	12.99	12.08	11.66	11.46
13¾	13.15	12.26	11.85	11.66
14	13.32	12.44	12.04	11.85
14¼	13.49	12.62	12.23	12.05
14½	13.66	12.80	12.43	12.25
14¾	13.83	12.99	12.62	12.45
15	14.00	13.17	12.81	12.65
15¼	14.17	13.36	13.01	12.85
15½	14.34	13.54	13.20	13.05
15¾	14.52	13.73	13.40	13.25
16	14.69	13.92	13.59	13.45

Disadvantages: This stability comes at a price. Interest rates usually run higher than starting rates on adjustable loans. In addition, the down payment requirement on a conventional fixed-rate loan is steep—up to 20%—and you may have to pay more points to get it.

While amortization costs (payments of principal and interest calculated so as to pay off the entire debt within a fixed time period) remain level over the loan term, monthly payments can increase over the years as property taxes and insurance costs go up.

Attractive (that is, low-interest) fixed-rate mortgages usually can't be assumed by subsequent buyers, since lenders want to take every opportunity to replace a low-rate loan with a higher-interest mortgage.

With the regular 20-to-30-year term, principal balance is reduced relatively slowly compared to loans with shorter terms. The total interest cost is high. For example, an $89,000, 30-year, 9.5% fixed-rate mortgage costs $180,409 in interest over its term. A 15-year, 9.5%, fixed-rate loan, on the other hand, has a total interest cost of $78,285—a savings of more than $100,000.

15-Year Fixed-Rate, Fixed-Payment Mortgage

Advantages: The 15-year loan permits you to own your home free and clear in half the time, and for less than half the total interest cost of a 30-year fixed-rate loan. Principal balance is reduced relatively rapidly compared to longer-term loans. Interest rates may be less than 30-year, fixed-rate loans. FHA offers low down payment, 15-year, fixed-rate loans, and the VA offers no down payment guaranteed loans.

Disadvantages: Higher monthly payments make these loans more difficult to qualify for than longer-term mortgages. You are locked in to making monthly payments roughly 15% to 25% higher than for comparable 30-year loans; this may limit the number of homes you would be able to afford. On an $89,000, 9.5% note, monthly payments would be $929 for 15 years and $748 for 30 years—a difference of more than $180.

The principal balance is paid off relatively rapidly compared to longer-term loans, thus reducing total mortgage interest payments—and the tax shelter benefits of homeownership.

HOW A 15-YEAR LOAN SLASHES INTEREST COSTS

The total interest cost of a 15-year fixed-rate mortgage at 8½% is less than half that of a 30-year fixed-rate loan at 9% on an $80,000 mortgage. (The 15-year mortgage is typically offered at an interest rate about a half-point lower than 30-year loans at any given time.)

Year	Payment Number	15-year fixed rate Payment	15-year fixed rate Principal Balance	30-year fixed rate Payment	30-year fixed rate Principal Balance
1	12	$788	$77,241	$644	$79,453
3	24	788	70,969	644	78,202
5	36	788	63,539	644	76,704
7	60	788	54,738	644	74,912
10	120	788	38,398	644	71,544
15	180	788	—0—	644	63,410

Total interest paid: $61,802 $151,731*

Total interest paid on 30-year loan by end of year 15: $99,330

Biweekly Fixed-Rate Mortgage

Advantages: The biweekly payment schedule of this kind of loan speeds up amortization, reduces total interest costs, and shortens the loan term—usually from 30 years to 18 to 22 years. You make 26 bi-weekly payments—which amounts to 13 annual payments—instead of 12 monthly payments. Conversion to a 30-year fixed-rate is usually permitted. Payments are made automatically from savings or checking accounts.

Disadvantages: Private companies and lenders usually charge for this service. Registration fees up to $500 and biweekly debit charges can make this a costly way to shorten the life of a loan and lower interest costs. The same objectives can be accomplished more flexibly with a 30-year mortgage by making an extra payment or two each year or by applying an additional sum to principal repayment when you make a monthly payment. As with other kinds of rapid-pay-off mortgages, you trade total interest cost reductions for reduced tax shelter benefits.

Growing Equity Mortgages (GEMs)

A fixed-rate GEM features payments that increase each year for a fixed number of years and then level off. Typically, the mortgage is calculated using a fixed 30-year note rate, say 10%. The initial year's monthly payment may be set much lower. Each year the rate is increased to the next predetermined level. Once payments exceed what would be necessary to amortize the 30-year 10% loan, the difference between what that monthly payment would be and the actual monthly bill is applied against the principal balance. That, in turn, cuts the life of the mortgage.

Annual increases are figured either by using a preset schedule—say 5% a year for seven years—or by using an index as a base from which to compute the increase. If, for example, the selected index rose by seven percentage points, a GEM might figure the new monthly payment by using 50% of the seven-point rise. GEMs are not promoted when other mortgages are easily obtained.

Advantages: The borrower saves on total interest costs. Interest rates charged by lender may be lower than for longer-term mortgages. Increases in the monthly payments are applied to principal, and loan term is shortened—most GEMs pay off in 12 to 17 years. Payment hikes can be determined when the loan contract is drawn up if a set schedule is used.

Disadvantages: Buyer's income must be able to keep up with escalating payments. Monthly payments typically are increased annually, but some loan contracts may call for adjustments every six months or two years. While rapid principal repayment lowers total mortgage interest cost, it also lowers the total amount of mortgage interest available as a tax deduction.

Graduated Payment Mortgages (GPMs)

Fixed-rate GPMs start out with low payments, which rise gradually (usually over five to ten years) and then level off for the remaining years of the loan. (See example on page 132.)

Advantages: Lower initial payments enable buyers to qualify for a larger mortgage loan than they otherwise would.

Disadvantages: The big problem is "negative amortization." Because low initial payments are not enough to cover fully the interest due on the loan, the difference is added to the balance, and future interest payments are calculated on the new higher loan balance. As a result, later payments must be higher than they would have been in order to pay off the loan.

If you sell after only a few years, you could wind up owing more on the home than you borrowed in the first place. With a GPM you gamble that appreciation in the value of the house will offset your increased indebtedness. If you hold on to the home for the life of the mortgage, you'll have to pay back the interest you borrowed in the early years—meaning the mortgage will be more expensive in the long run than a fixed-rate loan at the same interest rate without the graduated payment feature.

ADJUSTABLE-RATE MORTGAGES (ARMS)

ARMs may be called variable-rate loans, adjustable-rate loans or adjustable mortgage loans. Whatever the name, they all have in common an interest rate that can change periodically throughout the term of the loan.

The following are characteristics of ARMs; the first four are universal, and caps—both periodic and lifetime—are featured

GRADUATED-PAYMENT MORTGAGES
How they compare with fixed-rate loans

This graduated-payment mortgage for $90,000 at 9½% has a predetermined payment schedule and negative amortization. Monthly payments increase 7.5% every year for five years and then level off for the remaining term of the mortgage. The early payments start lower than a comparable level-payment fixed-rate mortgage, but then gradually catch up to the level necessary to amortize the loan. In this loan the last 25 years would be at a higher payment than a comparable level-payment loan. The monthly payment for a comparable loan on a straight 30-year fixed-rate mortgage (FRM), assuming the same 9½% interest rate, would be $767.77, for a total of $9,081.24 annually. (Lenders typically charge about ½% more for a GPM than a level-payment fixed-rate loan.)

Years	Payment	Difference from FRM	Total paid annually
1	$573.47	$183.30 less	$6,881.64
2	616.48	140.29 less	7,397.76
3	662.71	94.06 less	7,952.52
4	712.42	44.35 less	8,549.04
5	765.85	9.08 more	9,190.20
6–30	823.29	66.52 more for 25 yrs.	9,879.40

After the fifth year this borrower owes $94,230.37, or $4,230.37 more than he did originally. The payment is adjusted every year until the sixth year, when the final adjustment is made. The payment for years 6 through 30 is roughly 9% greater than it would be with a level-payment 30-year fixed-rate loan ($823.29 vs. $756.77).

The convenience of having smaller payments for the first four years does not come cheap:

Total payments on GPM	$286,958.16
Total payments on FRM	272,437.20
Extra cost of GPM	$ 14,520.96

on all adjustable mortgages sold on the secondary market.

1) *Initial interest rate*: The starting rate may be one to three percentage points lower than current fixed-rate mortgages. Lenders will offer the lower initial rate because the risk of higher rates in the future is being shared with, and shouldered primarily by, the borrower.

The starting rate of the ARM may be pegged especially low as a promotional gimmick, totaling less than the sum of the index rate and the added margin (see explanation of these terms below). Don't be taken in by this discounted rate; ask the lender to tell you what your new interest rate (and monthly payment) would be at the first adjustment date, even if the index rate doesn't change at all between now and then. You'll probably be told that the payment will be higher. (See "An ARM That Requires Caution," page 138.)

2) *Adjustment interval*: The changes in the rate to be charged on an ARM loan occur at the end of each adjustment period. ARM adjustment periods are equal in length and repeat throughout the term of the loan. The adjustment schedule is stated in the mortgage contract. Typically it is one, three or five years, depending on the index used. A loan with an adjustment period of one year is called a "one-year ARM," and the interest rate can change once every year; a "three-year ARM" will have its first adjustment three years after you get the loan.

3) *Index*: For each ARM loan, an index is chosen for calculating the changes in the loan rate at the end of each adjustment period. These indexes usually go up and down with the general movement of interest rates. The calculation is based on where the index rate stands at the time your rate is to be recalculated, which is typically one to two months before the anniversary date of your loan.

Among the most popular indexes are the rates on one-, three-, and five-year Treasury securities. Another common index is the national or regional average cost of funds to savings and loan associations.

Some indexes are more volatile than others. In certain circumstances the index with the most rapid ups and downs will prove to be the least expensive for borrowers over the long haul. While it will go up more quickly, it is less likely to "stick" at the high

ADJUSTABLE-RATE MORTGAGES
How payments could go up or down
(Figures in this and subsequent tables supplied by Fannie Mae)

Say you have a $90,000 one-year capped ARM loan at an initial rate of 7½% with an annual cap of two percentage points and a lifetime cap of six percentage points. Here's what the monthly payment would be on a fully amortized loan if interest rates rose 2½% every year and payments are adjusted every year.

Year(s)	Rate and amortization period	Monthly payment	Principal balance at end of period
1	7½% for 30 yrs.	$ 629.29	$89,170.35
2	9½% for 29 yrs.	754.44	88,562.16
3	11½% for 28 yrs.	884.61	88,108.03
4–30	13½%*for 27 yrs.	1,018.36	—0—

Maximum rate due to lifetime cap.

And this is what the monthly payments would be if interest rates dropped ½ of 1% every year for five years:

Year(s)	Rate and amortization period	Monthly payment	Principal balance at end of period
1	7½% for 30 yrs.	$ 629.29	$89,170.35
2	7% for 29 yrs.	599.34	88,189.10
3	6½% for 28 yrs.	570.60	87,040.40
4	6% for 27 yrs.	543.12	85,709.18
5	5½% for 26 yrs.	516.95	84,181.67
6–30	5% for 25 yrs.	492.12	—0—

CHECKLIST FOR COMPARING ADJUSTABLE-RATE MORTGAGE LOANS

Check types and lenders against each other. After you have been prequalified for the amount of money you may borrow, use these forms to compare ARMs. After you have identified the one or two that interest you, compare the terms and costs of several lenders.

Lender name: _____

Telephone number: _____

Down payment required:	_____%
Beginning interest rate (APR):	_____%
Points:	_____%
Beginning payment:	$_____
What is the lifetime cap on the interest rate?	_____%
Is there a periodic cap on the interest rate?	___ yes ___ no
What is the cap?	_____%
How often are payment adjustments permitted?	_____
Is there a cap on the payment?	_____
What is the cap?	_____%
Does loan permit negative amortization?	___ yes ___ no

Relative to the original loan amount, how much negative amortization is allowed? For example, can mortgage balance grow to 105% of original loan, 110%, etc.?   _____%

Loan is tied to which index?
   ___ 1-year Treasury securities
   ___ 3-year Treasury securities
   ___ 5-year Treasury securities
   ___ Federal Home Loan Bank Board (FHLBB) series for closed loans on
   ___ Other: _____

Loan calls for _____	adjustments.
1st adjustment occurs _____	months/years.
2nd adjustment occurs _____	months/years.
3rd adjustment occurs _____	months/years.
Can loan be converted to a fixed-rate?	___ yes ___ no
Under what circumstances?	_____
Cost of conversion option:	$_____
Can loan be prepaid in whole or in part at any time without penalty?	___ yes ___ no
If not, what are the conditions?	_____
Is loan assumable by a qualified buyer?	___ yes ___ no

level when interest rates fall. Thus, the volatile one-year Treasury securities index is ideal for adjustable borrowers when rates are falling.

A drop in interest rates does not automatically lead to a drop in monthly payments. Take a one-year 10% ARM with a 2% annual cap, for example. If the index to which it is tied rises 3% during the first year, the monthly payment will go up when the loan adjustment occurs, and the second-year rate will be 12%. At the second adjustment period, even if the index has dropped by one percent, your payment will remain at 12%.

You should ask what index will be used and how often it changes. Also find out how it has performed in the past and where it is published.

4) *Adjustment margin*: The loan rate and the index rate move up and down together, but they are not going to be the same rate. "Margin" is the additional amount the lender adds to the index rate—the smaller the better. Typically, it is 1 to 3 percentage points, and it usually doesn't vary over the life of the loan. The index rate plus the margin gives you the interest rate on your loan at each adjustment anniversary.

5) *Caps on interest*: Most ARMs today provide for limits or "caps" on rate increases or decreases. When interest rates are rising rapidly, caps protect borrowers from extreme increases in monthly payments.

There are two types of caps. Lifetime caps, required by law on all new ARMs and on assumptions, limit the overall interest-rate increase over the term of the loan. Periodic caps limit the interest-rate increase from one adjustment period to the next. For example, your mortgage contract could provide that even if the index increases 3 percentage points in one year, your rate can go up only 2 points. If you have a 5% lifetime cap, even if the index continued to rise each year, your rate could not increase more than 5 percentage points over the initial rate. In the secondary market, today, purchasers of mortgages typically will buy loans with lifetime caps of no more than 6 percentage points.

Many ARMs offer the possibility that rates may go down as well as up. In some contracts the lifetime caps apply to both decreases and increases.

6) *Caps on payment*: Payment caps limit your monthly payment

increase at the time of each adjustment, typically to a percentage of the previous payment.

Payment caps are not desirable, because they can result in "negative amortization" when rising interest rates would require payments higher than the cap permits. (See discussion above.) When the day for the amortizing payment adjustment finally comes, you could find (assuming that rates have kept increasing during the previous adjustment periods) that the new payment required to repay a larger loan over the shortened remaining loan term is very large indeed.

ARMs with caps on payments are not as common as they were in the late '70s and early '80s, when buyers and sellers were experimenting with every kind of new mortgage product. One reason is that secondary-market purchasers of mortgages have not been willing to buy uncapped ARMs because of their higher-than-average foreclosure rates.

Uncapped ARMs are safest when a buyer has unusually strong earnings security, can be sure of adequate increases in income at the time of the final adjustment, and when equity buildup in the value of homes is being fueled by inflation.

There are three other things you should ask about when you are shopping for an ARM. They are:

1) *Assumability*: Will you be able to transfer the mortgage to a prospective buyer with the same terms? By assuming the mortgage, the buyer takes on the primary liability for the unpaid balance of your existing mortgage or deed of trust against the property. Assumability is quite common with ARMs, because the lender has a more limited interest rate risk.

2) *Convertibility*: Will you be allowed to convert the ARM to a fixed-rate mortgage? Many ARM contracts permit this at predetermined periods—say, after one, three or four years. When you convert, the new rate generally is the current market rate for fixed-rate mortgages. This option means you may be able to lock in a low interest rate in the future. You may have to pay for the opportunity with a somewhat higher initial interest rate or front-end fee when you obtain the loan. In addition you can be charged a special fee at the date of conversion.

3) *Prepayment*: Will you have to pay a fee or penalty if you pay off the ARM early? Prepayment penalties sometimes are nego-

tiable, providing you do so before signing the loan documents. In many cases, however, you will be permitted to pay off the ARM loan at any time, in full or in part, without penalty.

An ARM That Requires Caution

"Discount ARMs" are offered at initial rates below the sum of the index and the margin. This introductory rate extends until the first adjustment period, which is set forth in the contract. Such loans often are combined with large initial loan fees (points), which increases their real cost.

Discount ARMs can cause payment shock. Even if the ARM has a periodic rate cap, it may apply only to adjustments that take place after the discounted rate expires. This means there is no limit to the size of first adjustment. Let's see what happens to payments in such a case:

loan amount: $72,000
index rate: 6.5%
adjustment margin: 2%
regular ARM rate: 8.5% with 2-point annual cap
discount ARM rate: 6.5% with no cap on first annual adjust-
     ment, 2% annual cap thereafter

Monthly payment:
1st-year discount ARM: $455
2nd-year discount ARM: $554

Even if the index rate stays the same, your monthly payment will increase almost $100 in the second year.

Suppose the index rate increases 2%. When the annual adjustment is made, the 2% will be added to the original index-plus-margin rate of 8.5%, making the new rate 10.5%. That will mean an increase of about $200 a month.

You can end up paying more on a discount ARM if the full rate (index plus margin) starts off higher than other standard ARM rates. If your discounted 6.5% ARM carries a full rate of 8.5%, compare that rate to other ARMs currently being offered. Remember, the discount period is relatively short and the full rate will apply during most of the term of the loan. Compare the cost of discount ARMs with standard ARMs by using the annual percentage rate (APR) for each.

Discount ARMs sometimes are called "buy-downs" when the seller pays the lender a lump sum at the time the loan is made in exchange for a lower rate to the buyer. The interest rate on a fixed-rate loan also can be bought down. Buy-downs can be permanent or temporary. The cost of a permanent buy-down frequently shows up as a higher price on the property.

FHA LOANS

The FHA (Federal Housing Authority) insures a wide variety of mortgages, including fixed-rates, ARMs, GEMs and GPMs. The maximum loan amount varies somewhat from one geographic area to another. It is calculated using a formula that takes into consideration the average cost of a home in that area. In 1989, the typical maximum was $67,500, with a $101,250 ceiling in the most expensive areas of the continental United States; the cap was even higher in Alaska and Hawaii. FHA-insured loans often carry an interest rate a bit below the going market rate. The rate no longer is set by the FHA, however, so borrowers will need to shop around for the lowest rate being offered by lenders. And, unlike VA-guaranteed loans, FHA mortgages do not restrict buyers from paying points.

Down payment requirements are lower—usually less than 5%—than those on conventional mortgages not carrying private mortgage insurance. The insurance premium, calculated as 3.8% of the loan, must be paid at settlement. Most buyers handle this by increasing the size of their mortgage by the amount of the insurance and making slightly larger monthly payments. If you prepay your loan, you are entitled to a refund.

FHA lenders qualify prospective buyers using a set of debt-to-income ratios similar to those applied by mortgage lenders making conventional loans. Family housing expenses may not exceed 29% of gross income and total indebtedness may not go over 41% of income. The rules permit lenders to make exceptions where there are "significant compensating factors." Just what those factors are isn't clear, so don't rule out a low down payment FHA loan without checking with more than one major mortgage broker in your area.

FHA loans are assumable by new owners. If the loan is less

than two years old, the FHA will run a credit check on the assuming home buyer, to verify creditworthiness.

Loans carry no prepayment penalty. You can make additional payments at any time during the life of the loan.

FHA loans are available from so-called FHA approved lenders. These include savings institutions, mortgage companies and commercial banks. Mortgage companies carry out the vast majority of FHA originations. Loan applications frequently take longer to process than those for conventional loans.

VA LOANS

The Veterans Administration "guarantees" lenders against losses on mortgage loans taken out by eligible veterans. VA loans are fixed-rate loans with long repayment periods. This may be as long as 30 years and one month. The interest rate usually is lower than conventional mortgage rates, and it is set by the Veteran's Administration.

No down payment is required by the VA unless the veteran is obtaining a loan with a graduated payment feature or the loan amount requested is more than the VA has determined the property is worth. While the VA sets no limit on the size of mortgage it will guarantee, lenders may limit the size of VA loans they make; the maximum portion that VA will guarantee was $36,000 in late 1989.

VA loans can be paid off in full at any time without penalty. There is no penalty for prepaying principal when you make your regular monthly payment so long as the amount involved is at least one month's installment (if the payment due is less than $100) or $100 (if the scheduled loan payment is more than $100).

The VA collects a one-time funding fee of 1% of the loan amount at settlement. This pays for the VA guarantee. (There may be an exception to this for certain disabled veterans.) In addition to the 1% funding fee, veteran buyers cannot be required to pay more than a 1% fee to the lender (usually called a "point" or "origination fee").

Conventional loans, by contrast, impose no restrictions on how points are to be divided between buyers and sellers. VA's limitation saves a veteran money, but it also may narrow his or her choice of homes during periods when lenders are charging several points to make VA mortgages. At such times, sellers may refuse to consider VA contracts once they realize that all points beyond the 1% cap will come from their pockets.

The VA sets minimum construction standards for new homes purchased with GI financing and requires the builder to provide each veteran purchaser with a one-year warranty indicating that the home has been built in conformity with VA-approved plans and specifications. A similar warranty also is required on new manufactured (mobile or modular) homes.

Regional VA offices can provide you with information on eligibility and other details. Look in the phone book under U.S. Government for the VA office nearest you.

OTHER TYPES OF FINANCING

When interest rates are so high that few people can afford a mortgage, how can buyers and sellers of homes still manage to make deals? In the late 1970s and early '80s, they did it with "creative financing"—unorthodox loan arrangements that most homeowners would shun in ordinary times. For the buyer, the seller's interest-rate subsidy provides relief from high market mortgage rates (and perhaps a chance to refinance if rates fall). For the seller, this kind of help to the buyer may make the difference between a sale or no sale. But it entails risks and possible tax consequences to both buyers and sellers not present in traditional mortgages.

Take-Back Mortgage

In this form of seller financing, the seller helps the buyer finance the purchase by taking back a mortgage for part of the purchase price. Take-backs often bridge the gap between the price of the property and the combined amounts of the down payment and first mortgage. The interest rate is negotiated between seller and buyer, and it is sometimes less than the rate on the first mortgage, if the seller is eager to make a deal.

Take-back mortgages can be attractive to sellers who don't need the entire proceeds from the sale right away and to buyers who are trying to work out a contract with terms they could handle. The seller often earns a yield higher than current money market rates—although in a buyer's market, the seller may have to offer a *lower*-than-market rate. As a second mortgage, the seller's loan is protected by a lien against the property, but the claim is subordinate to the primary lender's. If the buyer defaults and a foreclosure results, the second-mortgage holder will get reimbursed only after the first-mortgage holder's claim is satisfied. If the foreclosure doesn't yield as much as the original sale price, the second mortgage holder loses money.

Though payments on seller take-backs may be figured as though the loan would be paid back over a 25- or 30-year period, the loans often are due in full—with a balloon payment—three to ten years after the sale. This means the buyer will have to refinance by that time.

Purchase-Money Second Mortgage

In this deal, the seller agrees to finance part of the buyer's down payment through a second mortgage, usually of three to five years. The primary mortgage lender should be told of such an arrangement, since the payments on the second mortgage may affect the buyer's ability to meet payments on the first.

Wrap-Around Mortgage

This sort of deal involves an existing mortgage plus additional financing to complete the purchase. Say a house is selling for $100,000. The seller has an assumable mortgage with an outstanding balance of $40,000. A buyer makes a down payment of $20,000. He finds a lender, often the seller, who gives him a new mortgage that covers the old loan balance plus an additional $40,000. The buyer makes payments on the wrap-around mortgage to the lender, who uses part of the money to make payments on the old mortgage. The rate on the wrap-around loan is higher than the rate on the old mortgage, and the lender profits from the differential. Thus, by "blending" the rate on the old $40,000 mortgage with the rate on the new $40,000 mortgage, he can afford to offer a rate on the wraparound that is lower than prevailing rates. However, it may be difficult to find a lender for such an arrangement, since most mortgage contracts forbid it.

Land Contract

Also known as a conditional sales contract or contract for deed, this actually is an installment sale. The buyer doesn't get title to the property right away, but must wait until some point agreed upon in the contract—usually years down the road. The 1986 tax reforms impose penalties and restrictions on installment sales. Many sellers who might have considered such a deal under the old rules will find it no longer provides a financial benefit.

Much can go wrong with land contracts. As part of the deal, the buyer may agree to take over payments on the seller's existing mortgage—an arrangement that many mortgage lenders contend violates the "due on sale" provision of their mortgage contract. Lenders may be able to foreclose on such mortgages, leaving the buyer with nothing to show for his payments except a worthless contract. Neither buyer nor seller should draw up a land contract without expert legal help.

Equity Sharing

In a shared-equity arrangement, the home buyer and an investor—frequently a parent, relative or friend, but sometimes a stranger—buy a house together. This is a popular way for first-time homebuyers who otherwise could not afford to buy, or who would not qualify for a mortgage, to do so. For example, rather than making a loan or gift to help a child into homeownership, parents become part-owners and rent their share of the place to the child. As an investor, the parents share in the appreciation of the house. As landlord, they also get rental income and the tax deductions that go along with rental real estate. (For a discussion about the investment aspects of equity sharing, see Chapter 15.)

Both parties enter into a contract that specifies who pays what portion of the down payment, mortgage interest, property taxes and monthly costs, how much rent the child will pay, and how the equity will be split when the house is sold. The parents could pay the down payment and most of the mortgage interest and taxes. Or the equity can be split 50/50, with each party putting up half of the down payment and agreeing to pay half of the expenses. The possible combinations are practically endless.

MAKING A MORTGAGE CHOICE

Deciding which kind of mortgage is best for you requires a close look at your present circumstances, future earnings, and financial goals—not to mention some clear forecasting of economic conditions a few years down the road.

Do you want to put as little down as possible, carrying a big mortgage? Do you want the tax-sheltering effect of large monthly interest payments? Is getting the most house for the lowest possible monthly payment your primary objective, or is equity buildup more important?

For example, a 30-year, three-year ARM with a 2% periodic adjustment cap and a 6% lifetime cap might be a good choice for a couple expecting a job-related move within three to six years. Assuming equal points at settlement, if they can obtain this ARM with an initial interest rate 2 percentage points lower than a 30-year fixed-rate loan, the figures on the next page show how they would fare even with the 2% adjustment at the end of the sixth year.

In this example, monthly payments on the three-year ARM cost about $4,850 less than those on the fixed-rate loan over the six-year period, and our couple has reduced their mortgage balance by $829 more than they would have with the fixed-rate loan. If rates on the ARM increase less than the maximum 2% per adjustment period, savings would be even greater.

Three-year ARMs also can be worthwhile if refinancing calculations show that a lower initial interest rate is needed to justify the transaction costs. If interest rates on 30-year, fixed-rate loans have gone up during the loan application period, a three-year ARM may allow a deal to go through without higher monthly payments, at least initially.

Equity Buildup

If reducing the total cost of your home is a goal, and you aren't too concerned with the reduced tax benefit of shrinking interest payments, consider a shorter-term mortgage, or you can look for a longer-term loan that will allow you to pay off the loan early. On most 30-year mortgages, you can pay ahead on the principal as much as you like without penalty. Simply make

7.5%, 30-year, three-year ARM
$90,000 mortgage

Yr.	Interest rate	Payment	Balance
1	7.5%	$629	$89,170
2	7.5	629	88,276
3	7.5	629	87,312
4	9.5	749	86,583
5	9.5	749	85,780
6	9.5	749	84,898

9.5%, 30-year, fixed-rate
$90,000

Yr.	Interest rate	Payment	Balance
1	9.5%	$757	$89,445
2	9.5	757	88,835
3	9.5	757	88,165
4	9.5	757	87,428
5	9.5	757	86,618
6	9.5	757	85,727

heftier payments on a voluntary rather than mandatory basis. Once you have made your scheduled payment, anything extra is applied to the principal. Making extra payments doesn't mean you can skip a regular payment down the road, however.

If your loan documents allow the lender to charge a prepayment penalty, and you can't get it removed, chances are you'll do better not prepaying, but investing that extra sum elsewhere.

And before embarking on a major campaign of prepaying principal, give some thought to alternative uses of the money. How fast are houses in your area appreciating in value? Will you need that extra money back again? What kind of return on your money can you get these days in fixed-yield investments, stocks, or other kinds of investments? Remember, once you put that money into repayment of your mortgage, it will earn you no current income at all, and you can get it out only by borrowing it back, through some sort of refinancing.

CHAPTER 11

FINDING A LENDER, GETTING A LOAN

◆

AFTER YOU'VE studied the various kinds of mortgages and picked the one that suits your needs best, you're ready to find a lender who will make you the best deal.

As we said in the previous chapter, the identity and location of the lender is less important than the quality of the deal. Back a decade or so, finding a mortgage didn't require much comparison shopping; everything was fixed-rate financing, and rates didn't vary much, so most people dealt with a local institution they already had a relationship with. But things are more complex in today's competitive market.

Fortunately, shopping for mortgages has been greatly eased by the emergence in recent years of mortgage reporting services—firms that survey the major lenders in a given metropolitan area every week or two weeks and publish information sheets on who is offering what loans on what terms. These easy-to-understand grids make comparison shopping a breeze; use them to narrow your choices to a few lenders, and then call the lenders to confirm that a given deal is still being offered.

You can get the names of mortgage reporting services from real estate professionals. Some real estate agents will show you their fact sheets for nothing, but even if you have to pay $20 or so to buy the current sheets from a reporting service, it's still a bargain in time and trouble saved. (See the fuller discussion beginning on page 149.)

If there isn't a reporting service in your area, you can begin the search with your own bank or savings & loan, and real estate agents usually have extensive contacts in the local lending community. The local Board of Realtors probably has surveyed lenders in the community and provides rate information to member agents. Ask them for names of s&l's, banks, mortgage companies and mortgage brokers, but don't depend on them to find you the best deal. For that, you'll have to rely on your own efforts, lots of telephone calls and possibly some old-fashioned legwork.

If you went through a prequalifying process with a lender, of course you'll want to see if that firm is competitive on the kind of loan you want. If so, you'll save some additional paperwork and time dealing with the same company. But don't feel obliged to use their money, and by all means shop around before deciding.

SOURCES OF MORTGAGE MONEY

The major kinds of lenders are discussed below. The lender you choose will take your loan application, follow through on credit checks, property appraisal, and other details, and then disburse funds to the seller in exchange for a mortgage or deed of trust on your property.

Savings Institutions

Savings and loan associations and savings banks originate about half of all first home mortgages. Most are so-called conventional mortgages—those not guaranteed by the Veterans Administration (VA) or Farmers Home Administration (FmHA), or insured by the Federal Housing Administration (FHA).

Most mortgage loans made by savings institutions are sold to investors in the secondary market, through firms like Ginnie Mae and Fannie Mae. So if you want a loan, you probably will be expected to meet secondary-market standards covering appraisals, creditworthiness and down payment minimums.

Mortgage Companies

Mortgage companies make close to a third of all first mortgages and the majority of VA and FHA loans. Mortgage bankers continuously shop for the best available loans by working closely with the secondary market. When you borrow through a mortgage company, the mortgage banker is the lender of record. The company will make a loan commitment to you once your application is approved. Normally, even though your loan will be sold, you will continue to send your payment to the mortgage company after settlement. It also will set up and collect escrow funds.

Commercial Banks

Commercial banks are fairly active in residential lending. Many are affiliated with mortgage companies or operate their own mortgage banking subsidiaries. Banks also are a major supplier of loans for mobile home buyers. These institutions are generally more interested in making a mortgage loan to you if you already do business with them.

Mortgage Brokers

If you are having trouble locating a lender, consider using a mortgage broker. You may have to pay a flat fee for the service, although in many cases the lender pays the broker's fee as part of the total points collected at settlement; often the total points you pay will be more working through a broker than directly with a lender, but not always.

A mortgage broker shops the mortgage market and can refer a prospective borrower to a mortgage banker, savings institution, commercial bank or even an individual investor. Many brokers represent local, regional and national lenders, and may be able to locate a loan program that is not available in your area.

A broker is not the lender and does not approve the loan or make the loan commitment to a borrower. State and local boards of Realtors should be able to give you names of brokers active in a community. If not, contact the National Association of Mortgage Brokers, 706 E. Bell Rd., Phoenix, AZ 85022.

Credit Unions

Close to one-third of all credit unions now make first mortgage loans. You have to be a member of a credit union to get a mortgage from it, and membership is often based on some criterion of affinity—residency in a given city or state, employment, membership in an association or club, etc. Most mortgage loans are made by large credit unions in Massachusetts, New Hampshire, New Mexico, North Dakota, Rhode Island and Wisconsin. If you are already a member of a credit union, or even if you're just eligible to be a member, check out the rates and terms of its mortgages.

Public Agencies

State and local housing finance agencies make below-market-rate financing available to eligible low- and moderate-income, first-time buyers, through the sale of tax-exempt bonds. If you aren't able to locate the correct agency in your state, contact the Council of State Housing Agencies, Suite 118, 444 N. Capitol St., Washington, D.C. 20001, for assistance.

Buyers who cannot get credit from private providers of mortgage funds, but who meet certain income and rural residency requirements, may be able to buy a home through the Farmers Home Administration's rural housing program. Contact the Administrator, FmHA, U.S. Department of Agriculture, Washington, D.C. 20250, for information.

USING A REPORTING SERVICE

Most reporting services provide details on a variety of mortgages, including conventional, FHA and VA loans. Many also include rates on second mortgages and other types of loans. Information provided on each loan indicates the category (adjustable-rate or fixed-rate, for example), the term of the mortgage, interest rate, points, and how long the lender will guarantee the rate you're offered at application time. In the case of adjustable- rate mortgages, information is given on the index base, adjustment margin, and periodic and lifetime caps.

Reports usually are updated weekly, and single reports may

be available for purchase. In addition, many metropolitan newspapers publish a list of rates in weekly business or real estate sections. Often the data is supplied by a mortgage reporting service.

Use the reports and other resources to screen the local market. Then, thoroughly interview the most promising lenders before making mortgage application appointments.

Listed below are several firms that cover lenders in more than one state:

HSH Associates
1200 Rte. 23
Butler, N.J. 07405
(201) 838-3330

HSH surveys more than 2,000 lenders weekly in more than 30 states and many metropolitan areas. A two-issue subscription for $18.00 provides an extensive list of lenders and includes information from each on discount points, down payments, interest rates, annual percentage rate, terms and maximum mortgage amounts. The two-week subscription includes HSH's *Homebuyer's Mortgage Kit*; the kit contains a 32-page booklet, "How to Shop for a Mortgage." The booklet discusses the basics of mortgage financing, the mortgage process from application to closing, how to choose a mortgage that's right for you and the various types of mortgages and features available in the current market. *PC Mortgage Update*, an electronic version for IBM or IBM-compatible PCs, is available at the same price.

Gary Myers and Associates
308 W. Erie St., Suite 300
Chicago, IL 60610
(312) 642-9000

Myers reports mortgage rates weekly for Boston, Chicago, Cincinnati, Detroit, New York City, Washington, D.C., and all of California. A mortgage report for one city, or for California, costs $20. Myers also provides rate information to some 200 newspapers in more than 44 states.

National Mortgage Weekly
P.O. Box 18081
Cleveland, OH 44118
(216) 371-2767

NMW covers the metropolitan Boston, Cleveland, Columbus and Detroit areas. The company surveys about 70 to 80 lenders in each city. Subscribers pay $2.75 per week for one to 12 weeks, or $29.75 for 13 weeks.

Peeke LoanFax Inc.
101 Chestnut St., Suite 200
Gaithersburg, MD 20877
(301) 840-5752

Peeke provides mortgage reports for metropolitan Washington, D.C., including northern Virginia and suburban Maryland. The report lists rates offered by about 100 lenders. The first issue costs $20; reports for additional weeks are $15. Four consecutive weeks cost $50.

FINE-TUNING YOUR CHOICE

After you've selected the lenders who appear to have the best deal on the kind of loan you want, talk with them extensively on the phone or in person, before you apply to a particular lender. Make sure that the advertised terms of the loan are truly being offered. These discussions before applying for a loan shouldn't cost you anything.

Use the annual percentage rate (APR) to compare loans. APR is the cost of your mortgage loan expressed as a yearly rate. It reflects the effect of origination fees, points and (if applicable) mortgage insurance, by adding them to the loan rate as though they were spread out over the term of the loan.

Lenders will often promote a particular mortgage loan by advertising the interest rate or the monthly payment. By law, they also must divulge the APR of the loan and indicate whether the rate is fixed. This disclosure is required under federal Truth-in-Lending laws.

Before you apply, find out how long the currently advertised or stated rate of the loan is being guaranteed after application, if it's guaranteed at all. That is, if you apply tomorrow for a loan at that rate, will the lender assure you in writing that you can have that interest rate at settlement, whether that takes 30 days, 45 days, 60 days or longer?

In fact, many rate quotes are not guaranteed beyond a particular period of time, and some are not guaranteed at all, with the lender reserving the right to charge you whatever rate is generally current in the marketplace on settlement day. If the rate at closing is substantially higher, a buyer could be shocked with ''disqualification'' at the eleventh hour.

One way to lock in a rate is to pay a loan commitment fee—commonly 1% of the loan amount. This locks in the rate you're quoted at time of application as the highest rate you'll have to pay within, say, 60 days. If rates drop during your application period, you'll also be able to take advantage of that.

THE APPLICATION PROCESS

Now you're ready to apply for a mortgage. The application process costs some money—a charge that can run anywhere from $200 to about $350—and it is usually not refundable. Lenders assess it to cover the costs of credit reports, mortgage insurance applications, property appraisals and the like. Because of this cost, you'll want to avoid multiple applications, if possible. Only if you're shaky about the prospects of approval or speed of approval should you waste the fees on more than one application.

If you have paperwork from the prequalifying process, with this or another lender, take along those forms; lots of the information about your finances will be directly transferrable to this application process.

If not, take all the raw material for the application—income and balance sheet figures, plus copies of your last few income tax returns (which may be required by the lender). You should also take the title to your car, which will show it to be free of liens or encumbered by an auto loan.

Be prepared to give the name and phone number of someone who can verify financial information about you—most likely, your employer's personnel office. If you have substantial nonsalary income from investments, you'll be asked to substantiate this through an accountant, stock broker, trust officer, etc. If you are self-employed (a definition that could be triggered by as little as a 5% to 10% ownership stake in a closely held company you work for), you may be asked to submit financial information about the company.

Much of this information will be filled in on application forms during the interview, with the help of a loan officer, but you could also fill it in at home and return the forms.

For conventional loans carrying private mortgage insurance (PMI), check with your lender regarding the necessary documentation.

In addition to the application fee, you may be asked to pay a "loan origination fee" or "prepaid point"—typically 1% of the loan amount—when you apply, before approval is made. This is just another way of charging you prepaid interest, like the additional points you may have to pay at settlement.

Ask what will happen to your origination fee should you decide later to accept a mortgage from another lender. Also, what if the lender decides not to give you the loan—will the 1% origination fee be refunded to you? Get the answers to these questions *in writing* before paying this substantial amount.

Check whether the quoted interest rate is guaranteed, and for how long. If you think that interest rates may rise during the time that your application is being processed, consider paying a loan commitment fee, as discussed above. A useful brochure called *A Consumer's Guide to Mortgage Lock-Ins*, is available free from the Federal Reserve Board, Publication Services, MS-138, Washington, D.C. 20551.

The federal Real Estate Settlement Procedures Act (RESPA) requires a lender to provide you with a "good faith" estimate of closing costs once you complete a loan application or within three business days. The RESPA Statement reflects the lender's experience in the area where your property is located.

The estimate must include costs for such items as points, appraisal fees, title search, title insurance, survey, recording and attorney's fees. You can ask for a hypothetical calculation of such items as property taxes and hazard insurance, based on your anticipated closing date.

PRIVATE MORTGAGE INSURANCE

Lenders usually require buyers getting conventional loans with down payments of less than 20% to carry insurance provided by a separate private mortgage insurance company. The insurance is designed to protect a lender from losses in the event a borrower stops paying on a mortgage loan; premiums are paid by the home buyer.

Insured low-down-payment mortgages are more attractive—and less risky—investments than uninsured ones, and lenders who wish to sell such loans into the secondary market are generally required to have them insured. FHA-insured and VA-guaranteed loans also protect lenders against borrower default.

Insurance coverage is available for conventional fixed-rate and adjustable mortgages. Coverage of second mortgages may be difficult to locate, but at least one company, United Guaranty, Corp. in Greensboro, NC, was writing such policies in 1989.

Private mortgage insurance generally covers the top 20% to 25% of a first mortgage loan. This permits lenders to make loans of up to 90% or 95% of the appraised value of a home while taking about the same amount of risk they would assume in making a loan of about 71% to 72% of value. This so-called loan-to-value ratio (LTV or LV) expresses the relationship between the amount of a loan and the value of the property that will be pledged as security. For example, on a 90% loan-to-value ratio, a borrower makes a 10% down payment and therefore holds the first 10% risk of falling real estate values. The insurer takes 20% of the next 90%, or 18%, and the lender holds the remaining 72%.

Insurance premiums vary from company to company and according to the type of loan being insured. In most cases you will pay an initial premium at settlement and a renewal premium at the beginning of each year. First-year premiums typically range from 0.35% to 1.65% of the mortgage amount depending on, among other things, the loan amount, the size of the down payment, and whether the loan is a fixed-rate or adjustable-rate mortgage. Renewal premiums range from 0.25% to 0.75%.

When the loan is paid down to an acceptable LTV ratio (e.g. 80%), the lender usually has the option to terminate the coverage. However, premium payments are not automatically stopped. Find out at what LTV ratio point your lender will agree to release you from paying premiums and whether or not you will be notified once your loan reaches that level.

CREDIT LIFE INSURANCE

Your lender may try to talk you into buying some kind of credit life insurance that would pay off the mortgage in the event of your death. Even if your lender doesn't offer this to you, you will probably be deluged with mortgage life insurance solicitations after you buy your house.

Mortgage life insurance is a kind of decreasing-term insurance, in which the premium stays the same, but the amount of coverage declines each year, in lockstep with the declining balance owed on your mortgage. It is often promoted as valuable protection for your spouse and children, to keep them from losing the house if the primary breadwinner dies.

Mortgage life insurance does this, but there may be better and cheaper ways to provide the same protection. One problem with mortgage life insurance is that the beneficiary is the mortgage lender, not your heirs. Perhaps your heirs needn't and *shouldn't* pay off the balance on the mortgage, because the original interest rate is much lower than the prevailing rate when they inherit and there is sufficient income to keep making the payments. With mortgage life insurance automatically paying off to the lender, your heirs won't have a choice of how to use the insurance money. They would own the house free and clear, but they may have to refinance, possibly at a higher interest rate, to get their equity out for some worthwhile purpose, like college expenses.

Undeniably, any new homeowner with family to protect should boost his or her life insurance coverage, so that the insurance proceeds—if invested conservatively—would yield enough income to continue paying the mortgage and other basic expenses of living. For a young person, annually renewable term life insurance offers the most coverage for the lowest current cost, even though the premiums will rise each year. Before accepting an offer of mortgage life insurance, shop hard for the best deal in term coverage.

THE WAIT AND THE TENSION

From the time you submit a completed loan application and the appraisal and credit reports are in hand, a lender has up to 30 days to approve your loan request. If the lender turns you down, or refuses to meet your terms, you must be informed of the decision within 30 days. Moreover, the lender must tell you why your application was rejected.

When homes are selling briskly, the time between completing a loan application and the notification of approval from a lender can be all too long. Appraisers and credit bureaus get swamped. Harried mortgage loan officers slip problem applications back into the pile and move on to less troublesome applicants. It's not uncommon for the whole process to take 60 days.

Make sure you haven't been forgotten or put on a back burner. During the process, remind the loan officer of your settlement date and check on how everything is going.

Buyers with impeccable credit records who are able to make hefty down payments can take advantage of a new twist in mortgage lending: "no-doc" loans, so called because buyers do not have to provide the extensive documentation usually required to obtain a mortgage loan. Travelers Mortgage Services touts loan approvals in about an hour, while Citicorp Mortgage offers binding loan committments in as little as 15 minutes. With the latter's Power Plus, your loan information is entered into a personal computer by a local rep—usually a Realtor, builder or mortgage broker. The local PC "talks" to Citicorp's mainframe, which orders up an instant credit report even as it is printing out the necessary loan papers. If everything looks good, you get a legally binding commitment, contingent only on a property appraisal. And that should take about three to four days. Ask about these "no-doc" loans when you shop for a loan, or ask your real estate agent.

You should have assessed how long the application process will take back when you submitted your contract, making sure the settlement date was placed far enough into the future. If you goofed—by agreeing to a settlement that's looming before your loan is likely to be approved—you have a few choices now.

You can ask the seller for a new, later settlement date, explaining that processing delays beyond your control have made it necessary. Most sellers will agree to a good-faith postponement of settlement, and this kind of delay is generally not grounds for the seller to try to void the contract.

Or—if you already own a home—you can keep the original settlement date and go to the table without your mortgage money, instead relying on a hastily arranged bridge loan; this option isn't generally available to first-time buyers. If the bridge loan need not be repaid for several months (or longer), you now have the choice of either waiting for your mortgage approval currently underway, or re-shopping the mortgage and applying to another lender. Generally, all you'll lose is the loan application fees you've already paid.

During the tense wait between application and approval, as the settlement clock is ticking, you're generally at the lender's mercy. But in a climate of falling interest rates, you have some alternatives to chewing your fingernails.

If interest rates have come down since you agreed to a certain rate, remind the lender that they could lose money by delaying your settlement. If their slowness forces you to reschedule the settlement or get a bridge loan to keep the original date, you might be inclined to re-shop the mortgage and shift your business to another lender who will offer a new, lower rate or assure you of faster approval. If this is a real possibility (or even just a persuasive bluff), make sure they know you're considering it; it could motivate the lender to get moving.

THE ROLE OF THE SECONDARY MARKET

Three-fourths of all home mortgages are sold once they have been closed. The buyers—organizations with such names as Fannie Mae, Ginnie Mae and Freddie Mac, as well as a number of private firms—make up what is known as the secondary market.

It acts as a conduit, linking the world of the homebuyer to Wall Street by purchasing mortgages from lenders and reselling them, or securities backed by them, to investors.

Because it is so big, the secondary market affects what loans are available and what buyers have to do to get them.

By selling the loans they originate, savings institutions, mortgage companies and commercial banks get their cash back to reinvest, as well as fees for continuing to service the loans. Buyers, usually government or government-backed agencies or large mortgage bankers, get the right to receive the principal and interest paid by borrowers. They, in turn, package their mortgages and sell securities backed by the pooled loans. Pension funds and other institutional investors are the biggest market for mortgage-backed securities.

The secondary market helps redistribute available mortgage funds by buying mortgages in regions where the demand from homeowners outstrips lenders' deposits and selling them in other markets where available credit exceeds loan demand.

SERVICING YOUR MORTGAGE LOAN

The servicing of mortgage loans—collecting monthly payments, escrowing and periodic payment of taxes and insurance premiums—has become a big business quite separate from mortgage lending. It has also become a headache for many homeowners.

About one-third of all mortgage debt in America is being serviced by companies other than the originators of the loans. Not suprisingly, problems with loan service are common, especially after a loan is transferred from one mortgage company to another.

The new firm may not send you a new coupon book at all, leaving you in the dark as to where to send your next monthly payment. Or it might mess up the computation of your new adjustable-mortgage payment on the adjustment anniversary. Or it might fail to pay your real estate taxes or property insurance premium on time, causing you trouble with the local government or insurer.

If you suspect a problem, try to call the new servicing firm, if you can find its address and phone number; the previous servicing company or the original lender of your mortgage loan should be able to help with this. (If you are facing a possible late charge, the wisest course is to pay up, then dispute the amount you owe.)

If you can't straighten it out, try to find out from the original lender the name of the secondary-market firm—like Fannie Mae or Freddie Mac—that bought your loan. These giant companies, several of which are based in the Washington, D.C., area, have a strong interest in the proper servicing of the loans they buy and resell; they would appreciate learning of problems you're having with servicing firms that do business with them.

If Fannie Mae bought the loan, send a letter to your mortgage company that outlines the problem and send a copy to: Public Information Officer, Fannie Mae, 3900 Wisconsin Ave., N.W., Washington, D.C. 20016. The letter will be referred to the appropriate regional office. For Freddie Mac loans, call or write to the Regional Director of Loan Servicing at the regional office closest to your mortgage company. Regional offices are in Arlington, VA, Atlanta, Chicago, Dallas and Los Angeles. Be sure to include the company's name and your loan number and phone number.

CHAPTER 12

GETTING A GOOD TITLE

◆

IF YOU BUILT a new house and it burned to the ground, you'd still own the land, even if you failed to cover the house with insurance. But if you buy a home with a faulty title—perhaps due to fraud, forgery, conflict between long-ago heirs, unpaid liens from contractors, or just a title search error—you could lose everything.

When you buy a home, you are essentially buying the seller's title—his right to own, possess, use, control and dispose of his property. The written legal evidence that his ownership rights have been conveyed to you is a properly executed and recorded deed. Naturally, you want a deed that gives you the desired assurances and rights to your new property and conveys a marketable title, one you can in turn pass along to someone else. That's why you'll want the protection of title insurance, regardless of the customary practices in the state where you're buying.

The title examination goes on during the period between contract agreement and settlement. So it takes place concurrently with the processing of your mortgage loan application; the work is handled by attorneys or other title specialists, usually selected by the buyer.

If title problems turn up, they can usually be cleared up before settlement, but sometimes they can force a delay of settlement.

Clearing a title can require the release of a debt or use of a quitclaim deed. If the problem is the result of recordkeeping neglect, such as the failure to remove a paid-up second mortgage from the record, the task may be simple. But other problems, such as a contested will, can be nightmares. If really severe, title problems can lead a purchaser to seek to void his contract with the seller. Learning your legal rights in such a situation will require the advice of a skilled real estate lawyer. Don't try canceling without legal guidance. Such an action must be carried out exactly as the contract requires, or you could end up on the receiving end of a lawsuit.

Insist on being kept informed and on understanding each step in the title checking process.

If a title problem threatens to delay settlement, be sure to let your lender know how much time may be necessary to clear the title. Loan commitments often expire after 30 or 45 days, sometimes earlier than that. If you don't get a commitment extension in writing, you could lose your loan or at least the interest rate you were promised.

HAZARDS OF A CLOUDY TITLE

There are circumstances, such as assuming an old loan or using seller financing, in which you may be tempted to save money by forgoing a title search and new owner's title insurance. The amount you save is not worth the risk. Regardless of how great a deal you've found or the customs of the region, you should obtain owner's title insurance.

The wisdom of this should become more clear to you after you take a look at the following kinds of title problems that can arise. They are numerous and varied and not at all far-fetched. Some can be straightened out by the seller, but the buyer should have expert assistance in any event. In some, the problems may become so complicated or take so long to correct that the best solution may be to have your contract legally voided.

♦ You are buying a house from a supposedly single man or woman. The title search reveals two names on the ownership record and describes them as married: "John and Jane Clark, husband and wife."

♦ You are buying from a middle-aged brother and sister from

out of town. They are selling you a home their parents bought for their retirement. The father died several years ago and the widowed mother passed away just recently. A title search reveals that the property is in her name, but there is no will on file to direct what she wanted done with it.

◆ You are buying from a couple who borrowed $20,000 seven years ago to add a room to their house. They have long since paid back the loan but have forgotten that her parents recorded it as a second mortgage when they made the loan. A title search shows the second mortgage but no evidence of its having been paid.

◆ You are buying a house to which the owner added central air-conditioning two years ago. He had a fight with the air-conditioning contractor over some damage to a ceiling that occurred during installation. When the contractor refused to correct the damage, the seller refused to pay the final installment on his contract. The contractor filed a mechanic's lien on the property, and it's never been removed.

◆ You are buying a house at a great bargain from a man who is in trouble with the Internal Revenue Service. IRS has placed a lien on the property.

◆ You are buying a property that is beautifully landscaped. A title search shows that the landscaper has a lien on the property. The seller explains that several of the trees died and when the landscaper refused to replace them, he refused to make final payment.

◆ You are buying a house from an aged widow. She and her husband bought the property many years ago, and when he died last year, she thought she was the sole owner. Now a title search reveals that the deed by which she and her husband acquired title was defective. The deed says only "Horace and Henrietta Jenkins." It should have shown their relationship and the manner in which they intended to take title.

◆ You are buying a house that has a newly paved driveway. Your seller is proud of having improved the value of his property by converting his joint driveway into a private driveway. He bought his neighbor's half in a friendly deal last year when the neighbor built a new driveway on the opposite side of his house. There is just one problem: The expanded driveway doesn't appear in the public records.

♦ The paving, sidewalks and gutters in front of the house you have under contract are all new. A title search shows that your seller has not paid the city's special assessment for the improvements.

♦ You plan to build a garage on the west end of your lot as soon as you move in. A title search reveals an easement of eight feet over the length of your future yard, extending across the garage site. The gas company owns the easement, which was granted by the development company that built your house.

♦ You are planning to get away from it all on a piece of land 50 miles from town on which you are going to build a house. A title search reveals that your property was carved out of a large farm that was never legally subdivided. It was one of those down-home "from the apple tree on the southwest corner to the stone marker on the northwest corner" land descriptions.

That sort of inadequate land description and the resulting defective deeds occur in the city, too, when neighbors get together and swap bits of land. Sometimes an owner with an oversized yard sells off a rear 20 feet to the abutting neighbor with a short yard. Or neighbors buy a vacant lot between them and split it. They erect a fence along the newly created lot line and consider the job finished, never thinking to get a survey and a proper deed for their new half lot and have it recorded.

Sometimes it is the owner's financial manipulations in his business that cloud his title. In the case of a bankruptcy or an unincorporated business or partnership, the owner's personal residence may be attached to satisfy part of his business debt. Another business owner may not be in trouble, just expanding, and has pledged his personal residence as part of the security required to obtain a business loan. Until that lien is paid or he arranges with his creditor to substitute other property as security, he can't deliver a clear title to you.

The examples above show why you should never, never take title to a property—not even as a gift—without full knowledge of its legal and financial condition.

TITLE SECURITY

At closing time you want to feel sure that the title you're getting is what you expected and what it is represented to be. There are three basic methods of assuring everyone concerned that a title is good.

Title insurance: This is the most common and desirable form of protection. Before the insurance is issued, a title report is prepared, based on a search of the public records. The report gives a description of the property and shows the owner, title defects, liens or encumbrances of record.

Following examination of the title report, the company will normally insure the title. If problems are discovered, the company can still insure by requiring that certain conditions be met or by making the insurance coverage subject to certain specified exceptions.

Abstract plus an attorney's opinion: Title is usually in the form of an abstract, which is a historical summary of everything found in a search of public records that affects ownership of the property. It includes not only the chain of ownership but also recorded easements, mortgages, wills, tax liens, judgments, pending lawsuits, marriages and anything else that affects the title. When a property is sold, the abstract is examined by an attorney, who gives a written opinion as to the title—including who the owner of record is and his judgment on whether anyone else has any right or interest in the property. The opinion is often known as the certificate of title, and it does not include the financial protection of title insurance.

Attorney's record search and opinion: The attorney searches the public records and issues his certificate of title.

BUYING TITLE INSURANCE

No matter what state you live in or what the customary title assurance practices are, you can arrange to purchase title insurance for a one-time charge if you wish to do so. (In Iowa you can get lender's title insurance only through insurance companies located outside the state; owner's coverage is not available.)

Title insurance companies are regulated by state law, but in most states, rates can vary enough to make it worthwhile to shop around.

When you're checking the fees charged by different title

insurance companies, find out exactly what is covered in each case. In some locations, companies routinely make a single charge that includes the costs of handling the closing as well as the search, title report and insurance risk premium. Others include just the report and risk premium or, in a few states, only the premium.

If you are getting a new mortgage, the lender will generally require mortgage (lender's) title insurance. This protects his lien on the property and makes the mortgage more marketable in the secondary mortgage market.

The face amount on the lender's policy is the amount of the loan and will decline gradually as the debt is paid off. The lender's policy does not protect you. To protect yourself, you must buy an optional owner's policy and pay an extra fee, unless you live in an area where the seller customarily provides owner's title insurance for the buyer. You can buy this kind of coverage at any time, but it is usually considerably cheaper to purchase both policies at once.

Unlike the lender's policy, the owner's policy is for the purchase price and protects you and your heirs as long as you have an interest in the property. Your policy is the title insurance company's contract with you to make good any covered loss caused by a defect in the title or by any lien or encumbrance that was recorded in the public records and was not revealed to you when the policy was issued. The title company will also identify title problems and pay for a legal defense against an attack on the title in whatever manner is provided for in its policy.

Nearly all title policies follow the same standard format, regardless of the issuing company. Take time to read it, and if possible have someone knowledgeable go over the details with you before closing. Pay close attention to what it covers and to the exceptions and exclusions.

Ordinarily, you can expect an owner's policy to cover you against such things as loss or damage from forgery, failure to comply with the law, impersonation, acts of minors, and marital status and competency questions. Policies are sometimes amended by adding special endorsements or by removing exclusions. For example, the insurer may include a rider that will increase the face amount on the contract as your home appreciates.

One possibility for saving money and still receiving full protection is to find out whether the seller is carrying owner's title insurance and, if so, see whether the company that holds his policy offers a reissue rate. Companies in some areas will give a buyer a cost break when they reissue insurance on a title policy made four, six or possibly even ten years ago. In some cases a reissue can also be obtained from a company other than the original issuer.

You pay for title insurance at settlement. The cost for the required lender's policy is about $2.50 per thousand. Owner's protection, if purchased at the same time, will usually cost an extra $1 per thousand.

TITLE DOCUMENTS YOU'LL SEE AT CLOSING

You'll be wading through a dizzying number of legal papers at closing, and you'll find yourself signing your name over and over again, sometimes on several copies of the same document. Obviously, that's not the most auspicious time to be asking dozens of questions about deeds, titles and insurance protection—or for getting good answers. The time for that is before making a purchase offer. Get information and answers as you proceed. Here's a brief rundown on some of the common documents relating to title transfer:

Warranty deed: This document officially transfers title to the buyer. The seller, not the purchaser, signs it and thereby warrants that the title is free of defects that might come to light after closing. Generally, the closing agent will then have the deed recorded at the local courthouse and send you a copy.

In some states a different type of deed, such as a bargain and sale deed, security deed, grant deed or special warranty deed, is used in lieu of a general warranty deed to transfer title. Be sure you understand what kind of deed you will receive from the seller and what rights will be conveyed to you.

Quitclaim deed: This is a device often used to deal with title problems. Anyone with a potential claim against the property can sign it, thereby releasing any rights he or she might have. A seller who conveys with a quitclaim deed does not guarantee the title against claims, but merely gives the buyer whatever interest in the property the seller may have.

Mortgage or deed of trust: The basic purpose of both documents is to secure the loan. When a debt is secured by a mortgage, the borrower signs a document that gives the lender a lien on the property.

When a debt is secured by a deed of trust, the buyer conveys title to a third party who holds it until the note is paid in full. The lender does not receive title but only the right to request that the property be sold should the borrower default. Both documents should be recorded.

Owner's affidavit: The seller swears in this document that there are no unpaid liens, assessments or other encumbrances against the property. The affidavit protects the purchaser, lender and title company. If the seller is lying, he or she can be sued for damages.

Purchaser's affidavit: Sometimes the buyer is required by the lender to swear that there are no existing or pending suits, judgments or liens against him or her. If the buyer is lying, that is sufficient grounds for foreclosure.

CHAPTER 13

GET READY FOR SETTLEMENT

◆

T HERE IS NO way to ensure a smooth path from ratified contract to the settlement table, but you've done all the right things so far, and the process seems to be moving along well. Your loan application is in, and you are anticipating a written loan commitment. A title examination is underway. Things seem pretty much in order on your side of the fence.

Things can still go wrong and jeopardize your settlement date, if not the contract itself. Title problems are one of the more common causes of delayed settlements. Others include fairly frequent bureaucratic snags: slow appraisals, lengthy credit reporting requirements, delayed loan commitments and the like. In many cases, there isn't much you or anyone can do but wait.

If problems occur on your side—most commonly, a delay in mortgage approval that may cause you to miss the original closing date—contact the seller immediately and work out an extension, ideally at no penalty to yourself. A seller is unlikely to try to withdraw now, and neither are you.

While you're waiting on the completion of all the processes now in motion, there are a few more things to do, including:

◆ Decide how you want to take title to the house;

♦ Apply for homeowner's insurance on the new resident, so it's in place at settlement;

♦ Review the adequacy of your disability and life insurance;

♦ Contact the utility companies about starting service in your name;

♦ Get an exact accounting of settlement costs, and make sure the money and necessary documents will be there at closing;

♦ Arrange for a walk-through of the house a few days before settlement, and again just before the meeting.

♦ Arrange for electricity, gas, oil and water to be turned on the day of settlement and the accounts switched from the seller's to your name. That way there will be no interruption in service. Utility companies often require deposits, credit checks and advance notice, so make your arrangements a few weeks in advance.

HOW TO TAKE TITLE

Before you can take title to your new home, you'll have to decide what form of ownership you want.

If you're single, you'll probably buy the house in your name alone, but an increasing number of unrelated singles are buying houses together, using one of the methods discussed below.

The most common way for husband and wife to own property is through joint ownership, either in the form of joint tenancy with the right of survivorship or tenancy by the entirety.

Under either form, if one spouse dies, the other joint owner becomes sole owner of the property. This happens automatically, bypassing probate, avoiding delays and usually trimming the costs of settling the estate. For federal tax purposes, half the value of all property owned by a married couple as joint tenants is included in the estate of the first spouse to die.

The two kinds of joint ownership differ in some respects, and many states don't recognize tenancies by the entirety. You may want to have your lawyer's advice before deciding how to take title. If you live in a community property state (Arizona, California, Idaho, Louisiana, Nevada, New Mexico, Texas, Washington and Wisconsin), state law may affect the availability and treatment of certain joint ownership arrangements.

The advice of a good trusts-and-estates attorney is especially important if you are a member of a step family or are wealthy. For couples whose total wealth exceeds $1.2 million, if they die more or less simultaneously, there would be substantial savings on federal estate taxes if their property had been divided equally between them, so each spouse's estate gets the benefit of the $600,000 starting point for taxation.

So to save on estate taxes someday, you may want to put the new home in the name of one or the other spouse alone. But check that this is alright with your lender, too; it may not want the house owned by one spouse exclusively if all the earnings to pay the mortgage will be derived from the other spouse.

And consider this, too: If the house is put in one spouse's name alone, it could affect the division of property in the event of a divorce.

Other forms of ownership include:

Tenancy in common: Each owner has a separate legal title to an undivided interest in the whole property, and each can independently sell, mortgage or give away his interest.

It's wise for owners to have a written agreement setting out their rights to deal with their interest in the property. The agreement also should specify the percentage of ownership interest each person has in the property if, for example, they have not contributed equal amounts. When one of the owners dies, the others do not automatically get the deceased's share unless that person specifically provides for such an arrangement in his will. If the will doesn't cover this, or if he dies without a will, state law determines who gets the deceased owner's share.

Joint tenancy: Under this arrangement, each person has an equal interest in the property regardless of the amount contributed at purchase. If one owner dies, that person's share passes automatically to the others without going through probate.

Partnership: If title is in the name of a partnership, it is the partnership that owns the property, not the individual partners. This arrangement calls for an agreement that sets forth how each partner will share in the management of the partnership.

The death of a partner does not affect the partnership; that person's heirs would acquire the interest. This form of ownership is useful if one or more of the partners are investors who don't plan to live on the property. Another plus for a partnership arrangement is that you may avoid some problems that can arise with the other two forms discussed above, if one person goes into bankruptcy or has other legal problems that could cloud the title.

INSURANCE ON YOUR NEW HOME

Your lender will require you to take out a homeowner's insurance policy, something you'd want to do anyway. The lender is interested in coverage only on the amount of its mortgage, so it will get its money back in the event of a total loss; but you'll probably want full-value coverage, perhaps enhanced by an inflation-adjustment mechanism that keeps the coverage rising with home values. And you may want to consider other, special insurance.

Homeowners Insurance

The term "homeowners insurance" is to some extent a misnomer: Standard policies are packages that can cover almost everything you own, plus personal liability, credit card losses and even medical bills.

There are five basic types of homeowners policies, called prosaically HO-1, HO-2, HO-3, HO-6 and HO-8. (A sixth type, HO-4, covers renters.) The first three differ in the number of perils they cover and the degree of protection they offer. HO-1 affords basic protection, with many restrictions. HO-2, which costs 5% to 10% more, can protect you from costs arising from misfortunes such as burst pipes and exploding furnaces. An HO-3, or "all risk, policy, which can cost up to 30% more than an HO-1, covers everything not specifically excluded, including features that are part of the structure such as wall-to-wall carpeting and built-in dishwashers.

If you are buying a condominium, you will use an HO-6 form; and unique older houses may be insured with a special HO-8 policy available in some states.

All of these policies exclude floods, earthquakes, war and nuclear contamination. Policies may differ somewhat from company to company, and policy conditions may also vary according to state requirements.

A typical homeowner's policy combines two basic types of insurance with some additional coverage:

◆ *Property protection.*This part of the policy reimburses you for losses or damages to the house and its contents. The amount of coverage is based on the cost of replacing the entire structure, with coverage on personal property usually figured as a percentage of the cost—typically 50%. There are set monetary limits for specific classes of objects, ranging from $200 for currency to $1,000 for jewelry, furs and manuscripts, to $2,500 for silverware.

◆ *Liability insurance.*This protects you against personal liability, medical payments for injuries to others and damage to other people's property, and typically applies to you and other family members living in the house.

Liability coverage usually pays up to $100,000 to others for injury or damage that you or a family member might have caused, or for an accident that occurs around your home. You will be covered, for example, if the mailman falls through the front porch. If someone is injured at your home, medical payments coverage typically will pay at least $500 of the injured person's bills. Injuries to someone by a family member who is away from the home may also be covered. And the injury wouldn't have to have been your fault for the coverage to apply. You would also be covered for legal defense if you needed it.

Extended personal liability or umbrella insurance may be worth considering. It dramatically increases your personal liability coverage at comparatively little cost and extends your coverage beyond damages assessed for physical injury to such things as libel, slander, character defamation, shock, mental anguish, sickness or disease, false arrest, wrongful entry or eviction and malicious prosecution.

◆ *Additional coverage.*You can select a policy that will help cover costs, including provisions for housing and restaurant bills, should your home become uninhabitable. Many policies routinely pay up to $1,000 if a credit card is stolen or forged in your name.

Once you've pinned down the type of policy that suits your needs, the next step is to figure out how much coverage you want on the house and its contents. The basic building block of any policy will be the amount of coverage on the house. This should be based on the *replacement* value—that is, what it would cost to rebuild the structure.

Because you are unlikely to experience a total loss on your home, you usually will not need insurance for 100% of the replacement cost. You won't be fully protected for even a partial loss, however, unless your coverage at the time of the loss is at least 80% of replacement cost. That's unlikely to happen within the first few months of ownership, but it could become a problem as construction costs rise, or you improve the house.

One solution is to shift the responsibility for keeping replacement-cost coverage up to 80% from your shoulders to the insurance company through what is called a replacement-cost endorsement. Depending on where you buy, this option will cost from 10% to 15% of a year's base premium to three times as much as standard coverage. Or, you could check on the value of the house and contents at least every two years.

Most policies can be customized to meet your needs. You should be able to buy add-on coverage to insure valuable silverware or art not covered in standard policies.

Cutting costs. Prices for equivalent policies can vary by hundreds of dollars from company to company. As you shop, take these steps to insure that you're getting the most for your money:

1) Get price quotations from at least three companies.

2) Find out whether you'd get a price break if the insurer writes your home and automobile coverage.

3) For each policy, compare:

◆ the amount you wish to insure the house for and the cost of a replacement-cost endorsement.

◆ the cost of content coverage. Half the amount of coverage on the structure (less depreciation) is standard; decide if you want more.

◆ the cost of replacement coverage versus actual cash coverage on the contents. If possible, opt for replacement coverage.

◆ the deductible. As a general rule, don't ask for a deductible lower than $250; it's too expensive.

◆ the cost of floaters you may need for antiques, jewelry,

computer software and the like.

◆ the liability limits. $100,000 is standard, but $300,000 is desirable and not that costly.

Should you discover that the home you want can't be insured, you may be able to buy coverage under the Fair Access to Insurance Requirements (FAIR) plan. FAIR is in effect in over 25 states as well as the District of Columbia and Puerto Rico. You can find out whether it is available where you live by calling or writing the Insurance Information Institute, 110 William St., New York, NY 10038, or by calling toll free 800-221-4954. Or ask your real estate or insurance agent.

Flood Insurance

The most important risk universally excluded from homeowners policies is flood insurance. If you are buying a home in a flood-prone area, consider protecting yourself against a major disaster. Some 18,000 communities participate in the federal government's National Flood Insurance Program (800-638-6620). Insurance is available to individual homeowners in such communities through private insurance companies and independent agents. Protection isn't cheap; the average homeowner's annual premium is $260, and the average deductible is $500.

Earthquake Insurance

Although standard homeowners policies don't cover earthquake damage, you can get a special earthquake endorsement or a separate policy. In California, for example, earthquake insurance usually runs from $1.75 to $2.50 per $1,000 of coverage on wood-frame houses, equal to the cost of a typical homeowners policy. The deductible can go as high as 15% of the policy's amount, so the insurance pays off only on big claims.

California isn't the only area at risk. Parts of Arkansas, Colorado, Idaho, Illinois, Indiana, Kentucky, Massachusetts, Mississippi, Missouri, Nevada, New York, South Carolina, Tennessee, Utah, Washington and Wyoming are also considered to be at higher-than-average risk.

While most homeowners don't need earthquake protection, there are three conditions that should make you consider buying protection:

◆ Your home was constructed before World War II, when codes covering a structure's ability to withstand shifts in the earth were weaker; this is particularly important for homes not framed with wood.

◆ Your home is located within 10 miles of a fault.

◆ Your home is on unstable soil, such as a hillside, landfill or flood control plain.

Insurance on Your Life

If your new home represents a considerably higher financial burden than you've ever carried before, and if you have a spouse and children to protect in the event of your death or disability, this is a good time to review your insurance needs. Have an accountant, trusts-and-estates attorney, financial planner or trusted insurance professional review your situation on disability and life insurance.

Your best bet may be conventional term life insurance whose proceeds, if invested wisely, will produce enough annual income to pay the new mortgage and other basic living expenses. (See the discussion of credit life insurance and its drawbacks in Chapter 11.)

ON TO SETTLEMENT

You are only days away from becoming an owner. The search has been expensive in terms of both time and money. Now it's time for you to pay for the property, and for the seller to deliver the deed.

There is no standard name for this next step. Depending on where you live, it is known as title closing, settlement or closing of escrow. The closing officer in your area may be a title company, an abstract attorney or a regular real estate attorney. Occasionally, it is a broker or lender.

When closing involves an actual meeting, the process commonly is called settlement. If no meeting occurs, it's often known as escrow and is handled by an escrow agent. In escrow cases, the buyer and seller typically sign an agreement requiring each party to deposit certain funds and documents with the agent. When all the papers and monies are in, the escrow is "closed." The agent records the documents and makes the appropriate disbursements.

Settling on a home can be as serene as a treaty signing. Too often, it's as full of static as a debate at the United Nations. Planned closings stand a better chance of being peaceful closings. Each party knows what to expect.

As the buyer, you probably selected the person or firm to perform the settlement, so you can rely on their competence and integrity. If for some reason the seller specified the settlement agent, you might wish to take along your own attorney or have an attorney of your choice review the documents beforehand, at your expense. The cost of a few hundred dollars could give you added peace of mind.

The Costs You Face

The key to reducing shock at settlement is to know ahead of time what you'll have to pay. You had ballpark figures to work with when you started looking, and once your purchase offer was accepted, you received detailed estimates from the lender with whom you made an application.

Overall settlement costs are influenced by, among other things, where you live, your settlement date, how you finance your purchase and what the lender requires as an inducement to provide the loan.

It's difficult to say what closing costs run on a national basis, simply because there is no uniformity to how the costs are counted and calculated. But within local markets you generally can get a good estimate. For example, in Atlanta closing costs on conventional loans commonly come to about 3.5% of the loan amount. In California, 2% is closer to the mark. Neither of those estimates includes any discount points (equal to 1% of the loan amount) or the brokerage commission (usually paid by the seller)—and these, as you know by now, will make up the largest proportion of your settlement costs. When points are included, the total approaches 6% in some high-cost metropolitan areas.

The federal government's Real Estate Settlement Procedures Act (RESPA) covers most home loans, including VA, FHA, FmHA or other government-backed or government-assisted loans; loans eligible to be purchased by GNMA, FNMA or in other federally related secondary mortgage markets; and loans made by lenders who invest or make more than $1 million in residential loans each year. Assumptions and seller financing are not covered by RESPA.

When you applied for a new loan from a lender covered by RESPA, the law required that you be given a "good faith" estimate of fees when you made a written loan application—or within three business days—and that you be given a pamphlet titled *Settlement Costs and You*, put out by the Department of Housing and Urban Development. This contains a description of how the closing process works and explains terms you will encounter in your transaction.

The day before settlement, you are entitled to see the Uniform Settlement Statement. This is a copy of what you will get at settlement. In places where there is no meeting, the escrow agent is required to give you a copy when escrow is closed.

Use the worksheet on the following pages to check the lender's and agent's estimates against actual amounts as you get them. This may provide you with some advance warning if there are substantial changes before settlement. The worksheet, like HUD's Uniform Settlement Statement, breaks the total settlement charges into broad categories:

1) *Costs associated with getting a loan*: These can include the lender's charge for processing the loan, loan discount points and/or origination fees, appraisal fee, borrower's credit report, mortgage insurance, and if relevant, loan assumption fee.

2) *Items to be prepaid at closing*: Mortgage interest, property taxes, and mortgage and hazard insurance premiums are frequently paid in advance at closing.

Once you become an owner, you will pay interest on your monthly mortgage loan in arrears; that is, you will pay for the use of the loan at the end of each month. The loan is structured so that payments made on the first of each month cover the interest owed from the previous month. In order to make this work, the lender will collect interest in advance at settlement for the period between closing and the end of that month. For example, if settlement is August 15 and you must make your first regular mortgage payment October 1, the lender will collect interest through the end of August.

SETTLEMENT OR ESCROW COSTS
WORKSHEET

	Agent's estimate	Lender's estimate	Actual
Costs related to obtaining a loan			
Loan origination fee	_____	_____	_____
Loan discount, or points	_____	_____	_____
Appraisal fee	_____	_____	_____
Credit report	_____	_____	_____
Inspection fee	_____	_____	_____
Mortgage insurance application	_____	_____	_____
Assumption fee	_____	_____	_____
Items to be paid in advance			
Interest from _____ to _____ @ $_____ per day	_____	_____	_____
Mortgage insurance for _____ to _____	_____	_____	_____
Hazard insurance for _____ years to _____	_____	_____	_____
Items to be deposited with lender at settlement			
Hazard insurance _____ months @ $_____ per month	_____	_____	_____
Mortgage insurance _____ months @ $_____ per month	_____	_____	_____
City property taxes _____	_____	_____	_____
County property taxes _____	_____	_____	_____
Annual assessments _____	_____	_____	_____

	Agent's estimate	Lender's estimate	Actual
Title costs			
Settlement or escrow fee			
Abstract or title search			
Title examination or opinion			
Title insurance binder			
Document preparation			
Notary fees			
Attorney's fees			
(including the charges listed above)			
Title insurance			
(including the charges listed above)			
Lender's coverage			
Owner's coverage			
Recording and transfer charges			
Recording fees:			
Deed $_____			
Mortgage $_____			
Releases $_____			
City/county:			
Deed $_____ Mortgage $_____			
State:			
Deed $_____ Mortgage $_____			
Other costs			
Attorney's fee			
Buyer/broker fee			
Pest inspection			
_____			
_____			
Total Settlement or Escrow Charges			

In addition, lenders often require payment of as much as the first year's mortgage and hazard insurance premiums at closing. In some cases a buyer can arrange for the seller to transfer the remaining hazard insurance, paying the seller on a prorated basis for the remainder of the policy term.

3) *Reserves for insurance, taxes and assessments*: The borrower may be required to pay an initial amount at closing to set up a reserve fund, and each month a portion of the regular payment will be added to the reserve to assure sufficient sums to pay future taxes and insurance premiums.

4) *Title costs*: These pay for various transaction costs, notably the title search required by the lender. An examination is made of the public records to determine if the title you receive has any ownership or financial claims and restrictions on the use of the property. Other related charges include title insurance, document preparation, notary fees and the lender's attorney fees.

5) *Recording and transfer charges*: These cover the recording of the loan and property documents at the county courthouse, as well as related transfer taxes.

6) *Additional fees* for attorney and buyer broker services, property survey and pest inspection.

In general, items paid for in advance by the seller, such as property taxes, would be prorated in favor of the seller at closing. Items paid in arrears, for example, interest on an assumed loan, would be prorated in favor of the purchaser.

You may want to run through the worksheet and note which items are to be paid in full or in part by you. Local custom usually influences whether the buyer or the seller pays a particular charge. You can do things differently, but to avoid conflicts, make sure your purchase contract states clearly how each item is to be handled. Otherwise, it's not unreasonable for the seller to expect you to abide by the prevailing custom.

In some areas, for example, the buyer pays for a title insurance policy because the buyer's lender requires the protection. In other places, the seller absorbs the charge as one of the selling costs. In some areas, the buyer always pays the local tax for recording the deed; in others, the seller always pays it. (To see what closing costs might be involved in the purchase of a $150,000 home, see the example on the opposite page.)

HYPOTHETICAL SETTLEMENT COSTS

Location: Montgomery County, MD
Sale price: $150,000
Down payment: $30,000

Buyer's Costs

Credit report	$ 48.00
Loan origination fee (1%)*	1,200.00
Interest to Feb. 1'	936.90
Six months property tax†	640.50
Hazard insurance premium**	211.00
Two mos. insurance reserve**	35.16
Attorneys fees (Includes title exam fee and binder)	350.00
Recording fee	50.00
Survey	125.00
State recordation tax	660.00
State transfer tax	750.00
County transfer tax	1,500.00
Title insurance (Lender's coverage)	260.00
Title insurance (Borrower's coverage)	250.00
TOTAL:	$7,016.56

Seller's Costs

Sales commission (6%)	$9,000.00
Loan discount point (1%)*	1,200.00
Appraisal fee	250.00
Closing fees	125.00
Termite inspection	45.00
TOTAL:	$10,620.00

*The buyer is paying a 1% loan origination fee, and the seller has agreed to pay one point on the buyer's $120,000 mortgage.

'Because interest is paid in arrears—for the previous month—and because the buyer's first regular monthly payment won't be due until March 1, the lender collects interest for Jan. 2 through Feb. 1 at closing.

†Lenders frequently collect one-twelfth of the annual property taxes each month—along with the principal and interest payment—and hold them in escrow until payment is due. How much is paid at settlement depends on the closing date and when taxes are collected in a given locale.

**The lender is collecting and will be paying a full year's premium on hazard insurance covering at least the value of the mortgage; lender is also starting a reserve fund for future premiums.

In other locales and in other circumstances, the buyer's closing costs may include an assumption fee (if the buyer is taking over the seller's mortgage), mortgage insurance, and various other charges.

Total settlement charges are generally less if the buyer is assuming an existing loan or paying all cash, rather than getting a new mortgage.

(Settlement calculations provided by BANK ONE Mortgage Corp., Chevy Chase, MD.)

WHAT TO BRING TO CLOSING

In order for things to go smoothly, each person is responsible for bringing certain documents, and for being prepared to write the necessary checks. Many closing costs can be paid by personal check, but double check with the closing attorney. A certified or cashier's check may be required; find out to whom checks should be made payable—the seller or settlement attorney, for example.

Arrange to pay for discount points and loan origination fees with one check and other closing costs with another so that all your prepaid interest expenses will be clearly segregated for deduction from your taxable income in the year you pay them.

The seller and his attorney, or the settlement attorney you've both agreed on, are responsible for preparing and bringing the deed and the most recent property tax bill. They also will bring other documents required by the contract. This can include property insurance policy, termite inspection, documents showing the removal of liens, a bill of sale for personal property, loan documents and so on.

Your responsibilities include having adequate funds in your checking account, arranging for your attorney to represent your interests at the meeting, bringing your loan commitment and informing the lender of the meeting's time and place.

If your lender requires payment of the first year's mortgage and hazard insurance premiums at closing, you should be prepared to do so or to bring proof that they have already been paid. Finally, it's a good idea to bring a copy of the purchase contract. You may need to refresh your memory.

THE FINAL INSPECTION

The house you're buying must be handed over to you in the condition specified in the contract. (See the discussion of condition in Chapters 8 and 9.)

To verify this, schedule a walk-through of the house shortly before settlement; several days in advance is best, to allow time for the seller to correct any last-minute problems.

If the house is vacant, it should be empty of debris and in the "broom-clean" condition you specified in the contract. Take along a simple device for testing all the electrical outlets—a plug-in nightlight, for example. Turn on the furnace and air-conditioning. (If it's winter, you may not be able to turn on the AC, and an expert may have to verify that it's in working condition.) Flush the toilets and turn on faucets. In short, put the house through its paces.

If anything needs fixing or further cleaning (aside from things that were conveyed only in "as-is" condition), tell the seller immediately. Neither you nor the seller wants to postpone the settlement, but make it clear you won't go to closing until a second walk-through is satisfactory.

If the seller is staying on in the house after settlement, by leasing the house back from you the new owner, the seller will soon become your tenant. The contract should have spelled out the terms of this lease-back, including a security deposit (for example, one month's rent). You may want to have a formal lease with the previous owner, now your new tenant.

Under this arrangement, you will have two walk-throughs—one just before settlement (in which you check on all the things above except cleanliness) and another one after the seller moves out. Any difference in condition that occurs between the two inspections will have to be settled just as in a normal landlord-tenant relationship, with responsibility for repair determined accordingly. If everything is okay at the second walk-through, the seller will get back the damage/security deposit.

SAVE ALL THE DOCUMENTS FOR TAXES

With the completion of settlement proceedings, you're now a homeowner. Congratulations! The tax benefits of homeownership are considerable, but so too is the paperwork necessary to take advantage of all the breaks.

If you haven't read Chapter 3 carefully, do so after closing on your new home. Now is the time to begin keeping meticulous records of every cost incurred on your new home—from settlement expenses to improvements that add to the home's value. Some of these expenses can be deducted from taxable income in the year you buy the home; others will merely increase the tax basis, lowering the taxable gain when you someday sell the house, whether next year or 40 years hence. The better your records, the easier those calculations will be later on.

C H A P T E R 1 4

BUYING A VACATION HOME

◆

A SIMPLE LOG cabin in the Ozark mountains, or a weathered cottage on Cape Cod. A ski condo in Aspen, Colorado. A secluded mansion tucked into a cove on the Caribbean island of St. Lucia. A one-week timeshare at a resort in Pennsylvania's Poconos.

The words "vacation property" may be used by the owners of each of these, although the financial, legal and tax consequences of each can be as different as the beach and the mountains where the properties are located.

There are many reasons people buy a second home, some personal, some financial. Typically, they enjoy a particular vacation spot so much they believe they'll want to keep returning over and over. Rather than rent a different house or hotel room each time, living like nomads, they want to have a place where they'll be truly at home—where they can keep their vacation gear and summer (or winter) clothes, entertain friends, and feel like a part of the community.

If your desire is merely to lock in predictable vacation costs in a community where you like to go each year, a fractional interest or timeshare might make sense. Some kinds of timeshares are not real estate per se, but more like a prepaid right to use a given unit for a certain length of time each year. Keep your expectations of financial gain low or non-existent; it's often difficult to sell a timeshare for even your original investment. (See discussion beginning on page 189.)

Many people buy a vacation home where they think they will want to retire some day; at that point, their second home might become their primary residence.

For other vacation-home buyers, the primary motivation is financial. If this describes you, make sure you check out all the angles before succumbing to the fast talk of a resort sales person. Buying a vacation home to avoid rising rents might make sense in some communities, but not in others; it often costs the vacationer less to rent the nicest house in a given community for a month than it costs the owners to pay the mortgage, taxes and maintenance on that same house for a month, especially in the early years of the ownership period.

Price appreciation is another matter. Some people buy in a given vacation community because they've witnessed, first hand, a rapid rise in home prices (and probably rents, too) over the previous several years; they want to get in on the action. Carefully selected homes in the most sought-after communities can, in fact, appreciate nicely, making them good investments as well as nice places to spend a vacation. But appreciation is highly variable from region to region and resort to resort. Some people who hastily bought timeshares or resort houses from persuasive salesmen have found they can't even recover their original investment in a slender resale market. It takes a lot of study, cool analysis, and good guessing to make a smart decision.

STUDY BEFORE YOU BUY

In many ways, buying a vacation property is like buying a principal residence, so the preceding chapters of this book will be useful to you.

There are many special considerations, too. You have to define your needs very carefully, such as deciding how big a residence you need, its style, and how far away from your main residence is acceptable—a few hours drive? a long plane trip? Is the house exclusively for your own use, or will you want to rent it out for part or all of the year; if the latter, you have to curb your unusual tastes and buy whatever features the rental market wants most.

Keep these points in mind as you head out with your dreams, your maps and the classified ads:

A depressed price may not be a bargain. The property may have been grossly overpriced to begin with or severely inflated by a speculative orgy. If there's an abundance of listings, try to find out why from independent sources, such as the local tax assessor or a real estate agent. If a lot of people were burned, it could happen again. Or maybe the area is déclassé.

Location, location, location. That trilogy is just as important for a vacation home as it is for your principal residence. Overbuilding tends to run in cycles, and it generally happens in the bigger, better-known, heavily promoted areas with large numbers of builders and hard-charging chambers of commerce. You may find better prospects in older, quieter and less exotic family communities with a minimum of absentee owners. The more time you can spend looking and comparing, the better you're likely to do.

Beware of buying for speculation. You could make a serious mistake. Don't assume today's prices make appreciation a sure bet. Remember that many investors' hopes were dashed even when all the tax benefits were in place and prices were steadily moving up. Most of today's buyers are families who plan to use the property for vacations and weekend getaways. If a rental market does start to hum, overbuilding could soon spoil things.

Understand the remaining tax benefits. Albeit to a lesser extent than in the past, Uncle Sam will still subsidize your home away from home. You can probably fully deduct mortgage interest and property taxes you pay on a second home.

Buy for enjoyment. Buying a place where you can escape for fun, relaxation, tranquility and companionship could do wonders for your health and spirits, and could be one of the best investments you'll ever make. In terms of real value, a well-established, desirable, family-oriented community with good recreation facilities could be a far better choice than a neon-splashed strip of high-rise condominiums and cocktail lounges.

You shouldn't buy anywhere you haven't visited several times as a vacationer. Most of all, never buy a home on a first visit to a new resort community or timeshare resort that uses intensive sales pressure to convince people to commit themselves on the spot.

While on a vacation in the community you're considering, devote a few days to a thorough investigation of the market. Look at houses or timeshares for sale. Study the market, using actual sale prices, not advertised asking prices. Talk to the leading real estate brokers in the community. If you're intending to rent the house out, contact a firm that can manage your property—finding tenants, collecting rent, making repairs— when you're not around. Talk to all the year-round residents you can find, and drop by the offices of the local newspaper to learn what you can about zoning, future developments, and commercial growth in the area.

VACATION HOME STRATEGIES

Most would-be buyers soon have their choices narrowed by lofty price tags attached to the most attractive vacation properties. Here are various scenarios for personal use, renting out, and combinations of both, showing the kinds of properties that make the most sense in each circumstance.

Personal Use Only

The most affluent buyers are often looking for a unique or unusual property. They may want it to reflect their status in life. Such owners are not interested in rental income and intend to use the property for their own and their family's enjoyment. The vacation home may qualify as a second residence and, if so, mortgage interest will be fully deductible as long as the combined debt secured by the vacation home and principle residence doesn't exceed $1.1 million. Long-term appreciation and estate building are primary investment objectives.

Good bets include the most sought-after (and expensive) categories of vacation property: rural acreage near growing metropolitan areas; waterfront property; apartments or townhouses in cities that are hubs of international travel and cultural and recreational attractions.

Some Rental and Business Use

Another group of affluent, but more practical, buyers may look at vacation property with a sharper focus on potential medium-term investment return. They may own more than one property, to assure themselves a get-away place in the event one property is rented out. Using professional management, they actively seek rental income. Such owners may restrict personal use of a property in order to maintain deductions and tax shelter, although the tax law demands a careful analysis of that strategy. They may use property for business purposes, such as entertaining clients or customers. Appreciation and some tax shelter are financial objectives.

Their choices of vacation property might include condos or townhouses in popular resort areas, or perhaps a condo hotel suite in a sought-after area where weather permits either one long vacation season or two peak seasons.

Limited Personal Use, Heavy Renting

Less affluent vacation home buyers need rental income in order to carry their investment. They may manage the property on their own, or try to find a few prospects to supplement the rentals lined up for their property by a manager. Such owners may not use the property themselves, or may do so only out of season. (See the discussion below on the trade-offs between personal and rental use.) Cash-flow, appreciation and tax shelter are financial objectives. Owning in an area that becomes overbuilt—driving down rental rates and slowing appreciation—is a serious threat to those objectives.

Their best purchase prospects include resort property in areas with perennial popularity and with either one long rental season and/or two rental seasons (for example, a part of New England with winter skiing and summer camping).

LESS-THAN-FULL-TIME OWNERSHIP

Yet another segment of the vacation home market may dream of owning a beach cottage or a mountain hideaway, but cannot afford the down payment or the cash outlay an unrented property would drain from their budget. "You can't spend all your time on vacation, so why own a vacation place all the time?" they reason.

And, because so many people fall into this group, developers and sales people have spent hours upon hours trying to figure ways to help them own—ways that people probably wouldn't even consider for a primary residence but that might make sense to them for a vacation home.

If you fall into this group, consider fractional interests and timeshares in quality developments. Resort developers in such places as Florida, Texas, California, Hawaii and the Carolinas offer fractional interests in their properties.

Fractional Interest

Fractional interests may be sold as quarter-shares (13 weeks), fifth-shares (ten weeks) or tenth-shares (five weeks). Essentially, you're buying title to a number of weeks throughout the year. With a quarter-share, for example, you get to use the property every fourth week. Each year, the sequence shifts forward a week, giving you a chance to use all the weeks of the year within a four-year period. A mix of floating and fixed time periods sometimes is used.

Fractional interests are likely to offer better prospects for appreciation than timeshares. Pay attention to marketing costs, which may range from zero to 25%. Buyers paying a 25% premium in sales expenses (commissions, etc.) will have to wait some time before they can start counting paper profits.

The resort developer is the most likely source of funds to finance a fractional interest, and terms vary widely. Prices for "fractionals" range from $25,000 to $100,000 or more. Check with a knowledgeable accountant regarding tax consequences and interest deductions.

Timeshares

This is one of the most popular means of dividing up ownership of a vacation property, and often the cheapest way to buy into a resort. You become one of the owners of a property, typically a condo apartment. Usually, ownership is divided into 52 parts—one for each week of the year—and the parts are sold off one or more at a time. A one-week timeshare rarely sells for more than $10,000.

Timeshare ownership can be in the form of tenancy-in-common (sometimes called time-span ownership) or interval ownership. Tenancy-in-common gives you an undivided interest in a property, pro-rated according to the amount of time you purchase. Interval ownership lasts only for a specified number of years. When those years are up, you and the other interval owners become tenants in common. Under either type of ownership, you don't always get a specified unit for a fixed time period. Instead, you may choose from interchangeable units and floating weeks.

One form of timesharing—known as a vacation license, vacation lease or club membership—carries no ownership rights at all, only the right to use the property each year for a number of years. Ownership stays in the hands of the developer.

Whatever the form of purchase, you normally cannot get a mortgage to buy a timeshare. Financing typically is covered by a personal loan over a 5-to-10-year period with a 10% down payment, and the lender usually is the developer. Check with your accountant and attorney about the tax implications. Don't rely on assurances from a sales person.

If vacationing is your only motivation, then a timeshare may suit you. It locks in the cost of staying at a particular place, yet provides the flexibility to vacation elsewhere, too. For an annual fee, usually about $50 or $60, you can use a timeshare exchange that works out vacation-place swaps with other timeshare owners around the world.

But a timeshare doesn't make much sense if you're counting on reselling at a profit in the near future, especially if the unit is new and the developer still is selling others. Heavy marketing costs, which may include free airfare and lodging to lure potential buyers to the resort, push up the price charged for the units. Developers rarely devote time to reselling units until a resort is completed and sold out. According to the International Resale Brokers Association, most timeshares are resold for half—or less—of what their owners originally paid and take months to sell, if they can be sold at all.

BUYING WITH PARTNERS

Friends will often get together to buy a vacation home together, either as tenants in common or in a legally constituted partnership.

Owning as tenants in common, friendly as it sounds, can cause everyone a lot of headaches. Setting up a general partnership to own the place can head off many of those problems by anticipating and dealing with them in the partnership agreement. Use your real estate lawyer to draw up the agreement, but ask an attorney in the vacation area to check relevant regulations.

Make sure the contract addresses the following points:

◆ How ownership will be divided, which in turn determines who pays how much of the down payment, monthly payment, maintenance and repairs. The contract should also describe how any profits or losses from rent or sale of the place will be divided and how tax benefits will be distributed.

◆ Who gets to use the property when.

◆ What constitutes a deciding vote and under what circumstances such a vote is considered necessary.

◆ Which owner will act as managing partner and thus be responsible for signing checks and paying routine expenses.

◆ How much advance notice a withdrawing partner must give and how the buyout price will be set.

A partnership may also protect the existing mortgage when a new owner enters the picture if the lender agrees that it is an interest in the partnership—not an interest in the property—that is being transferred.

Ideally, a general partnership should try to find a lender who is willing to limit each partner's liability on the loan to his or her respective percentage of ownership, even though such agreements are unusual. Otherwise, each partner is responsible for 100% of the loan, so a lender could single out any partner to sue for the money if there's a default, instead of going through complicated foreclosure proceedings.

TAXES TAKE NO HOLIDAY

One thing you can't get away from at your get-away-from-it-all vacation home is taxes. In fact, the rules that apply have been declared "exasperatingly convoluted" by no less than an authority in the U.S. Tax Court.

When it's just for you and yours. First, look at the bright side. If your home-away-from-home is only that—a second residence that's never rented out—the tax benefits come with few complications. You can fully deduct mortgage interest on a second home just as you can on your principal residence.

Only two homes to a customer, though. Congress apparently figures that anyone who can afford more than two homes can handle the mortgage interest without the help of a tax deduction. Interest on any additional homes—and on any debt on the first and second homes that exceeds the $1.1 million cap —falls in the category of personal interest, the deduction for which is being phased out between now and 1991.

A motor home or boat can qualify as a second residence. To meet the IRS definition of a home, the boat or recreational vehicle must have basic living accommodations, including cooking facilities, a place to sleep and a toilet. (However, if you are subject to the alternative minimum tax, interest on a loan for a boat you use as a second home can't be deducted as mortgage interest.) Property taxes are deductible, too, regardless of how many homes you own.

However, points paid to get a mortgage on a vacation home are not deductible in the year paid. Instead, they're deducted proportionally over the life of the loan.

When you also rent. It's when you start renting the vacation home—as many owners do to help pay the freight—that things get tricky. The IRS does not care about any rental income you receive if you rent the place for 14 or fewer days a year. You can charge as much as you want, and as long as your temporary tenants stay no more than two weeks the rent you receive is tax-free. Rent for more than 14 days, though, and you become a landlord in the eyes of the IRS. You must report rental income, and you qualify to deduct rental expenses.

How much time tenants use the property versus how much time you enjoy it yourself controls whether the house is treated as a personal residence or a business property. The distinction is the key to the tax ramifications.

If your personal use accounts for more than 14 days during the year or more than 10% of the number of days the place is rented (26 or more personal days compared to 250 rental days, for example), the house is considered a personal residence. Hold personal use below the 14-day/10% threshold, however, and the house is considered a rental property.

The breakdown between personal and rental days is crucial because it determines whether or not the property can produce tax losses. Such losses—available only if personal use is limited so the property qualifies as a rental rather than a residence—can often be used to trim your tax bill by sheltering other income, such as your salary.

But limiting personal use no longer automatically opens the door to big tax losses. The law now limits the deduction of "passive" losses, a category that includes all losses on rental property. There is an important exception, though, that protects many vacation homeowners. If your adjusted gross income is less than $100,000, you can deduct up to $25,000 of rental losses each year. The $25,000 allowance is gradually phased out as AGI rises to $150,000. To sidestep the passive-loss rules, you must "actively" manage the property, a requirement you can probably meet as long as you're involved in such decisions as approving tenants, rental terms and repairs.

Expenses you can't deduct because of the passive-loss rules aren't lost forever. You'll be able to use them sometime in the future when you have passive income to offset or you sell the property. (See Chapter 15 for more details on the passive loss rules.)

Even if the $25,000 exception will protect your rental write-offs, there's another potential trap. Limiting personal use of your vacation home may mean giving up the right to some mortgage interest deductions.

Remember that the law now permits mortgage-interest deductions for loans secured by your first and second *residence*. If your vacation place is a business property, the mortgage isn't covered. Part of the interest would still be deductible—the portion attributable to the business use of the property—and the rest would be considered personal interest, which is losing its deductibility.

That rule has led some tax advisers to recommend that taxpayers intentionally flunk the 14-day/10% test by increasing personal use of vacation property. That way, you preserve the full interest write-off. Part of the interest would be deducted as a rental expense and the rest as personal mortgage interest. What you give up, of course, is the opportunity to claim a tax loss.

Allocation of expenses. To figure your vacation-home deductions, you have to allocate expenses between personal and rental use. There are two ways to do this—the IRS method and another approach that has been approved in court cases—and the one that's best for you depends on your circumstances.

According to the IRS, you begin by adding up the total number of days the house was used for personal and business purposes. Your deductible rental expenses are the same proportion of the total as the number of rental days is to the total number of days the place was used.

For example, assume you have a cabin in the mountains that you use for 30 days during the year and rent out for 100 days. The 100 days of rental use equals 77% of the total 130 days the cabin was used during the year. Using the IRS formula, 77% of your expenses—including interest, taxes, insurance, utilities, repairs and depreciation—would be rental expenses.

The IRS is also particular about the order in which you deduct those expenses against your rental income. You deduct interest and taxes first, then expenses except for depreciation, and then depreciation. The sequence is important, and detrimental, because of the rule that limits rental deductions to the amount of rental income when personal use exceeds 14 days or 10% of total use. Remember that property taxes and interest not assigned to rental use could be claimed as regular itemized deductions instead. But by applying those costs against rental income, the IRS method reduces the amount of rental income against which other expenses can be deducted.

By using a different allocation formula, though, you can limit the interest and tax expenses used to offset rental income and thereby boost the write-off of other rental costs. Courts have allowed taxpayers to allocate taxes and interest over the entire year rather than over just the total number of days a property is used. In the example above of 100 days of rental use, that method would allocate just 27% (100/365) of the taxes and interest to rental income. That would leave more rental income against which other expenses can be deducted. The extra taxes and interest can be deducted as regular itemized deductions.

Although the court-approved formula can pay off when the 14-day/10% test makes the property a personal residence, the IRS version can be more appealing if the place qualifies as a business property. Consider, for example, the result if you use your vacation place for ten days out of the year and rent it for 75 days.

The court-approved method would allocate 21% (75/365) of the interest to rental use. Under the new law, that would make 79% of the interest "personal" interest, only 10% of which is deductible in 1990—and none will be in future years. Using the IRS formula, though, 88% of the interest would be assigned to rental use (ten days personal use divided by 85 days total use). That would throw just 12% into the vulnerable personal-interest category.

Retirement Plans?

What if you want to buy a second home now with the idea of renting it out completely for several years and then possibly retiring to it? It would be classified as a rental property and you could deduct your expenses—including mortgage interest, property taxes, operating costs and depreciation—up to the amount of your rental income. Any excess expenses would be subject to the passive loss rules.

If you do sell your current home and retire to the rental unit after several years, you would not be able to roll over the profit from your old home. To qualify for the rollover, you must buy and move into the replacement residence within two years of the time you sell the old one. However, if you are age 55 or older when you sell your old home, and have owned and lived in it for at least three of the five years leading up to the sale, you could qualify for the special provision that permits taxpayers to exclude from income up to $125,000 of profit on the sale of a home. (See discussion in Chapter 17.)

FOR MORE INFORMATION

Periodicals and Newsletters

Island Properties Report (33K Water St., Guilford, CT 06437; 203-453-4345). Monthly newsletter on the Caribbean; eight islands are covered in depth each year, along with four quarterly reports covering the region generally. Thirty to 40 properties are featured in each letter, along with a list of real estate brokers.

Hideaways Guide (P.O. Box 1270, Littleton, MA 01460-9955; 800-843-4433). Directory of vacation homes for rent and for sale worldwide; published twice a year; newsletter is quarterly.

Timeshare Quarterly (816 S.E. Eighth Ave., Deerfield Beach, FL 33441; 800-874-6722); quarterly magazine lists about 1,200 timeshares and campgrounds for resale or rent in the U.S., Canada, Mexico and the Caribbean. Free to prospective buyers.

John T. Reed's Real Estate Investor's Monthly (Reed Publishing, 342 Bryan Drive, Danville, CA, 94526; 800-635-5425) Plain talk and cautionary counsel about real estate investment from an expert in the field.

Brokers, Clearinghouses, etc.

Condolink, 7701 Pacific St., Suite 300, Omaha, NE 68114; 800-877-9600.

Timeshare Resales International, 2122 Port Republic Rd., Harrisonburg, VA 22801; 800-368-3541 (east coast), 800-356-5277 (west coast).

International Resale Brokers Association, P.O. Box 617521, Orlando, FL 32861.

American Society of Real Estate Counselors, 430 N. Michigan Ave., Chicago, IL 60611; 312-329-8427.

CHAPTER 15

INVESTING IN RESIDENTIAL REAL ESTATE

S OME PEOPLE become landlords almost by accident, when they decide to keep and rent out a former residence rather than sell it—either because they can't sell it for a fair price or it makes sense as an investment.

Others are part-time landlords of a vacation property, which they rent to vacationers and also use personally.

Still other people are enthusiastic, deliberate investors in residential properties, whether single-family residences, condominium units or small multi-unit apartment houses.

The reason for the popularity of small-scale real estate investing is simple, and it's rooted in the track record of home prices since World War II. A well-chosen residence in an economically stable area has long been a pretty good investment, by at least holding its value and often appreciating at more than the rate of inflation.

In picking a good property for investment, you should be guided by many of the same criteria that affect value in a residence you would occupy yourself, especially the importance of a good location and a property that is in keeping with its surroundings.

Your rental property should be typical, not overly special. It should appeal broadly to the most renters in a given price range.

You want nothing that will disqualify major segments of the market. For example, it should be near public transportation, so its enjoyment is not dependent on owning a car; it should not have too hilly an approach or too many steps inside, which would turn away many elderly renters. Even that swimming pool that you're crazy about might not be appealing to a family with young, non-swimming kids, or people who don't want to tackle the maintenance.

CONVERTING YOUR HOME TO A RENTAL PROPERTY

This is how many taxpayers get into the landlord business—by deciding to hold on to their house when they move to a new home. That may sound like an easy way to do it; after all, you know the property and the neighborhood and probably have a good idea of what would be a reasonable rent. If you can afford it, why not turn the old homestead into a rental property? That way you could enjoy the rental income and tax benefits, not to mention the continued appreciation on the place.

Uncle Sam has a few special twists for homeowners-turned-landlords. You do qualify to write off all the basic rental expenses, and if those expenses exceed your rental income, you may be able to use the loss to shelter up to $25,000 of other income. But you fall under a unique rule when it comes to figuring depreciation and calculating the gain or loss when you sell the property.

Although your home probably appreciated—perhaps quite significantly—while you lived in it, you don't get to use the higher value for depreciation purposes. Your tax basis in such a converted residence is the lower of the house's value when you convert it to rental property or your adjusted basis. That means you're usually stuck with adjusted basis, which is generally what you originally paid for the place, plus the cost of improvements. If you rolled over the profit from a previous home—as discussed in Chapter 17—your basis is reduced by the amount of the profit on which you deferred the tax.

This rule can make a big difference in your depreciation write-offs. Say you bought your home several years ago for $50,000, $40,000 of which was the value of the building. Although you've made no improvements, it's now worth

$120,000, $100,000 of which is the value of the building. If you convert it to rental use, your depreciation is based on the $40,000 basis. If you bought your home after 1980, you depreciate the basis over 27.5 years; if you purchased before then, writeoffs are stretched out over a longer period.

Special vacation-home tax rules apply to a property you rent part-time and use personally, and these are discussed in Chapter 14. Also remember this about converting a home to a rental property: Doing so means forfeiting the right to roll over profit on the ultimate sale of the house into a new home. That tax break applies only when the home sold is your principal residence.

EQUITY SHARING

If you want minimal personal involvement in a real estate investment, you might try equity sharing. You as the investor and an owner-occupant agree on who pays how much of the down payment, mortgage interest, property taxes and other expenses such as insurance and repairs and on how the equity will be split when the property is sold. The owner-occupant also pays you fair market rent for your part of the house.

Setting a fair rent for your share of the house is a key to whether a shared-equity arrangement will pass muster with the IRS. If you charge a bargain rent, the deal can fall under the vacation-home rules, which would prohibit you from deducting any expenses that exceed the rental income.

But remember that the owner-occupant has to pay rent only on the part of the house you own. For example, in a 50/50 deal, if similar homes in the area generally rent for around $1,000 a month, you wouldn't need to set the rent above $500. And you might be able to set it even lower if the owner-occupant can be considered to be a particularly good tenant. These arrangements are often used by parents and children (see Chapter 10), and the U.S. Tax Court said that "fair rent" for a relative can be as much as 20% lower than fair rent for a stranger.

As the owner-investor, you get all the tax advantages of owning rental real estate. You report the rent you receive as income and deduct the mortgage interest and property taxes paid as a rental expense. You also deduct your share of the insurance bills, for example, and the cost of repairs. In addition, you can claim depreciation deductions based on the cost of your half of the house. If your expenses outstrip the rent you receive, you may be able to qualify to deduct up to $25,000 of your losses against other income.

The owner-occupant of the house gets all the tax advantages of homeownership, on a scaled-down level. The portion of the mortgage interest and property taxes paid are deductible, just as if he owned the house outright. (Like any tenant, of course, he can't deduct the rent he pays you.)

When the house is sold, you and the owner-occupant will split the proceeds. As an investor, your profit is taxable in the year of the sale. Since the house is the owner-occupant's principal residence, however, he or she may defer the tax bill by rolling the profit into a new home, as explained in Chapter 17.

The law requires that these arrangements be set up under a written "shared-equity financing agreement" that spells out the conditions of the deal, including each partner's share, which one will make the house a home, how expenses will be split and the fact that the owner-occupant will pay rent to the other owner. Because of the complexities, if you're interested in equity sharing, find a lawyer, real estate agent or mortgage-company official who is familiar with these arrangements.

RISKS AND REWARDS

This chapter is a guide for the small-scale, beginning investor in residential real estate, but the principles discussed are the same ones that the biggest investors are guided by, too.

Note that we call this "investing." Some purchasers of real estate are really speculators, and the distinction is largely one of risk. The speculator buys low-priced properties in decaying neighborhoods that he believes are poised for a rebound. The speculator buys foreclosed houses at auctions in cities suffering from economic distress, believing that when things get better, he'll make a killing on appreciation. Most investors won't touch situations like this. As in every kind of financial challenge, the rewards are commensurate with risks. The speculator who gambles correctly will make a lot of money, and he's willing to accept the possibility of losing a lot, too.

Before deciding to buy a property, you should consider not only the investment fundamentals, but also how such a choice compares with other possible investments. How does it fit with your long-range financial goals? And do you want to make the time commitment required to manage even a small holding? If you want to invest in real estate without active involvement, have you considered buying shares in a well-managed real estate investment trust, which buys and manages many properties for current income and appreciation, passing the gains on to its stockholders?

Whether residential real estate turns out to be lucrative for you—or just a costly ordeal—depends on when you buy, what you pay, where the property is located, how long you plan to hold it, and how diligently you study this business, among other factors.

THE ABC'S OF INVESTING

Start your inquiry by familiarizing yourself with some of the analytical tools needed to evaluate the economics of owning and renting a property.

Despite the complications, there are several relatively simple methods you can use to compute real estate gains and losses. Once you have developed your own predictions of inflation and real estate appreciation, the calculations require only straightforward arithmetic applied to the data normally used to prepare an income tax return.

Return on an investment property involves the interaction of four elements: on the positive side, there is rental income and appreciation, and on the debit side (in addition to maintenance expenses) there are the expenses of interest payments and depreciation, which can be used to offset income from the property—and may be used to "shelter" other income as well.

Loan Payments

Each mortgage payment consists of interest and principal amortization. The entire payment reduces the cash flow of earnings from a rental property, but only the interest is deductible for tax purposes. The amortization reduces the mortgage loan principal, thereby increasing your equity—your stake in the property.

During the first year of a loan, monthly payments consist almost entirely of interest. The proportion steadily declines thereafter. As a result, the tax break you get on mortgage interest drops off year by year until it disappears. Most investors sell or refinance their mortgages before that happens. By obtaining a new loan, you can draw money out of the property without selling it.

Depreciation

This is a noncash expense that can put money in your pocket. The law lets you depreciate rental property, claiming deductions that are supposed to reflect how the building is being "used up." You depreciate your basis in the building. The basis is basically what you paid for the property minus the value of the land. Depreciation is a key to many real estate investments because even if rental income fails to cover all out-of-pocket expenses, the tax savings of depreciation—by sheltering other income from the IRS—can make up much, if not all, of the difference.

Before 1987, buildings could be depreciated over 19 years (never mind the fact that a building would probably last much longer) using a method called the Accelerated Cost Recovery System (ACRS). It was "accelerated" because the write-off schedule bunched bigger deductions in the earlier years.

The law now demands that you use a straight-line method and stretches the write-offs over 27.5 years (31.5 years for commercial buildings.) The current rules apply only to buildings put into service in 1987 and later years. If you put rental property into service earlier, you continue to use the more favorable depreciation rules in effect at the time.

For new investments, the first-year depreciation deduction depends on the month you put the property into service and is based on what accountants call the midmonth convention: Regardless of what day of the month you start depreciating the building, you get credit for half of the first month. Put a rental house into service on July 1, for example, and your first-year depreciation write-off would be for 5½ months—half of July plus the rest of the year.

Figuring how much depreciation you can write off is fairly simple. Begin with the depreciable basis—which is the cost of the building itself. (That's less than you pay when you buy the place because you must subtract the cost of the land, which is not depreciable.) Divide the basis by 27.5 to find the annual depreciation amount. Divide that by 12 to get the monthly figure, and multiply that amount by the number of months it was available for rent, whether or not you actually had a tenant. On a property with a $100,000 basis a full year's depreciation would be $3,636 ($100,000/27.5). One month's worth would be $303.

After the first year, you deduct 3.64% of your basis each year, until the final year when the write-off would be slightly smaller depending on the first-year deduction.

Remember this about depreciation: Each deduction you take reduces your adjusted basis in the property. When you sell the property, it is the reduced basis that is compared to the sales proceeds to determine your profit on the sale. Thus every dollar you deduct as depreciation could result in a dollar of extra taxable profit when you sell.

If you make improvements to your rental property, the cost is added to your tax basis and can therefore trim the taxable profit when you sell. Such capital improvements should be depreciated separately from the building. Say, for example, that four years after you begin renting a duplex you add a $20,000 addition. You would depreciate that $20,000 over its own 27.5-year tax life rather than simply including that amount when figuring future depreciation write-offs for the building.

Other Rental Expenses

You can still deduct the costs of producing rental income. Uncle Sam demands a share only of your net income, so it's clearly in your best interest to tote up all the tax-saving expenses that can trim that figure. Be sure to count the following:
- Mortgage interest.
- Property taxes.
- Insurance premiums you pay.
- Fees paid to a management company.
- Cost of newspaper ads advertising the availability of the property.

◆ Legal or accounting costs connected with drafting a lease or evicting tenants.

◆ Cost of repairs to the property.

◆ Any utilities you pay for your tenants or while the place is vacant between renters.

◆ Salary or wages you pay to others to take care of the property, for cleaning or gardening, for example. This includes what you pay your child if he or she really works on the rental.

◆ The cost of travel to look after your properties. This can include the cost of driving across town to repair a leaky faucet or the expenses—including travel, meals and lodging—of visiting out-of-town rental property. The key to including such costs is that the principal purpose of the trip be to inspect or work on your property. For example, taking a two-week vacation to Florida and spending an afternoon checking on a rental condo won't qualify. A week-long visit, five days of which are spent on painting and repairs to prepare the place for a new tenant, would qualify.

Cash Flow from Rent

The rent you can charge is a function of supply and demand in your area in general, and rents on comparable properties in particular. One rule of thumb for estimating potential receipts holds that the annual rent should amount to about 9% of the market value of the property. That translates into $7,200 a year on an $80,000 home, or $600 a month.

Look for a property that, when rented, will produce a positive annual cash flow, however slight. That means the rental income will have to come close to covering mortgage payments, maintenance, taxes and insurance.

John T. Reed, editor of *John T. Reed's Real Estate Investor's Monthly* (342 Bryan Dr., Danville, CA 94526) recommends buying investment homes at the low end of the price spectrum. "The guys who have the positive cash flow buy at gross rent multipliers (GRM) of 90 to 110 times monthly rent. For example, a house that rents for $750 a month and sells for $80,000 has a gross rent multiplier of $80,000/$750, or 107. In general, the cheaper the house, the lower the gross rent multiplier."

As a buyer of a principal residence for you and your family, you might be willing to pay a premium for a very unusual house in a fancy neighborhood, carrying a high price relative to its square footage and number of bedrooms. But as a cash-flow-conscious investor, you should be wary of that kind of house. While it might appreciate more rapidly than the more modest house (the finest examples of every kind of asset tend to out-gain the average-quality items), it will probably not generate enough rent in the early years, relative to its high price, to generate a positive cash flow.

Appreciation Prospects

Single-family detached homes and condominiums often are overpriced relative to the rent they generate. This is because their market prices are influenced by the value buyers place on them as *homes*—including future appreciation. On the other hand, when the property is rented, tenants typically pay only for current *shelter* value, which is a function of space, number of bedrooms, etc.

Because the rent collected often does not cover the cost of holding the property, investors experience a negative cash flow—an operating loss. Not only must they dig into their pockets every month, but they must rely on a substantial increase in property value to offset that loss and to provide a good return on investment. And that means having a pool of prospective buyers seeking to purchase a home at the appropriate time (and willing to pay a price higher than would be justified by rents alone), as well as timing the sale to occur when mortgages are readily available and reasonably affordable.

Homes probably will remain a good long-term hedge against inflation, as they have been for decades. Nevertheless, counting on appreciation to turn a negative return into a positive one will be, on the whole, riskier than it was in other times such as the 1970s, when prices were going up by leaps and bounds almost everywhere.

FIGURING RATES OF RETURN

There are various standard methods of figuring rate of return on investments in small residential properties.

In all the methods described below, we'll examine two different properties, one costing $120,000 and the other $80,000. Each is bought with a 30-year, fixed-rate mortgage at 9.5% covering 80% of purchase price.

We'll presume that each property was sold after five years of ownership, and we'll assume each appreciated at a compounded rate of about 4% a year. However, we'll assume that rents, property taxes and maintenance costs did not increase during the five years; they probably will, but they could be considered self-canceling factors, and leaving them constant simplifies the equation considerably.

We'll see, by the end of our calculations and the sale of the properties, that the less expensive property—bought for $80,000 and sold for about $97,000—generated an average annual return of just over 9% over five years of ownership—a healthy return but nothing spectacular; many stock market investors get at least that return with far less effort.

The more expensive property—costing $120,000 and later sold for $145,000—showed an annualized return of 3%.

A note of caution: there are many variables that will affect your rate of return. For example, you'll do much better if your properties are located in high-growth regions where home prices (and possibly rents) might appreciate at 7% or 10% a year. Also, our examples presume agent-assisted sales with a 6% commission; a sale by owner with no commission would improve the rate of return.

On the other hand, our scenarios assume full rental of the homes for 12 months a year, with no rent lost to the transition between tenants; that's not always the case. Likewise, we assumed full owner management of the properties and rather modest maintenance costs. The bottom line would be worse if you hired a professional property manager or if maintenance costs were particularly high.

Our examples also assume a 20% down payment on each property—the standard amount that most mortgage lenders require. A smaller down payment—say, 10% or even 5%—and a larger mortgage would probably increase monthly out-of-pocket loss, but it might also improve your eventual return on a modest cash investment.

CASH FLOW BEFORE TAX

This tells you how much spendable cash the property yields for the year. Essentially, you match the anticipated gross income against overall cash outlay. Expenses typically include such things as taxes, insurance, maintenance and management fees.

The mortgage payment figure used for both properties in the illustration represents the first year's payments on a $96,000, 9.5%, 30-year mortgage for property A, and a $64,000 loan with the same terms for property B. It is assumed in both cases that the tenant pays the utility bills, so they are not included as operating expenses.

Because you are measuring cash income and expenditures, include as an expense the part of the mortgage payment that reduces the loan principal, even though that item is not tax-deductible, and exclude depreciation, which is deductible but requires no cash outlay.

CASH FLOW BEFORE TAX

	Property A	Property B
Purchase price:	$120,000	$80,000
Plus settlement costs	3,600	2,400
Cost	123,600	82,400
Minus mortgage balance	96,000	64,000
Cash invested:		
Downpayment + settlement costs	$27,600	$18,400

Gross income: Property A

Rent of $850 × 12 months:	10,200.00

Minus expenses:

Mortgage payment (interest + principal on
$96,000 at 9.5% for 30 years)

807.22 × 12 =	9,686.64	
Taxes:	1,000.00	
Insurance:	600.00	
Maintenance:	500.00	
TOTAL	$11,786.64	(11,786.64)

Cash flow before tax   ($ 1,586.64)

Gross income: Property B

Rent of $700 × 12:	$8,400.00

Minus expenses:

Mortgage payment (interest + principal on
$64,000 at 9.5% for 30 years)

538.15 × 12 = $6,457.80

Taxes:	800.00
Insurance:	500.00
Maintenance:	500.00
TOTAL	$8,257.80

(8,257.80)

Cash flow before tax: $ 142.20

Return on cash flow, before tax:

Property A:

$$\frac{\text{Cash flow before tax}}{\text{Cash invested}} = \frac{(1,586.64)}{27,600} = (.057) \times 100 = -5.7\%$$

Property B:

$$\frac{\text{Cash flow before tax}}{\text{Cash invested}} = \frac{142.20}{18,400} = .0077 \times 100 = .77\%$$

CASH FLOW AFTER TAX

Here, you measure current return after taking depreciation and taxes into account. Because loan payments that reduce principal are not tax deductible, adding the principal payment on the mortgage back into the cash flow before tax is a mechanical device for removing that item. It was subtracted from gross income to arrive at cash flow before tax, and adding it back merely cancels out the subtraction.

In the example, annual depreciation is computed by taking the depreciable tax basis and dividing it by 27.5. That figure is then divided by 12 to arrive at a monthly figure, and then multiplied by the number of months and half-months you held the property during the tax year. Regardless of the day of the month you buy, the law considers the property to be "placed in service" at mid-month. It makes no difference whether you become owner of a rental home on January 1, or January 31—you claim depreciation for 11.5 months of that year.

For the tax calculation, a 1989 marginal 28% income tax rate was assumed. If your analysis indicates that investing in a property will increase your income for federal income tax purposes, estimate the tax liability and subtract it from the cash flow before tax. It is likely, however, that you will come out with a negative figure.

In the past, real estate purchases often were arranged to produce just such a loss, which was then used to offset income the investor earned from other sources. An investor in the 50% marginal bracket paid $50 less in tax for every $100 removed from taxable income.

But beginning in 1987, the law broke all taxpayer income or loss into active, passive and portfolio categories, and severely limited a taxpayer's ability to offset gains or losses in one category against gains or losses in another. Your salary or the income you earn while actively involved in a business or trade on a regular and continuing basis is classified as active income. Money received from investing in a trade or business usually is passive income. Dividends on stock, interest from bank certificates of deposit, bonds and annuities are portfolio income.

Rental activity (other than very short-term activity such as would occur in operating a hotel, motel or country inn) is specifically labeled a passive activity. That could have been a knockout blow for a lot of landlords who count on claiming tax losses to make their real estate investments financially feasible. However, the law includes a major exception to the passive-loss rules that makes rental real estate an oasis in the otherwise barren tax-shelter landscape. If you qualify for this special exception, you can continue to deduct up to $25,000 of rental real estate losses against other income, such as your salary or interest and dividends.

To qualify you must *actively participate* in the management of the property. Fortunately, the demands for passing that test aren't particularly onerous. You don't have to be on call for middle-of-the-night repairs, cut the grass and collect rents. The IRS rules don't say exactly what you do have to do, but even if you hire a management firm to handle day-to-day matters, you

CASH FLOW AFTER TAXES

Property A

Cash flow before tax:	(1,586.64)
Add back principal payment:	591.98
Net:	(994.66)

Minus depreciation:
($121,000 − 30,250 = 92,750; 90,750/27.5 = 3,300;
3,300/12 = 275; 275 × 11.5 = 3,162.50) =   (3,162.50)

Taxable income (loss)	(4,157.16)

Property B

Cash flow before tax:	142.00
Add back principal payment:	394.69
	536.69

Minus depreciation:
($81,000 − 20,250 = 60,750; 60,750/27.5 = 2,209.09;
2,209.09/12 = 184.09; 184.09 × 11.5 = 2,117.04)   (2,117.04)

Taxable income (loss)	(1,580.35)

Tax liability or saving
taxable income × tax rate = tax liability
or
tax loss × tax rate = tax saving

Property A

Cash flow before tax:	(1,586.64)
Plus tax saving (4,157.16 × 28%):	1,164.00
Cash flow after tax:	(422.64)

Property B

Cash flow before tax:	142.00
Plus tax saving (1,580.35 × 28%):	442.49
Cash flow after tax:	584.49

can be actively involved as long as you approve tenants, set the rent and okay capital improvements.

The $25,000 exception isn't for fat cats, though, no matter how actively they're involved. It is phased out by 50 cents for every dollar of adjusted gross income (which is your income before subtracting itemized deductions, exemptions and rental losses) over $100,000, and is completely eliminated at $150,000.

The $25,000 allowance doesn't protect losses generated by a limited partnership or any rental property in which you own less than 10%. Passive losses that you can't deduct immediately are not useless. They are suspended rather than obliterated. You can store the losses for future years and deduct them when you have passive income to shelter. And when you ultimately sell the rental property that generated the passive losses, any unused losses are liberated to be deducted against any type of income, including your salary.

There are phase-in rules for passive activities begun or purchased under contract before the law was enacted. For 1990, 10% of losses outside the $25,000 exception still can be deducted from other income; after that, this deduction disappears.

TOTAL RETURN AFTER SALE

In this calculation, you compute the overall return, after tax, from selling the property. In the example, the sale takes place after five years. Accumulated passive losses (those carried forward in any given year because they could not be used to offset passive income in that same year) are used in full to offset gain when the property is sold.

The 1986 Tax Reform Act eliminated the special tax treatment of capital gains, which are profits from the sale of such assets as stocks and real estate owned more than six months. Prior law excluded 60% of those profits from taxation. Since only 40% was taxed, the top effective rate on profits ranged from 4.4% to 20%.

In the example, it was assumed for simplicity that gross income and costs—except for the interest deduction and annual income tax—did not change during the five-year period. The selling price, though, rose about 4% a year compounded— enough to produce a profit. In practice, your costs and income will change to some extent each year.

Property A:

Sales price:	$145,000
Minus sales expenses:	− 8,700
Gross sales proceeds:	136,300
Gross sales proceeds:	136,300
Minus mortgage balance:	− 92,391
Net sales proceeds:	$ 43,909
Cost:	$123,600
Minus total depreciation:	− 15,813
Adjusted cost:	107,787
Gross sales proceeds:	136,300
Minus adjusted cost:	−107,787
Taxable gain:	28,513

Taxable gain × marginal tax rate = tax

$28,513 × .28 =	$ 7,984
Net sales proceeds:	43,909
Minus tax:	− 7,984
Net sales proceeds after tax:	$ 35,925
Net sales proceeds after tax:	35,925
Plus annual cash flows after tax:	(2,113)
	33,812
Minus cash invested:	− 27,600
Total return:	6,212

Total % return:

$$\frac{\text{Total return}}{\text{Cash invested}} \times 100 = \% \text{ return}$$

$$\frac{6{,}212}{27{,}600} \times 100 = 23\%$$

Annual average return:

$$\frac{\text{Total \% return}}{\text{Years property held}} \times \text{Annual average return, or}$$

$$\frac{23}{5} = 4.6\%$$

Property B:

Sales price:	$ 97,000
Minus sales expenses:	− 5,820
Gross sales proceeds:	91,180
Gross sales proceeds:	91,180
Minus mortgage balance:	− 61,594
Net sales proceeds:	$ 29,586
Cost:	$ 82,400
Minus depreciation for all years:	− 10,585
Adjusted cost:	71,815
Gross sales proceeds:	91,180
Minus adjusted cost:	− 71,815
Taxable gain:	19,365

Taxable gain × marginal tax rate = tax

$19,365 × .28 = $5,422.20

Net sales proceeds:	$29,586
Minus tax:	− 5,422
Net sales proceeds after tax:	$24,164

Net sales proceeds after tax:	$24,164
Plus annual cash flows after tax:	+ 2,922
	$27,086
Minus cash invested:	−18,400
Total return:	8,686

Total % return:

$$\frac{\text{Total return}}{\text{Cash invested}} \times 100 = \% \text{ return}$$

$$\frac{8,686}{18,400} \times 100 = 47\%$$

Annual average return:

$$\frac{\text{Total \% return}}{\text{Years property held}} \times \text{Annual average return, or}$$

$$\frac{47\%}{5} = 9.4\%$$

OVERALL RETURN ON TOTAL CAPITAL

This measures operating income as a percentage of a property's worth and is calculated by dividing net operating income by current market value. Calculate net operating income by subtracting annual operating expenses, such as taxes, insurance and maintenance, from the total income from the property, which, in the example on the opposite page, comes entirely from rents. Do not include annual mortgage payments in operating expenses.

Overall return on capital, however, doesn't give you any perspective on whether the money you will keep tied up in the property each year (the down payment, settlement costs, repayment of principal and appreciation) could be earning a higher return elsewhere. Looking at return on equity will give you a better measure for making those kinds of comparisons.

$$\frac{\text{Net operating income}}{\text{Market value}} = \text{Overall return on capital}$$

Property A: $10,200 - 2,100 = \dfrac{8,100}{120,000} = .0675 \times 100 = 6.75\%$

Property B: $8,400 - 1,800 = \dfrac{6,600}{80,000} = .0825 \times 100 = 8.25\%$

THE RIGHT STUFF: RETURN ON EQUITY

Most investors, especially less sophisticated ones, tend to judge how well they are doing by their return on investment. By "investment" they typically mean the down payment they made when they bought the property in the first place. When you calculate it that way, return on investment usually goes up every year. As a result, the investor thinks he or she is flourishing, when in fact, actual investment performance probably is deteriorating a little bit every year that the property is held. Why? Because the value of the property may be increasing faster than the income.

The down payment you made on the property when you bought it is irrelevant after the purchase. What matters is your equity in the property—the difference between what the property is worth and the balance owed on the mortgage. The equity represents your stake in the property, because it is money you could realize—and use for some other investment—by selling the property. Return on equity provides a more valid measure of investment performance than return on original investment.

$$\frac{\text{Cash flow before taxes}}{\text{Current equity}} = \text{Return on equity before taxes}$$

The table on the next page shows how the two return figures differ. Say you buy a rental property for $100,000. After covering the mortgage payments and operating expenses, you have $1,000 left over at the end of the year—the before-tax cash flow. Your down payment was $20,000. Assume the before-tax cash flow and the value of the property both increase 10% per year, and that you pay off $400 on the mortgage each year. The table demonstrates what your return on the $100,000 investment would look like, before taking selling costs into account.

Return on investment

Before-tax cash flow:	$ 1,000	1,100	1,210	1,331	1,464
Investment:	20,000	20,000	20,000	20,000	20,000
Return on investment:	5%	5.5%	6.05%	6.7%	7.3%

Return on equity

Assuming 10% price and income growth each year

Before-tax cash flow:	$ 1,000	1,100	1,210	1,331	1,464
Property value:	100,000	110,000	121,000	133,000	146,400
Loan balance:	80,000	79,600	79,200	78,800	78,400
Equity:	20,000	30,400	41,800	54,200	68,000
Return on equity:	5%	3.6%	2.9%	2.5%	2.2%

Notice that the return on investment increases each year. But look at return on equity. As you can see, it goes down, not up. In a rising real estate market, where equity in the property increases as fast or faster than the income, returns will fall.

Even if property values increase only modestly and the demand for rental homes permits rents to rise substantially, returns on equity still fall, but more gradually. In the example below, cash flow is increasing at the same 10% each year, but the market value of the property is going up by only 4% a year.

Return on equity

Assuming income up 10% a year, value up 4%

Before-tax cash flow:	$ 1,000	1,100	1,210	1,331	1,464
Property value:	100,000	104,000	108,160	112,486	116,986
Loan balance:	80,000	79,600	79,200	78,800	78,400
Equity:	20,000	24,400	28,960	33,686	38,586
Return on equity:	5%	4.5%	4.18%	3.95%	3.79%

THE BENEFITS OF IMPROVING A RENTAL PROPERTY

One way to improve the return on equity is to renovate or otherwise improve the property, boosting both the rental income it can generate and the market value for resale.

Keep in mind, however, that the same warning applies to improving a rental property as a principal residence: Don't over-improve it relative to comparable homes in the same neighborhood, or you'll get neither higher rent nor appreciation sufficient to offset your additional investment.

Landlords, even more than homeowners, must investigate what kinds of improvements and additions yield the best return on investment and stick to those guidelines. For a landlord, for example, adding two bedrooms or finishing the basement into another rental unit will immediately enhance rental income, while building a garage might not.

Return on equity

Refinancing for improvements and to hike rent

Before-tax cash flow:	$ 700	700	2,000	2,200	2,420
Property value:	100,000	104,000	150,000	156,000	162,000
Loan balance:	80,000	79,600	120,000	119,600	119,200
Equity:	20,000	24,400	30,000	36,400	42,800
Return on equity:	3.5%	2.86%	6.66%	6.04%	5.67%

PULL OUT EQUITY, PUT IT TO BETTER USE

One sure way to deal with the decline in the return on equity is to pull some of it out of the property, with a full or partial refinancing. The proceeds of the loan can be used for other investments—either additional down payments on more real estate or financial investments likes stocks and bonds. This is how many small-scale real estate investors used inflation and leverage (borrowed money) to snowball their wealth in the 1970s. It's harder to do in a low-inflation environment, but the techniques are the same.

Most investors realize their return can be magnified by borrowing a large portion of the purchase price when they invest in real estate. But the same investors who are eager to use leverage when they buy a property often forget about it after the purchase.

Most investors hate to make a down payment of more than 20% or 25%. But those same investors too often let their equity grow well beyond that level. (In the first return-on-equity example above, the investor's equity rose from 20% to 46% of the property's value, and the return plummeted.)

The reasons for using leverage when you buy a property apply equally to the period when you hold the property. Some investors make it a practice to set and maintain an equity target—say 20% or 25% of the property's value. Theoretically, you could achieve this by refinancing periodically with a second mortgage or a new first mortgage.

The decline in return on equity and the difficulties and expense that may be encountered in refinancing create, in effect, a penalty for retaining property for long periods. But, the loss of special capital gains tax treatment and lower tax rates counter the pressure to sell—at least for properties producing income on a before-tax basis.

Returning to Properties A and B above, let's calculate the return on equity at the end of the first year, using before-tax and after-tax cash flows. We'll assume that each property appreciated 3% over its total cost of $123,600 and $82,400, respectively.

Return on equity before tax:

	Property A	Property B
Before-tax cash flow:	(1,587)	142
Property value:	127,308	84,872
Loan balance:	95,408	63,605
Equity:	31,900	21,267
Return on equity:	(4.97%)	.67%

EQUITY DIVIDEND AFTER TAX

This recognizes the tax savings resulting from the mortgage interest and depreciation deductions of real estate investments.

Remember, though, that these figures are projections, not results. Use them to assist you in making investment decisions, and then at least once each year, to see where you stand.

Return on equity after tax:

	Property A	Property B
After-tax cash flow:	(132)	695
Equity:	31,900	21,267
Return on equity after tax:	(1.00%)	2.00%

BEYOND BASICS

Two More-Complex Calculations

Most small-scale investors in single-family houses will find the calculations above adequate. If you study real estate books written for professional investors in multi-family housing and commercial properties, however, you may encounter two other ways of figuring return: internal rate of return (IRR) and adjusted rate of return (ARR). To use these, you'll need a financial calculator and computer spreadsheet . . . plus lots of patience. The IRR assumes cash flows are reinvested at the IRR rate, whereas the ARR allows you to choose a reinvestment rate—typically an after-tax rate. In general, the ARR will be lower than the IRR.

Using an IRR or ARR allows you to interject the time value of money into your analysis. It is a sophisticated measure of return that takes into account the fact that the money made on the sale is earned not in equal annual amounts (as an annual return assumes) but in a lump sum at the end of the holding period. The calculation factors in expenses, income, beginning equity, tax savings from interest and depreciation deductions, appreciation, income taxes, and the timing of payments and receipts.

This time-value factor is significant. It's not hard to grasp that the after-tax cash flow you earned three years ago counts more than the same amount earned one year ago. That's because the money, if invested, could earn more interest for you in three years than it could in one. By the same token, the reverse is true of cash you won't receive until next year: the same amount would be worth more to you today because you could put it to work earning interest. Both the IRR and ARR take these differences into account.

IRR/ARR also properly values appreciation. Unlike the measures of profitability used on the preceding pages, it doesn't assume that money made on the sale is earned in equal annual amounts. Instead, the IRR/ARR assigns the after-tax sales proceeds to the after-tax cash flow in the year of the sale, thus crediting earnings when they are actually received.

What the IRR or ARR tells you is the percentage rate of return it would take to make your initial cash investment equal to the present value of all the benefits associated with the property, accounting for the time value of all costs incurred and income received along the way. A respectable IRR on major residential and commercial properties is thought to be 15% to 18%.

If you're boggled by the complexity of the IRR or ARR, an accountant probably can run the numbers for you. Members of the American Society of Real Estate Counselors, an affiliate of the National Association of Realtors, will advise investors on all aspects of a deal, including IRR. You can get a free directory of members by writing the Society at 430 N. Michigan Ave., Chicago, IL 60611.

Buying a Foreclosed Property

You may be able to buy a house in the final stage of foreclosure, when the lender has title to the property. At this point, the price may be attractive—possibly below market value—and the lenders may offer good financing terms. Mortgage institutions, such as Fannie Mae, FHA, VA, savings and loans and commercial banks acquire properties when borrowers default on their loan obligations. Obviously, buying a home that has been foreclosed involves a higher-than-normal level of risk. You'll want to assure yourself that the property can be mortgaged, and that the seller will be able to close the deal in a timely manner and provide you with clear title when you become the owner. For more information about foreclosures, refer to Andrew McLean"s *Foreclosures, How to Profitably Invest in Distressed Real Estate* (Contemporary Books, Chicago). In addition to studying the subject, you'll want to use the services of an experienced broker and real estate attorney.

Installment Sales

Installment sales are a popular method for selling property, particularly rental real estate, because the seller can help grease the deal by providing at least part of the necessary financing for the buyer. Rather than demanding the full price up front, with an installment sale you agree to have the buyer pay at least part of the price in the future. And, wonder of wonders, the IRS doesn't tax your profit on the sale until you actually get the money.

If you will receive at least one payment in a year after the sale, you can use the installment method to report and pay tax on the profit as you receive it. Each year, the payments you receive will have three components:

♦ Return of your basis, which is nontaxable.

♦ Profit, which thanks to tax reform's elimination of the capital-gains exclusion is fully taxable.

♦ Interest on the "loan" you made by financing the sale. The IRS demands that you charge interest on the unpaid balance. This, too, is taxable.

Depreciation recapture. This is a complication—one of many—that may make you wonder whether the benefit of delaying the tax bill is worth the hassle. As mentioned earlier in this chapter, because depreciation reduces your basis, it translates into higher gain when you sell. The law demands that all depreciation recapture be taxed in the year of the sale, regardless of when the income is received. When considering an installment sale, consider the impact of depreciation recapture. You'll probably want to be sure the down payment on the sale is at least enough to cover the tax bill that's due on the sale.

Minimum interest. The law requires that you charge an "adequate" amount of interest on the installment sale, and it's not because the IRS is worried that you'd otherwise have an unfair advantage over banks and other lenders. The rationale is to prevent the price from being set artificially high to make up for interest-free or below-market financing. The IRS cares about the price of the sale, of course, because it affects the seller's gain or loss and the buyer's basis for depreciation in the building.

You can meet the IRS definition of adequate and still give the buyer a break on the interest rate. What the agency demands is that you charge a rate at least equal to the "applicable federal rate" (AFR) at the time of the sale. The AFR is determined by the IRS and is basically what it costs the government to borrow money. Regardless of how high the AFR goes, however, you don't have to charge more than 9%, compounded semiannually, on your installment sale. If the AFR at the time of the sale is less than 9%, you can write a lower rate into the contract, but the IRS can't demand that you charge more than 9%.

If the contract fails to provide for adequate stated interest, the IRS has ways—very complicated calculations—for figuring what part of each payment is "imputed" interest—that is, what part will be treated as interest no matter what you call it. This affects not only your gain or loss and the buyer's basis but also the amount of interest income you report each year and the amount the buyer gets to deduct. It's much easier to check with the IRS before finalizing a deal to be sure you include an adequate interest rate.

Tax-Free Exchanges

You may have heard of a "tax-free exchange" of real estate, a concept that has definite appeal. This maneuver allows you to dispose of rental property without triggering an immediate tax bill on the gain. What it demands is that you find an amenable owner of similar property. Although that's not easy, some brokers specialize in real estate exchanges.

If you trade property for property of a "like kind," the IRS does not treat your disposal of your property as a sale. Like kind is liberally defined. Clearly, exchanging a rental house for another rental house is covered, but so is trading raw land for an apartment building. The advantage is that you hold off the tax bill on your profit from the first property.

Consider an example. Say you have a rental house with an adjusted basis of $50,000 and that it is now worth $150,000. You'd like to expand your rental activities by buying a duplex with a price tag of $250,000. If you sell the first house, you'll owe tax on $100,000 of profit. That will cost you $33,000 if you're in the 33% bracket. Instead, assume you persuade the owner of the duplex to trade—his $250,000 duplex for your $150,000 house plus $100,000 in cash. As long as the deal qualifies as a tax-free exchange, you avoid that $33,000 tax tab.

Avoid is really too strong a term. Defer is more accurate. Your basis in the new building would not be its $250,000 price but rather your old $50,000 basis plus the $100,000 in cash you had to put into the deal. When you later sell the duplex—assuming you don't work another tax-free exchange—the gain would be based on your $150,000 basis. That would give the IRS its delayed shot at the $100,000 of profit that built up in the first house.

Since, in this example, the owner of the duplex received cash as well as like-kind property, it's not a totally tax-free exchange for him. Part or all of his profit—the difference between his basis in the property and the $250,000 value of your building plus cash—would be taxable. He would owe tax on the lower of his total profit or $100,000 (the amount of cash received). His basis on the rental house would be reduced by any part of the $100,000 that wasn't taxed in the year of the trade.

Like-kind exchanges have disadvantages. Your depreciation deductions on the new property will be held down because you carry over the basis from old property. Also, if you use a like-kind exchange in a year you have suspended passive losses (discussed on pages 208–211) you'll miss the chance to absorb some of those losses.

To qualify as a tax-free exchange, the trade must take place within a specified time frame. You must identify the property you're going to receive within 45 days of transferring your property, and the trade must generally be completed within 180 days.

PROPERTY MANAGEMENT: MORE IMPORTANT NOW

In its crackdown on shelters of all kinds, Congress severely limited the ability of investors in "passive activities"—the definition includes real estate rentals and limited partnerships—to deduct losses from those investments.

Under the old law, you could deduct the mortgage interest, depreciation, property taxes and other expenses of rental property, whatever their total. Under current law, deductions are limited to the amount of rental income you receive. Any excess deductions are considered a passive loss and—with some exceptions—can be used only to offset income from a similar activity, such as another rental house.

The exceptions are designed to protect small real estate

investors. If you "actively manage" the property, and your adjusted gross income is under $100,000, you may deduct as much as $25,000 of rental losses against other income, including your salary. The loss allowance is phased out between $100,000 and $150,000 of income.

Disallowance rules apply for passive activities begun, or purchased under contract, before the law was enacted. For 1990, 10% of losses outside the $25,000 exception still can be deducted from other income; after that nothing can.

Stay Active

If your property generates a loss, and your income is less than $150,000, be sure you qualify as an "active" manager to protect the loss allowance.

You don't have to cut the grass and unplug drains to qualify. You'll probably pass the tests, even if you pay a management firm to handle day-to-day matters, as long as you're involved in approving tenants, setting rents and okaying repairs and capital improvements.

Managing a rental home, duplex or triplex takes a lot of time, and novice investors nearly always underestimate how much— at least initially. Too often, they also discover that collecting rents and getting repairs done at reasonable costs can be a big headache. This scenario is played out often enough that professional managers consider such "self-managers" a good source of business.

What can you do to avoid taking on a commitment you will end up despising? For starters, stick close to home. The first property you buy and manage should be located no more than 30 minutes away.

Even if time will not be a pressing factor, ask yourself whether you have the skills, toughness and perseverence to handle the job in a business-like manner. Can you do a thorough job of screening prospective tenants? Can you handle phone calls? Respond calmly to emergencies? What kind of liability insurance will you need? Where will you get good contracts?

In addition to answering these questions, you will need to be prepared to tackle the following:

Setting an attractive rent: One that is not too high or too low.

Advertising: A well-placed sign and classified newspaper advertising are effective ways to advertise your property.

Showing prospects: You can't rent a home without showing it to prospective tenants. Be prepared not only to take them through, but also to have the property cleaned, painted and in good repair. As you take tenants through, you may need to help them visualize what it will look like once they have moved in.

Screening: Rejecting a potentially troublesome tenant can save you endless grief. Finding a tenant who will use the property as if he owned it is your goal. Use an application form that gives you all the information you need to check out the prospect thoroughly. Be sure to obtain written permission to check an applicant's credit history with the local credit bureau. Then follow through: Check all references, talk with former landlords, obtain new credit reports, and verify income and job history with employers.

Lease negotiations and renewals.

Collecting security deposits: You will need to know what the law requires of landlords in your state and community.

Move-out and move-in inspections: A major source of conflict between owners and tenants centers around property condition and what constitutes ordinary wear and tear.

Maintenance and repairs: You will have to do them yourself or hire someone else to do them. Finding reliable, honest repair people willing to do small jobs on short notice is not easy.

Problem tenants: Remain a landlord for long, and, at some point, you will encounter a tenant who does not pay the rent. If you become too friendly with your tenants or sympathetic to their personal problems, you will have a harder time collecting and raising the rent.

Record keeping: You may have an accountant, but you nevertheless will need to keep good records and detailed accounts.

Many individual investors successfully manage their own properties. Many also get themselves leg-tied in legal squabbles or hobbled with horrible tenants.

Professional property manager Ralph Tutor urges investor/owners to consult with their insurance agents about liability protection. In many situations, owners can purchase substantial protection with a rider on their homeowner's policy. This coverage should be reviewed annually and increased in tandem with net worth.

Another problem area, Tutor notes, is failing to screen tenants adequately. Landlords may ask for all the pertinent information on an application form. They frequently get the necessary written permission needed to verify creditworthiness and employment. But then they don't check, relying instead on intuition. One solution is to hire a firm that will find you a qualified tenant. Such outfits, often called "lease only" companies, take on the job of advertising and screening tenants for a fee, commonly 50% of the first month's rent.

Tutor also suggests that landlords develop an inventory and condition report, which should be filled out in detail when the first tenant moves in. This report establishes a baseline against which future property inspection reports can be compared. Give a copy of this report to the first tenant when he moves in. Allow 48 hours for changes or additions. Then repeat this inspection process when the tenant moves out, using the report records as a basis for determining whether all or part of the security deposit will be returned. Repeat with each tenant.

USING A PROFESSIONAL MANAGER

Good professional management can be a boon to an investor. For example, if you will be living overseas, or if you own rental property in a distant resort area, trying to do without hands-on local management is just plain risky. Even investors with local properties decide they don't want the hassle of dealing with tenants. So weigh your options and be realistic about your capabilities. If you decide to go with professional management, select carefully.

You will pay anywhere from 8% to 14% of your monthly rental income for the services of a property manager. On top of that, each time the property is leased or the lease is renewed, there will be a leasing fee of 20% to 50% of the first month's rent. On a home that brings in $900 a month in rent, that amounts to $1,350 each year, assuming a 10% monthly management fee and a 25% leasing fee. And, if you want the manager to handle mortgage or insurance payments, you also could pay a one-time set-up fee.

What should you expect in return? For starters, a property manager should be more than a rent collector. A good one will see that your property is rented and cared for in a way that maximizes income and enhances value. That means selecting good tenants and keeping turnover low. It means maintaining the property and charging the right amount of rent.

Questions to Ask

When you look for a property manager, get answers to the following questions before you hire one:

1) What kind of experience do they have? Look for a manager with at least five years of full-time property management experience. Look for experience with properties similar to yours. Ask about educational background and professional affiliations. The Institute of Real Estate Management, for example, designates qualified individuals as Certified Property Managers (CPMs) and Accredited Resident Managers (ARMs).

2) What kind of properties do they manage? To whom do the properties belong? Can you look at them? Can you speak with the owners?

3) How many properties do they manage? What kind and how many support staff do they have? A property manager may be able to handle a large residential apartment building with very little help. That is not the case when managing dozens of single-family dwellings scattered over a metropolitan area. (What's a good ratio of support staff to properties? Ideally, a manager should have one support staffer for every 50 to 75 properties under management.)

4) Are record-keeping and bookkeeping handled on a computer? You wouldn't automatically reject a manager for not having this in place, but, these days, it is a sign of efficiency and service capability. And better to have the system up and running before you come on board than to be involved in a "transition," with its inevitable glitches and gaps.

5) What kind of reports will you the owner get, and how often? Monthly accounting statements and an annual property condition report are minimal service. Look for routine property reports every six months and then again each time the lease changes. How often will drive-by inspections occur?

6) How will repairs and maintenance be handled? Does the firm have repair people under contract? On retainer? Are they licensed and bonded?

7) How do they handle vacancies? Advertising? Tenant screening and credit checks?

8) What kind of insurance do they carry?

9) How does the fee structure work?

10) Under what circumstances can you be released from your contract? Under what circumstances would the manager terminate your contract? Will the contract be automatically renewed? If so, what action must you take to terminate the agreement?

11) May you have references?

The Management Contract

Ultimately, everything should be laid out clearly in a management contract. You are appointing the property manager as your attorney-in-fact and giving him the authority to negotiate leases, collect rents, hold security deposits and, if necessary, evict tenants, on your behalf.

On-the-ball property management firms already have modified the language in their contracts to ensure that investors will be treated as "active" managers for tax purposes. But don't take it for granted. Discuss the matter with prospective managers and double check the contract wording. Remember, too, that should you be audited, the IRS will look beyond the contract for evidence of correspondence, telephone calls, and the like to verify your involvement.

Many management contracts commit you to using the property manager as broker should you decide to sell your property. That may suit you fine if you are satisfied with your property manager. The manager may even be willing to charge you a lower-than-market commission if it appears that you may be able to sell to your tenant or to another investor with properties under the same management.

But where do you stand if you believe your investment has been badly managed and has been allowed to run down? You don't want that manager handling the sale. You can cancel your contract and manage the property yourself for the next three months, then put it on the market. Suppose, though, that the current tenants are uncooperative or destructive? Then, you'll have to decide which is worse: paying a sales commission to a broker you think did you wrong or taking the risk that the property will be worth considerably less by the time you can sell it. And, if you don't sell it yourself, you'll wind up paying a sales commission anyway.

FOR MORE INFORMATION

In addition to sources cited elsewhere in this chapter, see the following materials for information on investing and managing residential real estate:

◆ *Investing in Residential Income Property*, by Douglas M. Temple (Contemporary Books, Chicago).

◆ Articles on single-family property management published by the Institute of Real Estate Management, in its *Journal of Property Management*. You can get single copies free by writing to the institute at 430 N. Michigan Avenue, Chicago, IL 60611. Also inquire about their seminar and book on managing single-family rental properties.

◆ *How to Make Big Money Managing Small Properties*, by Ralph Tutor (Real Estate Software Co., 10622 Montwood, Suite D, El Paso, TX 79935). It covers all the important aspects of property management, including leases, credit investigation, tenant/manager relationships, property maintenance, rent collection, cost control and choosing a computer system. It also has an excellent selection of model contracts and forms that can be reproduced or adapted for use by individual owner/managers.

◆ *How to Find and Manage Profitable Properties*, by Robert Irwin (McGraw-Hill Book Co., N.Y.).

◆ *The Home Equity Kit*, By Andrew James McLean (John Wiley & Sons, N.Y.).

◆ *How to Manage Residential Property for Maximum Cash Flow and Resale Value*, by John T. Reed (Reed Publishing, 342 Bryan Drive, Danville, CA 94526).

PART TWO

FOR SELLERS

CHAPTER 16

ALTERNATIVES TO SELLING

◆

T HERE ARE as many reasons for selling a home as there are for buying. Some people sell because they are being relocated in their jobs, and they believe they must sell their current house to get back equity they'll need to buy a home in their new area. Others sell because they need more space for a growing family—or less space because the children are grown. Still others sell because they need the capital tied up in their home for living expenses, due to retirement, ill health or a reduction in income.

Whatever the reason you're thinking about selling your home, stop for a minute to consider possible alternatives. There is frequently a way to meet your objectives without selling. Don't expect to hear about them from a real estate agent, though. In a business fueled by commissions on sales, it's a rare agent who will advise you not to sell. Nor *should* an agent advise you on something that is really a financial-planning decision. If you're unsure about selling, check with your lawyer or accountant—or seek advice from a financial planner.

But *you* should consider whether there's a way to accomplish your goal without selling. For example, if your present home is too small, consider remodeling or adding on. Moving to another home is usually the most expensive solution to the tight-space problem. With sales commissions, closing costs, moving expenses and decorating costs, picking up and relocating is a formidable effort both financially and emotionally.

Would remodeling make sense in your situation? Do you like the neighborhood enough to want to stay long enough to justify the cost and hassle of a major building project? Is your lot big enough for an addition? Would your improved house be too big or fancy for the neighborhood, making it difficult to recover the cost of your improvements if you have to move?

Even if you have to move for a job change, you don't necessarily have to sell. Examine the housing markets in your current and future hometowns. If houses are appreciating in value rapidly where you live now, but less so where you're moving, perhaps you should convert your home to a rental property and either buy or rent in the new community. (See Chapter 15 for a discussion of the implications of turning your home into a rental.)

But where on earth would the money come from—to pay for remodeling or for the downpayment on a place in the new hometown? It's right under your nose. You can tap the equity in your current home, by refinancing the mortgage, using a traditional second mortgage or opening a home-equity line of credit. Those alternatives are discussed next. Beginning on page 242 is a discussion of special options for older homeowners who want to stay in their homes but need the money they could get by selling the house.

TAPPING YOUR HOME EQUITY

Your equity in your home is the difference between what the place is worth and any amount you owe on loans secured by the house. If your home would sell for $100,000 and the balance on your mortgage is $60,000, for example, your equity is $40,000.

Most homeowners see their equity increase each year, as home values appreciate and monthly payments reduce what's owed on the mortgage. For many, home equity represents one of the largest chunks of net worth. And, in recent years more and more homeowners have been dipping into that equity by borrowing against it. The appeal of this kind of debt—whether via refinancing, a second mortgage or a home-equity line of credit—is that interest paid on the loan is generally fully deductible on the borrower's tax return, while interest paid on other consumer loans is not. (Only 10% of such interest is deductible in 1990; none after that.)

In other words, the government will subsidize the cost of borrowing *if* the loan is secured by your home, but offers little—and soon no—help with other personal loans. Consider what that means on a $10,000, 10-year loan at 10.5%. In the first 12 monthly payments, interest totals $1,022. If the loan is secured by your home and the $1,022 is deducted in the 28% bracket, the federal government effectively pays $286 of the interest. (Your state government might help, too, assuming you also get the benefit of the deduction on your state return.) Over the course of the loan, or when larger amounts are involved, you can see the enormous appeal of deductible home-based debt over nondeductible personal borrowing.

Home-Equity Line of Credit

This is the latest, and the hottest, method for tapping home equity to get money for home improvements, college expenses, a new car or almost any other need. Unlike a traditional second mortgage (discussed later), home-equity lines are a form of revolving credit, somewhat like a credit card. Your home serves as collateral for the home-equity line. The lender sets a credit limit and you may borrow up to that amount by writing checks. That flexibility, along with the tax-deductible status of interest paid on the loan, give these loans great appeal. But remember that casual use could lead to draining your home equity or, in the extreme, the loss of your home.

How the loan works. With a typical equity loan, the maximum credit limit is based on what is called the loan-to-value ratio. If a lender uses an 80% ratio, for example, the most you could borrow is 80% of the appraised value of your home. If you own a $100,000 home free and clear, for example, you would be eligible for a credit limit of up to $80,000. If you still owe $60,000 on the mortgage, though, the limit would be $20,000—$80,000 minus the $60,000 already borrowed against the house.

The loans usually carry a variable interest rate, figured by adding one to three points to a floating rate, commonly the prime rate. The rate can vary as often as monthly. And, although home-equity loans must have a cap on how high the interest rate can go, there is no limit on how high a lender can set that cap.

You pay interest only on the amount you borrow, not the amount of credit available, and will be required to make at least a minimum monthly payment on any outstanding loan amount.

Home-equity lines are usually structured to expire far sooner than 30-year mortgages, although some come due only when you sell. Generally, the loan period is divided into two segments—a "draw" period and a "payback" period. During the draw period, which is typically five years or so—you can borrow at will simply by writing a check. As you pay back any or all of the loan, your credit limit is restored accordingly. The length of the draw period is set out in the contract with the lender, along with minimum withdrawal amounts and any restrictions on how often you can tap the credit line.

The contract also spells out what happens when the draw period ends. You may be able to renew the credit line, for example, or you may be required to pay the outstanding balance at once. Another plan might call for repayment of the outstanding balance over a fixed period—over ten years, perhaps.

What to look for when you shop. When lenders are competing hard for home-equity loan business, temporary low teaser rates may be dangled before homeowners, or lenders may reduce application and closing charges to "cost." A few may even offer to set up equity lines free of all closing costs.

But more often, appraisals, title searches, credit reports and the like are added to the cost of the loan. Few banks or thrifts dare dump all these costs on you, but many will levy whatever the competition or market will bear. Lenders generally calculate closing costs as a percentage of the credit limit, or charge a flat fee plus actual costs. As a rule, the larger the line of credit, the more you pay. That is so because the amount charged is based on the maximum loan available, not on what you actually borrow. Generally, you pay these costs when you open the credit line, although in certain cases you may be able to roll them into the first loan advance.

The shorter the borrowing term, the more critical it is to hold up-front costs to a minimum. On the other hand, if you're using the loan to pay for major home improvements, you'll probably be repaying over a period of five years or more. In that case reasonable up-front fees and transaction costs are less important than the interest rate and the index to which the rate is pegged.

In the past, indexes have strayed far afield from one another, with drastically different results in the interest charged on home-equity line advances. The table below shows how two popular indexes behaved during the 1980s. On the left is the prime rate as published in the *Wall Street Journal* for January of each year. On the right is the average cost of funds for the 11th District Federal Home Loan Bank in each January.

	Prime rate	FHLB Cost of Funds
1980	15.25%	8.76%
1981	20	10.45
1982	15.75	11.95
1983	11	10.46
1984	11	10.03
1985	10.5	10.22
1986	9.5	8.77
1987	7.5	7.40
1988	8.75	7.62
1989	10.5	8.13

Remember that although equity-line rates are tied to an index, lenders usually add one to three points or more to the index rate. Also, as you consider various offers, don't overlook the fact that an index that responds quickly to rising rates, such as the volatile index of short-term Treasury bills, will also reflect a drop in rates much more quickly than a slow-to-rise more stable one. The lender should provide you with an historical example showing how changes in the index rate in the past would affect minimum payments due on the home-equity line.

Here are other issues that demand special attention as you shop. Compare each loan you consider on these terms:

◆ *Payment terms.* These must be spelled out clearly. For example, you might be told that your line of credit is good for ten years, with a minimum monthly payment of $100 or 1/360 of the loan balance plus finance charges, whichever is greater. After this ten-year draw period, you'd have another five years to pay any remaining balance. Minimum terms during the repayment period would be 1/60 of the outstanding balance plus finance charges.

◆ *Payment example.* You must be given an example of what the minimum monthly payments would be if you borrowed a certain amount—$10,000 say—and the interest rate reached its maximum level.

◆ *Lenders' fees.* These include loan application fees (typically around $150), one or more "points" (each at 1% of your credit limit) and a maintenance fee (often around $75).

◆ *Third-party fees.* Fees usually include amounts for home appraisals, credit reports and lawyer fees and might total between $500 and $900.

◆ *Variable-rate features.* As noted earlier, you must be told what interest index is used, along with the maximum rate that can be applied to your loan.

As a rule, a lender is barred from cutting off your credit line, accelerating payments or changing any terms once the line has been opened. The index used for setting the variable rate must be one that is out of the lender's control. Banks won't be allowed to use their own cost of funds as an index or change the index at their own discretion. Also note this: You have three business days to back out of the loan if your principal residence serves as collateral.

Once you've found a good home-equity loan, compare the deal with a traditional second mortgage (see page 239) before you commit. But you can't simply compare the APRs on the two loans. The APR on second mortgages—as with first mortgages—takes into account the interest rate charged, plus points and other finance charges, while the APR on a home-equity loan is based only on the periodic interest rate and excludes points and other charges.

Paying off the loan when you sell. You may be required to advise the lender when you put your house on the market. In any case, at settlement you must repay the home-equity loan along with your original mortgage. You'll face minor additional fees since clearing title involves an extra step. Your settlement attorney must prepare a release, which can cost from $10 to $50, and file it, usually at a cost of another $10 to $25.

Second Mortgages

Lenders typically offer second mortgages—also called second trusts—of up to 15 years. Unlike an equity line, second mortgages usually involve a fixed amount of money to be repaid over a fixed period of time. You generally can borrow up to 75% or 80% of a home's appraised value; if you can find a lender willing to count the value remodeling will add to the property, you may be able to borrow more.

The stated interest rates on such loans usually are one to two percentage points above those on conventional first mortgages. Adjustable-rate versions start a little lower.

Comparing the cost of second mortgages is complicated by the points charged by lenders. Here's a rule of thumb that can help: On a 10-year, fixed-rate remodeling loan at 11.5% to 12%, one discount point adds about one quarter of a percent to the rate.

The application process for a second mortgage is similar to that for a first. You won't get approval until your home is appraised, your credit checked and title insurance written. Turnaround time for approval can be fairly short; you could close within two or three weeks of applying.

You'll also have to pay closing costs, which typically amount to 2% or 3% of the loan. For second mortgages of less than $15,000, lenders are often satisfied with a drive-by appraisal and verification of existing title insurance and an in-file credit report. As with home-equity loans, lenders may allow you to finance the closing costs as part of the loan.

Even with a higher interest rate, adding a second trust on top of a first mortgage usually costs far less, over the whole term of your homeownership, than refinancing with a new first.

FHA loans. If you need to borrow $17,500 or less, consider an FHA Title I home improvement loan. Since these are guaranteed by the federal government, you should get a break on the interest rate. FHA loans of less than $2,500 are treated as unsecured personal loans, so the interest is losing its tax deductiblity. Larger loans are secured by your home, however, so interest paid can be fully deductible. Title I loan terms run from 6 months to 15 years. Contact your local Housing and Urban Development (HUD) field office for a list of the Title I lenders in your area.

Full Refinancing

Refinancing means getting a new first mortgage. It also generally means paying origination, appraisal and credit check fees and points. A home-equity loan or second mortgage provides a more direct means of tapping your equity, but refinancing can also free up funds. Say, for example, that you home is worth $200,000 and the balance on your mortgage is $75,000. You could refinance for $125,000, using $75,000 to pay off the old loan and putting the freed $50,000 of home-equity to whatever use you choose. (The tax consequences of the interest on the larger loan depend on how you spend the money. See Chapter 3 for details.)

If interest rates are lower now than when the original mortgage was written, its possible that you can get a bigger loan without a big increase in monthly payments. For example, a $100,000 30-year mortgage at 12% carries monthly payments of $1,029. Say you want to refinance now for $130,000 and use the extra money to pay for home improvements. If rates have fallen to 9%, the payments on the new loan would be $1,046—just $17 a month more than on the old loan.

Consider the 2% rule. Refinancing can make sense even if you don't need to tap the equity in your home. In fact, you should consider refinancing any time there's a difference of two percentage points or more between your fixed loan rate and current rates. The 2% rule assumes you'll stay in the house for at least four to seven years after refinancing, long enough for the lower monthly payments to offset the costs of refinancing. You can get away with less of a differential if you plan to live in your home for a long time and can spread out the expense of refinancing over many years. A 1.5% spread is likely to make refinancing pay if you'll be in your home more than seven years.

Figuring the difference when refinancing from an ARM to a fixed loan is not as tidy because ARM rates change; the longer you plan to live in your home, the more uncertainty you face.

A lucky interest rate guess could save you thousands of dollars in an ARM-to-fixed refinancing, but a mistake could be just as costly. Loantech, a mortgage consulting firm based in Gaithersburg, MD, analyzed a 30-year, $80,000 refinancing from a 10% adjustable-rate loan to a 9.75% fixed loan, plus $3,400 of closing costs, given various interest rate scenarios and assuming the owner would sell the house and pay off the loan in seven years.

In a high-rate scenario that saw ARM rates climb to 13% in three years and stay there, the refinancing decision saved $7,074 in interest payments, although some of the saving is illusory since your tax deduction will be smaller.

However, if ARM rates remain unchanged at 10%, a refinanced fixed-rate mortgage costs $1,837 more than sticking with the ARM, because the changeover costs more than the accumulated savings from 0.25% difference in interest rates. And if ARM rates dropped in three years to 6%, the switch to a fixed mortgage would cost $12,571 over seven years (although you would get some of that back through bigger tax deductions for interest payments).

Note: The penalty for making a wrong guess isn't as fierce as these examples suggest, because even if rates do decline, you still have the option of refinancing again. Presumably, you'd do just that if rates dipped to 6%.

In 1989, the Federal National Mortgage Association (Fannie Mae), the biggest investor in home mortgages, eased refinancing rules for homeowners and lenders under certain circumstances. If you refinance with your current loan servicer, the streamlined rules means saving $250 to $300 on the typical 3% to 5% of loan principal charged in refinancings, and in some cases allow loan processing in a snappy one to two weeks rather than a few months.

Many lenders, following Fannie Mae's lead, have adjusted their policies to conform to these changes:

♦ Homeowners don't need a new home appraisal when they refinance into a fixed-rate loan with the same lender—provided the lender vouches that the property hasn't declined in value since the original loan was made.

◆ A full-blown credit report isn't necessary—just a check of your existing electronic credit file and a simplified income verification. Your mortgage payment record must be good but not necessarily perfect.

◆ You can roll up-front refinancing costs into the new loan and you need not wait any minimum time before refinancing.

Unfortunately, the rules won't work for those considering refinancing as a means of tapping their equity, rather than just to secure a more favorable interest rate. Borrowers are allowed to take no more than 1% of the loan amount out as cash.

Refinancing points—unlike points paid to buy your principal residence—are not necessarily deductible all at once in the year you pay them. If you're refinancing to get money for home improvements, you can deduct the points immediately; otherwise, this expense is considered prepaid interest to be written off over the life of the loan. See Chapter 3 for details.

SPECIAL HELP FOR SENIOR CITIZENS

Many elderly homeowners are in the awkward position of having too little income for comfortable living, but plenty of value in their paid-up homes. Three out of four Americans 65 years and older own their own homes, and over 80% of those have paid off the mortgage. Total home equity held by America's senior citizens may be as much as $2 *trillion*.

But many of these elderly people have only modest incomes; they wouldn't benefit from conventional means of tapping home equity, because they couldn't handle the monthly repayment schedule for a new mortgage or home-equity loan. If you face such a dilemma, you may want to look into ways to unlock that equity and convert it into monthly income.

The Home Equity Kit, by Andrew McLean (John Wiley & Sons), evaluates the income-producing benefits of various home-equity conversion options. McLean analyzes how much surplus income (additional yearly income from equity conversion, less annual housing costs) would result from: a cash sale and purchase of a replacement home; cash sale and rental; installment sale and purchase of a replacement home; installment sale and rental; reverse mortgage; sale-leaseback; and renting out a room.

Sale and Leaseback

In a sale-leaseback, the homeowner gives up title to become a renter. In a typical situation, parents sell their house to a son or daughter, who immediately leases it back to them for life. The parents, assuming they are 55 or older, can qualify to treat up to $125,000 of profit from the sale as tax-free income. Since the child owns the house and rents it out, he or she can depreciate it and deduct the expenses that go with being a landlord.

Most sale-leasebacks are seller-financed. The parents receive a down payment and take back a note for the remainder of the sales price. Things can be arranged so that the buyer makes monthly payments, providing a steady income stream to the parents. Some advisors suggest that the parents use the down payment to purchase a deferred annuity, which insures that the parents will continue to receive the same amount of income if they outlive the payments on the note.

Sale-leasebacks are designed for people who want to spend the rest of their lives in the house, and they can work well when the primary objective is to keep the house in the family. The main drawback is that these arrangements are complicated. Four separate contracts may be involved: a sale contract, a rental contract, a mortgage contract and, usually, an annuity contract. Moreover, the terms of the contract are interrelated and open to negotiation.

Tax considerations should figure in a choice between a sale-leaseback and other options, such as a reverse mortgage. (See the discussion beginning on the following page.) The IRS requires that the landlord charge a market rate of rent, or it could decide the deal is a tax dodge and nullify some of the tax advantages. Charging the same rent for 12 years, for example, won't meet the test. It's advisable to put an inflation clause in the rental agreement—raising the rent annually according to a specified index.

Parents also generally want some assurance they can rent "their house" for as long as they live. You must accomplish this indirectly or the IRS may decide that no sale took place. A lease term that exceeds the parents' life expectancies and a clause that guarantees the seller the right to renew the lease each year may fill the bill.

Special-Purpose Loans

A far simpler option is to take advantage of special-purpose loans available from many local government agencies and a few state governments. These loans are usually restricted to homeowners with limited incomes. The loans most often carry low- or no-interest, and can be used for property taxes or pay for home repair, health-related modifications or in-home services. They need not be repaid until the house is sold or the homeowner dies.

The loans don't necessarily involve cash; property taxes can be charged to an account that establishes a lien against the property. With other deferred-payment loans, the homeowner gets a lump sum that must be used for a specific purpose, such as installing ramps, railings and grab bars.

Reverse Mortgages

These special mortgages allow you to live off your nest egg and in it, too. Reverse mortgages mirror the cash flow of a regular mortgage: Instead of making monthly payments, this loan is advanced to you in monthly increments. You pay nothing back until the term is up, when the advances plus interest must be repaid, presumably from the proceeds on the sale of your home. Monthly income is tax-free.

FHA-supported loans. This program run by the Federal Housing Authority (FHA) provides government-backed insurance to local, private and public lenders who make approved reverse mortgages to older homeowners. You are eligible if you own your home debt-free or nearly so and you are at least 62. If you're married, your spouse must also be at least 62.

The FHA sets the maximum payout that can be made through the mortgage, basing its decision on your life expectancy and the equity in the home—up to the maximum FHA-insured loan in the area. You can use the reverse mortgage to obtain regular monthly income or as a periodic line of credit to take out cash when you need it. As you receive payments from the lender, they create a debt of principal and interest that eventually must be repaid. At an agreed-upon point—often when the house is sold after death or if you move to a nursing home—the full debt must be paid off.

The agency collects an insurance premium on each reverse mortgage. The insurance protects lenders against losses in situations where borrowers outlive their equity—that is, they live so long and their homes appreciate so little that final loan balances exceed the value of their homes. In such cases, the FHA insurance pool compensates the lender.

FHA-insured loans offer three initial payment options:

♦ *Tenure.* With this payment option, you get equal monthly checks so long as the house is your principal residence.

♦ *Term.* You receive equal monthly payments for a fixed term. You choose the term.

♦ *Line of credit.* You determine when you need to borrow money and the amount. You may borrow up to the permitted limit.

Whatever option you choose, you can alter the pattern in the future should circumstances change. If you select a loan with a tenure- or term-payment option, you may want to combine it with an agreed-upon line of credit that will permit you to tap a portion of the loan for unanticipated needs. Say you sign on for a tenure loan that pays $300 a month. A year later, you find you need to add a bath on the ground floor of your home for your husband, who has become too frail to use the only existing bath on the second floor. You could contact your lender and request a lump-sum payment to make the improvement—so long as your request would not exceed the maximum claim amount.

Once you reach that maximum amount, you could no longer receive monthly payments. You can remain in the home until you move, sell or die.

FHA-insured reverse mortgages can be fixed- or adjustable-rate loans. Lenders, are permitted to offer reverse adjustable rate mortgages with no monthly interest-rate adjustments and no annual limitation on interest increases, providing they also offer capped loans, which must carry a lifetime interest-rate cap of no more than five percentage points and an annual limit on rate increases or decreases of no more than two points.

You can negotiate a lower rate in exchange for granting the lender a percentage of any future appreciation on your house. With a reverse ARM, the payments don't change when interest-rate adjustments are made to the loan, but adjustments have an effect of increasing or decreasing the rate at which your equity is used up.

For additional information about these loans, send a stamped, self-addressed envelope to the National Center for Home Equity Conversion, 348 Main St., Marshall, Minn. 56258.

CHAPTER 17

TAX ANGLES OF SELLING A HOME

◆

SO YOU WEIGHED all the alternatives to selling your home, and you decided it's the right thing for you to do. Take a close look at the tax ramifications of selling.

You don't have to file any forms with the IRS when you buy your home or to report improvements that hike your basis. But when you sell, the government wants to know the details. After all, there might be a tax to be collected, although there is a good chance—if you re-invest the sale proceeds in another home of comparable or greater value (see below)—the transaction won't add a dime to your current tax bill.

DETERMINE YOUR BASIS

When you sell your home, you will realize how clever you've been to keep meticulous records of every improvement to your home over the years of your ownership. To determine the tax consequences of the sale, you have to know the adjusted basis of your home, a value you can compute easily with the information in your files. Your adjusted basis is what you paid for the house plus the cost of all improvements, minus any casualty losses on the property you claimed while living there—for fire or storm damage, for example. The basis is also reduced by any gain from a previous home you rolled over into the house being sold.

Your profit or loss on the sale is the difference between that adjusted basis and the amount you realize on the sale. Since nothing involved with taxes is easy, the amount realized is not simply the selling price. That's the beginning point, from which you subtract costs connected with the sale such as real estate commissions, points paid for the buyer, advertising and legal fees. Not included, however, are amounts you spend for repairs or other efforts to make the place more attractive to buyers.

If your adjusted basis is more than the amount realized, your loss is not deductible. In the more likely event that your home sale produces a profit, your gain may be taxable in the year of the sale, sometime in the future or perhaps never at all. The opportunity to put off or completely avoid tax on the profit has long been one of the most valuable tax benefits enjoyed by homeowners.

DEFERRING THE TAX BILL

Fortunately, it's easy to defer the tax bill almost indefinitely. To do so, all you have to do is buy a new principal residence—costing at least as much as you get from the sale of the one sold—within a specified time period.

To qualify, you must buy or build *and* occupy the new home within two years—before or after—the sale of the old one. (If you are in the armed forces or living outside the United States when your home is sold, you may qualify for a longer replacement period that gives you up to four years to buy and occupy a new principal residence.)

Be warned that the IRS is inflexible about the replacement period. In a case in which a serious illness prevented a taxpayer from occupying the new home before the deadline, the IRS prohibited the rollover. What if you're building a new home and it burns down just before you're planning to move in? Again, the IRS says you forfeit the rollover privilege.

To defer the tax on all the gain on the sale of one home, the replacement home must cost at least as much as you realized from the sale of the old one. Assume, for example, that the adjusted basis of your home is $70,000 and you sell it for $100,000. Within the replacement period, you buy and move into a new home that costs $125,000. The tax bill on your $30,000 profit is deferred. Rather than report it as income in the year of the sale, you reduce the basis of the new home by that amount. The basis of the new home becomes $95,000—the $125,000 purchase price minus the $30,000 of deferred gain.

If you later sell that house for $150,000, in the eyes of the IRS the profit would be $55,000—the combination of the $30,000 gain from the first house and $25,000 from the second. Of course, you could put off the tax bill again by buying a replacement home within two years that costs $150,000 or more. Its basis would be reduced by the $55,000 of rolled-over gain.

You don't have to invest the actual proceeds of the sale in the new home to qualify to defer tax on the gain. Say you sold a house for $200,000 and bought a new one for $210,000. You can roll over all the profit from the first house, even if you made a minimum down payment on the new house and used the remaining proceeds for some other purpose. The key is that the new home cost at least as much as the one you sold, not how you pay for the new house.

What if you and your fiancé each own a home, sell both of them and together buy a new home? You can defer the gain on both of the old homes if the price of the new house exceeds the combined sales prices of the old ones. Any profit left out of the rollover, though, would be taxable in the year of sale. However, if one taxpayer sells a home to move in with a new husband or wife in a home the spouse already owns, you cannot defer tax on the gain. But if the seller is over age 55, he or she might qualify for the exclusion discussed on page 252.

The law does provide for a situation in which a jointly owned home is sold in connection with a divorce and each spouse buys a separate home. If each spouse invests his or her share of the proceeds of the sale in a new principal residence—within the rollover period—the tax bill on the profit is deferred.

In any situation, if you choose a replacement home that costs less than the one you sold, you will owe tax on the profit to the extent that the adjusted sales price of the old home exceeds the cost of the new one.

The adjusted sales price is usually the same as the amount realized on the sale, but it can be less if prior to the sale you incurred qualifying fix-up expenses, such as the cost of painting or repairs to make the home more attractive to buyers. Those are costs that can't qualify as improvements to boost your basis. They come into play for tax purposes only if your replacement home costs less than the one you sold. (Although real estate agents encouraging you to spruce up the place may suggest that such costs are deductible, they are not. If you don't buy a replacement home, or if you buy one that costs enough that you can roll over all your profit, fix-up costs have no tax power.)

To qualify for this limited tax benefit, fix-up expenses must be for work done during the 90 days before you sign a contract to sell your house and must be paid for within 30 days afterward.

Trading down without tripping up. It is possible to buy a less expensive home without incurring a taxable profit in the year of the sale. Anything you spend on the new place that qualifies as an improvement—such as the cost of renovation or adding an addition or a swimming pool—can serve to raise the new home's "price" for rollover purposes. The key here is that the expense must be incurred and the bill paid within the two-year replacement period.

This provision can prove especially rewarding if you're transferred from an area of the country with high home prices to an area of more modestly priced homes.

Say the "adjusted basis" of your old house is $100,000. You sell it for $150,000, after expenses. Thanks to a transfer to a less expensive part of the country, your new home costs just $120,000—the amount that sets the ceiling for rolling over the proceeds of your home sale. That leaves $30,000 of profit out in the cold, taxable in the year of the sale. In the 28% bracket, the bill is $8,400.

You can hold down or eliminate that tax bill, though, by investing more in the new place. If you spend $30,000 or more on improvements within two years after the sale of the first house, the entire profit could be rolled over.

The rollover provision applies only to your principal residence, not to a second home, say, or rental property. And if you use part of your principal home for business—by renting out a room, say, or having a home office for which you claim deductions—part of the profit from the sale will not qualify for rollover treatment. If you claim 10% of your home as a home office, for example, 10% of the gain on the sale won't be eligible for the deferral.

There is no limit on the number of times or the amount of profit you can roll over from one home to the next. In fact, the profit from the first home you own is likely to affect the tax basis of the last place you live, a point that emphasizes the importance of detailed record keeping.

There is a restriction, however, that generally prevents you from using the rollover provision more than once every two years. If during the replacement period you buy or build more than one new principal residence, only the last one can be treated as your new home for figuring the rollover. That restriction does not apply if the sale of your home is connected with a job-related move that qualifies you to deduct moving expenses.

Reporting home sales. In the year of the sale, you must file a Form 2119, *Sale or Exchange of Principal Residence,* with your tax return. The form must be filed whether or not you owe tax on the sale. It's a relatively simple form, and it includes a section for determining the adjusted basis of your new home by subtracting from its cost any rolled over profit from the sale. Since each sale will affect the basis of your next home, you'll want to hang on to a copy of every Form 2119 you file throughout your homeowning career.

What if you plan to buy a replacement home but haven't closed the deal by the time your tax return is due for the year of the sale? You can still postpone the gain. Just file a Form 2119—reporting only the date your old home was sold—with your return. If the replacement home you buy costs enough to defer all of your gain, just notify the IRS Service Center where you filed your return and file a completed Form 2119 at that time. If the new house doesn't cost enough to permit a rollover of all the profit—or if the replacement period expires before you buy—you'll have to file an amended tax return for the year of the sale. In addition to the tax on the profit, you'll have to pay interest on the tax due.

You handle things the same way if you follow the "trading down without tripping up" strategy discussed earlier. You report the sale of the first home for the year of the sale and, after you complete your major improvements on the new place, file a completed Form 2119.

You'll also have to file an amended return if you report the profit from the home sale—under the assumption that you won't replace the house—and later decide to buy a new home. If you occupy the new place within the replacement period, you can retroactively defer the gain and reclaim the tax you paid on the original sale.

THE $125,000 EXCLUSION

So over the years you keep packing your profit with you from one home to another, holding the IRS at bay by purchasing more and more costly homes. But what happens when you finally decide to cash in on all that profit that has built up? When you retire or for some other reason decide not to buy another house, is the IRS going to swoop down and demand a healthy share of your nest egg?

Not if you qualify for the homeowners' icing on the cake: the right to escape tax entirely on up to $125,000 of profit. The same $125,000 exclusion is available whether you're married and filing a joint return or single and filing an individual one. If you are married and filing separate returns, the limit is $62,500 for each spouse.

The value of this tax break is enhanced by the fact that it usually comes around retirement time, when extra cash often comes in particularly handy. In the 31% tax bracket, sheltering $125,000 of gain saves you $38,750!

With such a rich reward at stake, it's essential that you know how to claim it.

To qualify, you must be at least 55 years old when you sell your home and you must have owned and lived in the home for at least three of the five years leading up to the sale. If you are married and the house is jointly owned, you can qualify as long as either you or your spouse meet all three requirements: age, ownership and residency.

Unlike the rollover rule, which applies only if the house sold is your principal residence at the time of the sale, you don't have to be living in the house when it is sold to qualify for the exclusion. If you move before the place is sold, you can still dodge tax on the profit as long as the sale occurs before so much time has passed that you no longer meet the three-out-of-five-year residency test.

Assume, for example, that you are at least age 55 and have owned and lived in your home for at least three years. You retire and move to an apartment. As long as your home is sold within two years of the move, you will meet the three-of-five-year test and qualify for the exclusion. That applies whether you rent your old home or leave it vacant prior to the sale.

Married couples are limited to a single $125,000 exclusion, and if one spouse used the exclusion before marriage, that scotches the other spouse's right to it as long as they are married. Say that you own a home and plan to marry someone who also owns a home. Assume, too, that both of you meet the age, ownership and residency tests. If each of you sells your house before marriage, you each qualify for up to a $125,000 exclusion. Wait until after the ceremony, though, and together you can exclude only $125,000. Similarly, if you plan to marry someone who has already used the exclusion, selling your home before the wedding can protect your right to the exclusion.

The exclusion can also come into play in divorce. If you're planning a divorce, in some circumstances it may make sense to hold off selling the family home until after the split. If the profit will exceed $125,000, postponing the sale until you are both single co-owners of the place can permit each ex-spouse to exclude up to $125,000 of gain.

You don't necessarily want to use the exclusion the first time it is available to you. In fact, that can be a costly mistake. This is a once-in-a-lifetime opportunity. You can't use part of the exclusion to shelter $50,000 of profit on one home, for example, and later use the rest of it to avoid tax on the sale of another. Use any part of the exclusion and you use it all.

Your best bet will usually be to hold off using the exclusion until you sell what you expect to be your last home or until you can take advantage of the full $125,000. Don't worry about shortchanging your heirs by forfeiting the tax break if you die before using it; the tax on all profit that builds up during your life is excused when you die.

You claim the exclusion on Form 2119, the same form you use to report home sales and the deferral of gain.

OWNER FINANCING

Sometimes, particularly when mortgage rates are high, the sale of a home goes through only because the seller helps finance the deal. If you wind up holding a note of some sort, your tax picture is sure to be complicated.

The selling price of your home—for purposes of determining the gain to be rolled over, excluded or taxed—includes the face value of any mortgage or note you receive, as well as cash. If you are deferring tax on the gain or using the exclusion to shelter it from the IRS, however, you basically report the sale just as you would if you received all cash.

Payments on the note may be a combination of return of your basis (nontaxable), part of your gain (deferred or excluded) and interest on the loan (taxable). You should report the interest as income on Schedule B, the same form you use to report interest on a bank account. There's even a special line for reporting interest on seller-financed mortgages.

If gain is taxable in the year of the sale and you help finance the deal, you may report the profit on an installment basis. That permits you to pay tax on the profit as you receive it over the years.

What if you can't sell? It's a homeowner's nightmare: You move to a new home but can't find a buyer for the old homestead. Not only might you have to get a bridge loan to finance the new house, you also face the prospect of making two mortgage payments month after month. Few family budgets can handle that financial burden.

One solution is to rent your former residence to generate cash to help pay the bills. But that can lead you into a maze of tax complications.

The part of the tax law that permits homeowners to defer the tax on the profit from one house by rolling it over into a new home applies only to your principal residence. Can a house that's being rented to someone else when you finally sell it qualify as *your* home? If not, the vagaries of the housing market could force you to pay tax on the profit rather than roll it over.

If you can show the rental was temporary, the house still qualifies as your principal residence and the gain can be rolled over—as long as you sell the old house within two years of the time you buy the new home. If the old home hasn't sold within the rollover-replacement period, you're out of luck.

The IRS demands that you treat the rent you receive as income. Temporary or not, you become a landlord in the eyes of the IRS. You may be able to completely offset the tax bill on the rental income, however, with deductions for rental expenses including the continued mortgage interest and tax payments on the house, the cost of repairs and even depreciation.

Permanent rental. If you are unable to sell your old house within two years, you may want to consider making the rental arrangement permanent. After the replacement period ends, any profit on a sale—including any gain from previous homes that had been rolled over into the house—will be taxed. Neither the rollover nor the $125,000 exclusion provision will protect you.

Some homeowners plan from the outset to hang on to their old homes, a move that can be among the easiest ways to become a real estate investor and latch on to the tax benefits discussed in Chapter 15.

There's a potential catch to converting your home to a rental property, however, beyond forfeiting the chance to roll over the profit into a new home. The value of the house for figuring depreciation deductions—a key write-off for real estate investors—is your adjusted basis or the fair market value of the house, whichever is less. The basis may be far less than what the house is worth when you convert it, particularly if you have pushed it down by rolling over profit from previous homes.

Assume, for example, that your house is worth $150,000. You bought it for $100,000 several years ago and, at that time rolled over $30,000 in profit from your previous home. If you convert the house to a rental property, your basis for depreciation purposes is a skimpy $70,000. Because you cannot depreciate the value of land, you must subtract its value to determine the amount on which to base your depreciation write-offs. (If someone else bought your home for $150,000 and turned it into a rental property, the new owner's basis for depreciation purposes would be $150,000—minus the value of the land—and he or she would enjoy depreciation deductions more than twice as large as you are allowed.)

HOUSE-HUNTING AND MOVING EXPENSES, TOO

Buying a new house is often part of a move to take a new job. If your purchase is connected with a job switch, you can rack up additional benefits; some of the cost of selling your old place and buying the new house may be deductible. To qualify to write off moving expenses, your new job must be at least 35 miles farther from your old home than your old job was. If your former job was 10 mile away from your old home, for example, the new job has to be at least 45 miles away from that old home. It doesn't matter how far the new home is away from your new job. (If you are moving to take your first job, the 35 mile test applies to the distance from your old home to your new job location.)

In addition to the distance test, to be eligible to deduct moving expenses you must work full time for at least 39 weeks during the 12 months after the move (or at least 78 weeks out of the first 24 months if you are self-employed). If you qualify, here's what you can deduct.

◆ The cost of trips to the area of the new job to look for a new house. There's no requirement that the house-hunting expedition be successful for the cost to be deductible.

◆ The cost of having your furniture and other household goods shipped, including the cost of packing, insurance and storage for up to 30 days.

◆ The cost of getting yourself and your family to the new hometown, including the cost of food and lodging on the trip.

◆ The cost of food and lodging for up to 30 days in the new hometown if these temporary living expenses are necessary because you have not yet found a new home or it is not ready when you arrive.

◆ Certain costs associated with the sale of your old house and purchase of the new one. These expenses—including real estate commissions, legal fees, state transfer taxes, and appraisal and title fees—are the same costs discussed earlier as potential additions to the basis of the house you buy or reductions in the amount realized on the home you sold. If you qualify to write off moving expenses, you can choose whether to deduct these costs or use them as adjustments to your basis. It's almost always beneficial to count them as deductible expenses.

There is a dollar limit on the amount you can deduct for certain expenses. The cap for house-hunting trips and temporary living expenses is $1,500, and those costs plus buying and selling expenses can't exceed $3,000. There is no limit on how much you can deduct for the cost of shipping household goods or travel expenses. Any reasonable amount you pay can be deducted.

If your employer reimburses you for moving expenses, the amount should show up on your W-2 form for the year. You include the amount with your income and offset it by claiming your moving expense deductions. These deductions are considered itemized deductions to be included with other miscellaneous deductions on Schedule A. Although other miscellaneous expenses are deducted only to the extent they exceed 2% of your adjusted gross income, that restriction does not apply to moving expenses. You may deduct your qualifying expenses in full, without regard to the 2% threshold.

CHAPTER 18

POLISHING THE MERCHANDISE

◆

BEFORE YOU make any decision on how to sell your home—through an agent or by yourself—or even what price to ask for it, put your property in the finest possible condition to impress buyers, agents, appraisers and inspectors.

How your house looks and functions will have a lot of impact on your bargaining power as a seller. Nothing can help a sale more than a thorough spit-and-polish campaign, so now is the time for cleaning, touch-ups and postponed maintenance. Repair the torn screen in the basement window, reset the loose tile in the bathroom, fix leaking faucets, and repaint the scratched front door.

Real estate agents have a phrase for a well-maintained, nicely decorated home: they say it "shows well." Other things being equal, this kind of home will sell faster and for a higher price than a comparable house that isn't as attractive.

Do not, however, undertake a major redecorating or remodeling of your house just to prepare it for selling. Why? Because your tastes may not coincide with the tastes of the buyer, and the work will just have to be redone anyway—and at the buyer's expense. Rather than crediting you with work already done, the buyer is instead going to factor the costs he'll incur to redo the work into his offering price.

So stay away from such things as fancy new curtains, wallpaper, and wall-to-wall carpeting over otherwise good floors (plank hardwood, parquet, etc.).

As for the decorating that you deem necessary for making your home look good—new paint, replacement of worn linoleum or wall-to-wall over unfinished flooring, etc.—choose neutral colors and simple patterns that are likely to harmonize with the tastes of most prospective buyers; they'll view these improvements as savings to them in both money and time.

FIRST IMPRESSIONS COUNT

Start with a curb-to-door cleanup. Prune shrubs and tree branches, edge the lawn and if the season permits, add a show of color with annual bedding plants. Paint the front door and put out a new welcome mat.

Inside, make your home look as spacious as possible. Get rid of everything extraneous, admit as much daylight as possible, and keep things shipshape. Inventory what you want to sell, give away or throw away when you move. Then do it now, *before* you begin showing your home. Clutter turns buyers off, so empty out crammed closets, pack away extra books and rarely-used china and sort out attic and basement storage spaces to avoid the flea-market look.

Depersonalize your space. Reduce distractions, and help would-be buyers visualize making themselves at home. Tuck away the family pictures covering your bedroom wall. The display of family roots may fascinate some shoppers and embarrass others. A home that appears to be stamped indelibly with your personality and style can be harder to sell.

Neutralize it ideologically. Remove obvious clues to your political, religious and social sentiments. Store away banners, bumper stickers and partisan literature, including magazines.

Packaging Your Home for Profit, by Bruce Percelay and Peter Arnold (Little, Brown and Company), provides comprehensive advice on what you can do, both inside and outside your home, to enhance its value and make it easier to sell. It includes tips on using color and smell, and suggests which improvements will yield the highest returns on your money.

GET THE PLACE IN SHAPE

Walk through your home making a list of everything that needs to be done. During your inspection, jot down the problems and what can be done to make each room attractive. Taking down dark curtains and opening a room to sunlight may change its character completely. So can repainting.

You can't anticipate what will catch the attention of a prospective buyer. Plaster walls and a new furnace may get only passing notice, while the cracked toilet tank top elicits several questions. Or hours may be spent evaluating the heating and plumbing, while fresh paint, refinished floors and brand-new windows are overlooked.

Use this inspection guide to see your home as buyers might:

Inside

Attic. Check underside of roof for leaks, stains or dampness. Look around chimney for condensation or signs of water. Clean and clear ventilation openings if necessary. Clean out stored junk.

Walls and ceilings. Check condition of paint and wallpaper. Repair cracks, holes or damage to plaster or wallboard.

Windows and doors. Check for smooth operation. Replace broken or cracked panes. Repair glazing. Check condition of weather stripping and caulking. Examine condition of paint. Test doorbell, chimes, burglar alarms. Wash windows and woodwork, if necessary.

Floors. Inspect for creaking boards, loose or missing tiles, worn areas. Check baseboards and moldings. Test staircases for loose handrails, posts, treads.

Bathrooms. Check tile joints, grouting and caulking. Remove mildew. Repair dripping faucets and shower heads. Check condition of painted or papered walls. Test operation of toilet.

Kitchen. Wash all appliances. Clean ventilator or exhaust fan. Remove accumulation of grease or dust from tiles, walls, floors.

Basement. Remove clutter. Check for signs of dampness, cracked walls or damaged floors. Inspect structural beams. Check pipes for leaks.

Electrical system. Check exposed wiring and outlets for signs of wear or damage. Repair broken switches and outlets. Label each circuit or fuse.

Plumbing system. Look for leaks at faucets and sink traps. Clear slow-running or clogged drains. Bleed air off radiators if needed, and check for leaking valves.

Heating and cooling systems. Change or clean furnace and air-conditioning filters. Have equipment serviced if needed. Clear and clean area around heating and cooling equipment.

Outside

Roof and gutters. Repair or replace loose, damaged or blistered shingles. Clean gutters and downspout strainers. Check gutters for leaks and proper alignment. Inspect flashings around roof stacks, vents, skylights and chimneys. Clear obstructions from vents, louvers and chimneys. Check fascias and soffits for decay and peeling paint. Inspect chimney for loose or missing mortar.

Exterior walls. Renail loose siding and check for warping or decay. Paint siding if necessary. Check masonry walls for cracks or other damage. Replace loose or missing caulking.

Driveway. Repair concrete or blacktop if necessary.

Garage. Lubricate garage door hinges and hardware. Inspect doors and windows for peeling paint. Check condition of glazing around windows. Test electrical outlets.

Foundation. Check walls, steps, retaining walls, walks and patios for cracks, heaving or crumbling.

Yard. Mow lawn, reseed or sod if necessary. Trim hedges, prune trees and shrubs. Weed and mulch flowerbeds.

THE RADON QUESTION

Radon wasn't a household word until a few years ago, when a Pennsylvania nuclear-power-plant worker set off radiation alarms at work because he had been exposed to extraordinarily high levels of radon at home. A colorless, odorless radioactive gas produced by decaying uranium, radon exists naturally in soil and rock. But when it seeps into homes where it cannot diffuse as quickly as in open air, the lung-cancer causing gas can accumulate to dangerous levels.

The Environmental Protection Agency (EPA) and private testing companies have detected unsafe levels of radon in nearly every state, but that shouldn't be cause for panic. Although the EPA found unsafe levels in about 20% of the homes tested in ten states, only 1% registered levels above 20 picocuries per liter, defined by the EPA as the equivalent of smoking two packs of cigarettes a day. Nor has the link between indoor radon and lung cancer been conclusively proven.

But once you decide to sell your home, you may have to test anyway. In some areas many home buyers are including contingency clauses in sales contracts that require a test for, and sometimes correction of, radon problems before they will buy.

An initial three- to seven-day charcoal-canister test can alert you to dangerously high radon levels. The test can be repeated. Or you can use an alpha track detector over an extended period, since readings often vary at different times. Before you pay a private company $10 to $50 for the charcoal test, check with your state or local environmental office; some government agencies provide free or low-cost testing.

An EPA report available from your state's radiation-control or radiological-health office lists companies that test for radon. For more information, also request one of these booklets: *A Citizen's Guide to Radon* and *Radon Reduction Methods*.

C H A P T E R 1 9

SELL THROUGH AN AGENT OR GO IT ALONE?

◆

THE VAST majority of homes are sold through a listing contract with a real estate agent, with the seller paying the typical 6% commission on the sale price. But for the other homes, the sellers apparently asked themselves, "Why pay someone thousands of dollars for doing something I can do myself, with the help of a few professionals I'll compensate on a flat-fee or hourly basis?"

Saving $9,000 on a $150,000 home sale is plenty of motivation for a "fizzbo," or FSBO (For Sale by Owner)—a term real estate agents use somewhat disdainfully. The urge to try selling one's own home is especially strong in a seller's market, when qualified buyers are plentiful, listings are relatively few, and everything that's fairly priced gets snapped up fast.

Agents can reel off a dozen or more arguments against trying to sell your own home, among them that you could set the wrong price, accept an unqualified buyer, and lose out on the cooperation of agents, who won't bring their clients by to see your home. Sure, all of those things can happen—but some of them might happen even if you list your home with an agent.

AN AGENT'S STRENGTHS

The fact that most people do use an agent to sell their homes suggests that a lot of homeowners believe they get good value for the 6% commission. Selling a house by oneself is hard work, and it requires time, savvy, and a knack for selling.

The benefits of good sales agents are many. They are experienced at the proper pricing of a property and writing of effective ads. They'll advise you on sprucing up your home for an easy sale. In a slow market, they will beat the bushes for buyers. They can help screen buyers on financial qualifications. They'll review the buyers' offers and negotiate the best deal they can get for you. They'll help locate financing for your buyer and shepherd both parties through the twisted maze toward settlement.

Another important benefit of selling through an agent is getting your home listed in a multiple listing service—the computerized clearinghouse of properties listed with professional brokers. You can't use the agent's MLS on your own, and you'll have to make up for this with your own advertising efforts.

Finally, if the agent can get you a sale price that is at least 6% higher than you could get selling your home yourself without paying a commission, then the agent's skills cost your nothing, theoretically. That's a big "if," however. (See Chapter 21.)

GOING IT ALONE

Without denying the real estate agent his or her due, all the tasks of selling a house can be accomplished by an energetic, imaginative seller aided by a few professionals—appraiser, inspector and real estate attorney—who will charge on an hourly or flat-fee basis, rather than commission.

You don't need a license or any kind of official permission to sell your own property. But you will need these resources:

Time: Finding a buyer can take time, even in a feverish market. A house or condominium unit may not move quickly if it is unusual in some way, in disrepair, in a deteriorating neighborhood or equipped with extras not every buyer wants, such as a swimming pool or tennis court.

Going it alone is risky if you must sell in a hurry. You might speed things up by telling prospects that you will cut the price by a percentage of the amount of a sales commission. Still, the odds are an agent with access to a multiple listing service and other contacts would get faster action.

Flexibility: You will need plenty of time to show your home during the day, as well as at night and on weekends. You can decide to show it by appointment only, but you probably can't afford to be too rigid about that either. If you can't be at home, arrange for a responsible, interested adult to be there. It's not enough to make your home accessible by having a painter, babysitter or child open the door. That may be okay if an agent is coming to show it, but it's not good enough for a FSBO. You have to *show* your home to prospects, not just allow them to wander about.

Patience: Unless you are used to dealing with the public, it is easy to underestimate the amount of patience you'll need to handle telephone calls, answer questions, give directions and show the property—again and again.

Information: You will need to know all about your neighborhood, your property, your appliances, furnace, roof, plumbing and electrical systems. You must be willing to get the facts you need to assist prospects with financing. You should be thoroughly familiar with all comparable properties in your area.

Knack for selling: If the prospect of displaying the merchandise, fielding questions, overcoming objections and solving problems in order to make the sale impresses you as indelicate or undignified, reconsider handling this project without a real estate agent.

Intuition: Will you be able to sniff out a genuine candidate from a window-shopper? Time spent with individuals or couples who haven't really decided to buy is time not spent with those who have—and who only need to be sold on your home.

A little money: You will need to pay upfront for advertising, the copying of fact sheets, and hiring a lawyer to draw up a contract and buyer qualification forms. An appraisal isn't required but could be well worth the $175 to $350.

Elbow grease: Make your place gleam, even if it means hiring a cleaning crew. Use a paint brush and make other improvements. Everything said in Chapter 18 about getting your home ready goes double if you are selling it yourself. A glib agent can talk a client past a plaster crack or dirty wallpaper, but it will be much harder for you to do so.

Keep track of what you spend in getting the place in shape. If you buy a replacement home that costs less than the one you sell, fixing-up expenses incurred in the 90 days before the sale can be used to shave the tax on any profit.

STEPS TO SUCCESS FOR THE FSBO

Price It Right

The single most important task in the selling of a house is the proper pricing of it—right at the market value, neither too low nor too high. This requires either your own careful study of comparable transactions in your neighborhood, or the services of a professional appraiser, who will do the same thing for you.

The FSBO must decide whether to price the house right at full market value and try to pocket the commission savings himself, or share these savings with the buyer, settling for a little less than the full asking price but more than would result from an agent sale at asking price minus commission. For a full discussion of pricing, see Chapter 21.

Prepare Fact Sheets

Prospects seldom take notes as they are being shown around. They may be reluctant to appear too interested, or they may find writing distracts them from looking. But they rarely refuse to accept a printed fact sheet.

These fact sheets are important; they tell at a glance what you're selling, highlight the best points, and later on can refresh the memories of lookers who may have seen a dozen other offerings. For added impact, attach a snapshot of the place—one that shows it to advantage in its best season of the year.

The sheet should include all relevant facts about the property—age, construction, square footage, room dimensions, mechanical systems (heat, air conditioning, etc.), appliances that go with the home, amenities, lot size, and proximity to schools, public transportation, shopping and such. Add to that the price, taxes, maintenance and utility costs, and any relevant information about the current mortgage (if assumable) and seller financing help, if any. You may want to include the appraised value and a drawing of the layout.

Arrange all this in logical order and type it up, preferably on a single page. Add a statement that the "information is not guaranteed but deemed accurate to the best of my knowledge." Make copies to give to each prospect.

Inform potential buyers about known problems or defects. You're legally obliged to, and failing to do so could cause you to lose a sale or become entangled in a lawsuit.

Get Contract and Buyer Qualification Forms

Preprinted contract forms, which vary from state to state, generally are available from office supply stores, stationers, real estate boards and lawyers. Alternatively, arrange for the attorney who will represent you to draw up a contract to meet your requirements and protect your interests while conforming to state and local laws—particularly with regard to disclosures about your property's physical and structural condition. Some real estate lawyers may help clients negotiate a deal and assess the creditworthiness and financial abilities of prospective purchasers.

Qualification forms, which you can draw up yourself or with your attorney's assistance, will help you decide whether a prospective buyer is financially able to follow through on his or her offer. When an offer is submitted, have the person fill out the form, listing annual income, debts, assets, place and length of employment, credit references and such.

Gather Documents You May Need

Questions may come up that could be answered by a site plan or surveyor's report. If you're selling a condominium unit, have handy the declaration or plan of condominium ownership (also called the declaration of covenants or the master deed), the bylaws of the owners' association and the rules governing property use. Have handy your actual stubs or photocopies of utility bills and recent tax bills.

Bone Up on Mortgage Financing

Offers usually are made contingent on the buyer's ability to get financing. It is in your interest to be helpful to buyers who find the prospect of getting a mortgage more intimidating than finding a home. Remember, this is the sort of service that a real estate agent provides to prospective buyers, and you must do the same if you're serious about selling your house yourself.

Draw up a list of lenders and check weekly on financing rates and terms. Your local newspaper may publish such information, or you can subscribe to a mortgage reporting service. (See Chapter 11 for names and addresses of some of the larger services.) You might even keep an interest-rate table and calculator handy so a prospect could calculate on the spot what the monthly principal and interest payments would be.

Be prepared to answer questions on VA and FHA loans if your home is likely to attract veterans and first-time buyers. Albert Santi's *The Mortgage Manual (Questions & Answers for FHA, VA & Conventional Loans)* provides extensive coverage. The book is available from Probus Publishing Co., Chicago.

You may be asked by some prospective buyers whether you are willing to assist them by taking back a second trust on your house. Before the issue arises, study the various kinds of "creative financing" discussed in Chapter 10 and decide whether you want to offer anything like this, and see Chapter 22 for mistakes to avoid when offering seller financing.

Generally, in an economy where interest rates are not unreasonably high and there are many qualified buyers, you don't have to help the purchaser with financing, and most sellers would rather not bother with it. If possible, go for a sale that will give you the total cash value of your property, for you to invest as you wish, in your next house or some other investment.

Put Up an Attractive Sign

Create a good impression by putting up a bright new sign in the front. Look in a hardware or sign shop for a "For Sale by Owner" sign that has a place below the main message for an add-on sign (or have one made professionally). During the week, you can hang out a phone number. And, if you have an open house, you can remove it and hang an "Open" sign.

Signs are effective sources of clients for both amateur sellers and real estate firms. A response to a sign is a more valuable inquiry than a response to a newspaper ad. The sign caller is already in the neighborhood. He or she probably knows and likes the area and obviously likes the look of your home well enough to want to see the inside. You are two selling steps ahead of a classified ad caller. That person is responding to general information, and may or may not like your area or the external appearance of your home when and if a viewing appointment is made and the prospect arrives.

Study Effective Real Estate Ads

Read the Sunday paper and study the ads written by the professionals. The best ads have very full descriptions of the house, not sketchy write-ups with so much abbreviation that they're hard to decipher. The strong points are played up, the weak points are omitted or put in the best possible light. (A small house becomes "cozy" in a good ad.) Avoid exaggeration and overly cute writing. Always put in the price. List the address (with some general directions) if it's an ad for an open house. Otherwise, you may wish to list only your phone number, to get calls for an appointment. Run the ad in the Sunday paper; to ensure the most accurate ad, deliver ad copy to the newspaper, rather than calling it in by phone.

Give Good Directions

All the good advertising money can buy won't get people into your home if they get lost trying to get there. Prepare maps and directions. Anticipate where prospects will be coming from, and route them along the simplest, most direct and most attractive route you can devise.

Put up a large map by the telephone to answer questions and redirect turned-about buyers who care enough to call.

Hold an Open House

Sunday open houses are a ritual among house hunters. You'll

get a lot of serious buyers, a lot of curiosity lookers, and a few neighbors who like to keep abreast of the local market. Any of these could lead to a successful contract, sooner or later.

Have a visitor register handy—a simple pad of paper will suffice—so you can get names and phone numbers. Some people will gladly sign it, while others will decline, preferring anonymity; don't press the point.

Most buyers like to go through a house by themselves, so that they can discuss its strengths and weaknesses without embarrassing the owner. Station yourself in the front hall or the dining room, greet visitors warmly, and hand them a fact sheet that they can take through the house with them. But don't escort them until they ask you to. (If you're worried about security, make sure any small objects of value are locked up or stashed out of sight.) Before they leave, ask them if they have any additional questions. Remember that you're a salesman for your house; try to engage visitors in conversation so you can make your best points.

If both spouses of a couple feel comfortable showing the house together, it's a good idea. If one gets into a deep discussion (or even an unexpected negotiation) with a serious prospect—in a private place, out of earshot of other visitors—the spouse can continue to greet new visitors.

Be Ready to Negotiate

Some interested buyers will want to sleep on their first impressions and return to your house one or more times, ideally getting more and more comfortable with it each time.

But the highly prepared buyer—who knows just what he wants and thinks he has found it in your property—may want to get right into a negotiation, especially if the market is tight and he's afraid your house will go fast.

It isn't unheard of for a visitor to an open house to take one of your prepared contract forms, go home and fill it out, and return to submit it before the day is out.

If you have a "live wire" buyer in your midst, be ready to deal. There are some questions about your acceptable contract terms that you would be happy to discuss verbally, such as an ideal settlement date, occupancy date (if different from settlement), your willingness to finance part of the deal yourself, etc.

But the most important element—price—should not be negotiated verbally, nor your intentions telegraphed. While still in your home, some buyers will ask questions like, "Is your price firm?" or "What are you really willing to accept?".

Don't answer directly, but try to deflect these questions in a courteous, noncommittal way that keeps the buyer interested, with an answer like, "The house is fairly priced for the market right now, but all offers will be considered," or "The price, like other aspects of your offer, can be negotiated; please make us your best offer."

For a fuller discussion of seller negotiating strategies, see Chapter 22.

DEALING WITH AGENTS

As soon as you start advertising or hold your first open house, you'll get calls from agents asking for a listing. They will often tell you that your home is priced way too low, and if they help you sell it, they'll get you enough more to more than cover the commission and net you more than you'll get selling by yourself.

Of course, they might be right, but then, their judgment isn't exactly objective. If you've proceeded on your course with care and have priced your house according to comparable values in the market, stand your ground—at least for a while. Tell inquiring agents you intend to try it yourself first.

Be wary of anyone who attempts to get a sales listing on your house by claiming to have a hot prospect who is looking for a home just like yours. If the agent's prospect is truly motivated, he or she probably checks out the Sunday real estate ads and will see your ad; at that point, you will get a direct inquiry from the buyer. (The main exception to this assumption, which makes the agent's claim more valid, is the out-of-town buyer who is relying totally on the agent to find houses.)

While you're holding firm to your own sales effort, don't allow agents on your property with prospects. If you allow the agent to bring a prospect without a written agreement, you may have—in effect—granted an open listing to the agent. And, if the prospect buys, you may end up paying a commission, even without a written agreement. (But some states have tried to avoid misunderstandings—and suits—between FSBO sellers and agents by enacting laws that effectively bar an agent from collecting a commission unless there was some sort of written agreement with the seller.)

While holding eager agents at bay, set a time limit on your own brokering, exactly as you would with a professional broker. Give yourself 30, 60 or 90 days, depending on the current selling climate and how quickly you must sell your house. Then, during your time period, be clear and firm with agents seeking a listing: "No listings until I've taken a crack at it myself." Do your best to sell the home, but if you don't succeed, back off and turn the job over to an agent of your choice.

GETTING HELP

You don't have to go it entirely alone to bring off a sale. There are a number of ways to get professional help and still pay less than full commission.

Temporary Listing Contract

If you think a particular agent has a buyer who might not see or buy your house without the agent's cooperation, you might be persuaded to give the agent a shot at selling your house, but for less than a 6% commission. This calls for a short-term, custom-tailored listing agreement.

Tell the agent to come *alone* to your house (even if the prospective buyer just waits in the car at the curb) and sign a temporary listing agreement that contains the name of the agent, the amount of the commission (generally just 2% or 3%, since you've done most of the work yourself), the name of the prospective buyer and the asking price for this particular transaction. The price will probably be higher than what you've been asking for a FSBO transaction, to cover the commission you're going to pay if the deal goes through.

You should limit the time an agent has to bring you a purchase offer from this buyer, so the agreement—covering only the particular named buyer—should be valid for only one or two days at most.

Open listing: 3% deal for all agents

Since many house hunters do their searching with agents, who get compensated for those efforts only by sharing in the sales commissions, it's understandable that the agents will try to steer their clients away from FSBO listings. A FSBO who refuses to pay any commission will, in effect, be trying to split house hunters away from the agents who may have given them considerable help in the search.

If, as described above, you are willing to pay 3% to an agent who brings in the final buyer, you should let other agents know. They will probably be more than willing to cooperate—a 3% commission is about as much as they make on most home sales, since the 6% commission is usually split between the listing broker and the broker's agent. Agents will ask you to draw up a listing agreement—called an open listing—that guarantees them their commission if the deal goes through.

You should be willing to sign such a listing, one for each agent. Unlike the agreement above, it need not identify a particular buyer. It can cover as long a period as you wish, but writing in a finite expiration date is essential, because you may not legally sign an exclusive listing agreement with one agent while you have any open listings like these still floating around valid.

If you decide to try this partial FSBO method, make sure you put the words "sale by owner; brokers welcome at 3%" in your ads.

Discount agents and counselors

Some real estate brokers offer bare-bones service, charging flat fees or lower commissions in exchange for specific services that can run the gamut from the most basic—renting a sign—to service barely distinguishable from full-service brokerages. Most offer something in between. HELP-U-SELL, a real estate company based in Salt Lake City, Utah, for example, unbundles some of the services they sell to buyers. The company offers three prepackaged deals to home sellers. With their basic service, they agree to post the property in a proprietary listing system, advertise the home through direct mail and in the newspaper, put up signs and help prospective buyers write up their offers. The seller is responsible for showing the property and for paying HELP-U-SELL when the house is sold. The cost is roughly half that of a full-service broker (including showing and holding open houses).

If you are considering a discount broker, apply all the same standards you would if you were selecting a full-service broker. (See the next chapter.) One service you probably shouldn't pass up is having your home advertised to other agents through the MLS in your area. Make sure any discount broker you're considering can list your home with the service.

There also may be real estate counselors or broker-consultants in your community who help owner-sellers for 1% or 2% of the selling price or work on an hourly basis. For names, check with large real estate firms in your area and watch for advertisements in the real estate section of the paper. In some communities, title companies will help you close the deal once you have a contract agreement with a buyer.

CHAPTER 20

PICKING A BROKER, LISTING YOUR HOME

◆

FOR MOST Americans, their home is their principal asset. If you want to turn the work of selling this asset over to a broker, choose one who will help you get the highest price for your home and perform the task efficiently, honestly and quickly.

You will pay the broker and his agent thousands of dollars at settlement. While any broker can list, advertise and show your home, brokers and agents are not unlike lawyers, doctors and car dealers—they come in every variety, bringing with them different economic backgrounds, personalities, resources and levels of skills and integrity. Two out of three sellers hire the first agent they contact. Needless to say, that's not the best way to do it.

Select one or two brokerage firms in your area with a reputation for integrity and a proven track record selling homes comparable to yours. Then interview at least three successful agents at those firms whose personalities and selling styles are compatible with yours.

Consider hiring a discount broker—a firm that will help you sell your house for less than a full 6% commission, in exchange for your doing some of the work that the listing agent normally does. (See the discussion in Chapter 19.)

SELECTING THE FIRM

Find out how intensely the firm works your area. How many listings does the firm carry, both in and out of season? What percentage of those listings are sold by the firm's agents? One indicator is the frequency of the firm's name in the by-neighborhood listings in the Sunday paper and the number of the firm's signs you see in your area.

Check the company's reputation and experience with lenders, lawyers and former clients. When you sign a listing agreement, you are employing a firm or a broker to find a buyer for your property. If you pick a brokerage firm because you want to work with a particular agent, keep in mind that you are still relying on the firm's experience, contacts and reputation. While most of your contact may be with the agent, satisfy yourself that behind that agent is strong supervision and plenty of expertise. To whom will an agent turn for advice should problems arise? In most firms the managing broker is responsible for resolving financial problems, supervising complex contract preparation and counseling agents.

In your initial telephone contact, ask whether the 6% commission will be reduced under special circumstances—for example, if the buyer is found by the listing broker, with no sharing of commission with another firm. While brokerage commissions are officially negotiable, in practice, most firms hold tight to their stated commission.

Find out how the firm is staffed. How many agents are full-time? How many are part-time? How experienced is the group as a whole? Do most agents concentrate on selling homes, or do they dabble in commercial real estate and property management as well? Do agents have access to administrative and secretarial help?

How will telephone queries about your property be handled? Call the firm as though you were a prospective buyer, and ask a few friends to do the same. When you call as a seller, you're almost assured of a warm welcome; but the reception could be less enthusiastic for purchasers, especially in a seller's market when agents are busy.

Does a would-be buyer get an alert and enthusiastic response? How long does it take to get a call returned? How carefully are messages and phone numbers taken? Does the answering agent have listing information available, and is he or she able to tell you what you want to know about the property?

Does the firm participate in the local multiple listing service? An MLS provides a computerized master list of all the homes for sale in a marketplace through its member real estate companies. Agents use this information extensively to match up buyers and sellers.

Is the firm hooked into a nationwide referral system? If your home could be attractive to corporate transferees, find out how many referrals the office received during the past 12 months. How many referrals resulted in sales and what was the average selling price?

FINDING THE BEST AGENT

Ask the head of the firm you select to give you the names of the agents in the office who have the most experience in your neighborhood and price range. An agent who does a lot of business with sellers in the area may work at developing a list of interested buyers, or may maintain close contact with agents who have such clients. Select one who knows the community's price history and one who has weathered bad years as well as profited during good ones. Look for an agent who can not only answer a buyer's questions about recently sold homes, but who frequently can say, "We made those sales."

Interview your former neighbors. Track down at least two who sold within the last six months to a year; ask them about the agent they used and those they chose not to use. The following is a list of suggested questions:

♦ How long was the house on the market?

♦ Did it sell for the original price, or did you have to reduce the price substantially?

♦ With how many agents did you have your home listed? If more than one, what happened to the other one(s)?

♦ Did the agent withdraw voluntarily, or did you refuse to renew the listing? Either way, why?

♦ Do you think your agent got you the best available deal in both price and terms, or did you accept the offer because you had to make a decision without more delay?

◆ Did the entire office push your home, or did the job fall almost entirely to the listing agent?

◆ Do you think your agent and his firm made it easy or hard for other firms to cooperate?

◆ Did the firm maintain a strong selling push, or did you have to keep prodding it?

◆ Do you think the property could have been sold faster? For more money?

◆ Did the agent see you through closing?

◆ Were the people you dealt with courteous?

◆ Did they call for appointments to show your home and call to cancel when they had a change of plans?

◆ Knowing what you know now, would you use the same agent again?

INTERVIEWING THE AGENTS

To save time, you may wish to hold an informal open house for agents, during which several agents will come to tour your home at the same time. Later, select two or three to give you a full "listing presentation." The agent's presentation should include:

◆ Information about the agent's experience, education and background.

◆ Advice on repairs and other improvements that would make your home more appealing.

◆ Information about the housing market in general and current activity in your neighborhood.

◆ Market analysis showing all recent comparable sales in your area. An analysis should show properties currently on the market. It also should specify the selling price and date of sale for the sold homes, and date of listing for the unsold ones, along with detailed descriptions of each property.

◆ Suggested asking price, based on how quickly you wish to sell your home.

◆ Discussion of the kind of advertising and promotion to expect.

◆ "Net proceeds" sheet, illustrating what you might realize on the sale under varying financing arrangements and with various levels of commission.

♦ Explanation of various kinds of listings and listing agreements.

After all the presentations, select the one agent you want to do business with first. Your decision should be based on everything from professionalism and knowledge to the intangibles of personal chemistry.

You might very well receive from the agents you interview a wide range of suggested asking prices. You will be very tempted to list your home with the agent who confidently suggests the highest asking price. Take this with a grain of salt, and examine how the suggested price relates to comparable recent transactions.

Just as some agents will try to talk you into a low asking price to assure themselves a quick, easy sale (and sure commission), others will give you an inflated estimate of your house's value to get the initial listing. Only later, after your home has sat unsold for too long, will they suggest a price reduction.

KINDS OF LISTINGS

After you select an agent, decide on one of the several kinds of listing agreements. A listing agreement, whether oral or written, exclusive or nonexclusive, is a legally enforceable contract. Review each prospective agent's listing agreement form while you are still going through the selection process. Once you've picked the agent you want to work with, you may want to modify certain parts of the contract.

With any kind of listing, if the agent brings you the deal that the listing calls for (full price and exact terms offered by a buyer who is ready, willing and able to buy), you are obliged to pay a commission *whether you accept the deal or not*.

These are the most frequently used arrangements:

♦ *Exclusive right to sell*. This is the most common agreement. The listing agent is entitled to a commission no matter who sells the property, including you. If another agent produces the buyer, you still owe only the one commission, which will be split between the listing broker and the broker who found the buyer. This type of agreement usually assures you the most service. The agent is guaranteed a commission if he produces a sale, and you have an agent to hold responsible for making all "reasonable" or "diligent" efforts to find a purchaser.

If your employer has guaranteed to buy your home at a discount if you can't get a better offer on the open market (usually in cases of a transfer), be sure to amend an exclusive-right-to-sell agreement to prevent an agent from claiming a commission on your company's purchase.

◆ *Exclusive, or exclusive agency.* You don't pay a commission if you find a buyer without help from the agent. If you sign an agreement like this, you're in effect competing with your own listing agent; if you get direct queries about your property, handle them yourself and don't refer calls to your agent.

If you have a good prospect who expressed an interest in your home before you listed it with an agent, use this kind of agreement and add a clause that says you may sell the house to this named party—and any other whom you find yourself—without paying a commission.

◆ *Open.* You agree to pay a commission to any agent as long as he or she is the first to produce an acceptable buyer. Again, you don't owe any commission if you are the first one to find a buyer.

This type of listing is most common when there is no multiple listing service. It's also the kind of listing often used by sellers who want to do most of the selling work themselves but want the cooperation of agents in finding buyers.

The commission is typically half of the standard rate—say, 3%. The seller should notify agents of such an offer by putting the words "Brokers welcome at 3%" in newspaper ads. Then the seller signs a simple open-listing agreement with each of the agents who expresses an interest in bringing a buyer to see the home.

Make sure you specify an expiration date (not too distant) on every open listing, because you can't sign an exclusive listing with one agent if you have open listings still in force.

ELEMENTS OF THE LISTING CONTRACT

Expiration Date

Knowing the average and median length of time it takes for

homes to sell in your neighborhood should influence your choice of a listing expiration date. Thirty to 90 days is common. Generally, the shorter the better, but it isn't reasonable to insist on a 30-day listing when homes like yours are taking three to six months to sell.

A relatively short listing will give you the option of switching agents if friction develops with your first agent, or if you feel he or she isn't working hard to sell your home.

You can extend a listing beyond its original life, but don't inadvertently sign an agreement containing an automatic extension. If you wish, substitute a provision that extends the listing as much as 60 days if a buyer reneges on a signed sales contract.

You also may want to add a clause reinforcing your right to cancel the contract should the agent fail to do a good job. If you exercise that option, however, you may find that you are still liable for certain expenses that were incurred by the agent. Moreover, in some listing contracts, you may have to pay a penalty for canceling.

Protection Period

If, after the listing expires, you sell your home to someone your former agent had a hand in finding, there may be a clause in the contract that entitles the agent to a commission anyway. Naturally, no agent wants to lose a commission because the listing agreement expires while he is still working with a prospective buyer.

Typically, protection clauses give commission rights to agents for 30 to 60 days after a contract ends. If a listing agreement contains such a provision, it also should provide, in fairness to the seller, that the agent give the seller the names of prospective buyers *before* the listing expires—and require written purchase offers from any such buyers within a reasonable time *after* the listing expires.

Commission

Commissions are negotiable. They are not set by law or by industry rules—something most sellers don't realize. A listing agent usually gets a commission based on a percentage of the final sales price of the property—typically 6% to 7%.

As a practical matter you won't get very far negotiating a lower rate unless you have special circumstances that make your property more economical to sell than others. You can make a strong argument for a lower commission or other concessions in the following cases:

Easy sale: The property is fairly priced, and it's in the right location. The mortgage carries an attractive interest rate and is assumable, and the house is in immaculate condition.

Volume discount: You have other properties to put on the block with your home.

Double score: Another agent from the firm listing your property delivers a buyer, so the commission won't be shared with another broker.

Scaled-back Service: You take on some of the burden of selling and lower the commission accordingly. You also may be able to find a "discount" real estate broker. In either case, be sure the listing contract is clear about what will be done for you in the way of advertising and promotion. Keep in mind that if the commission cut is too deep, cooperating brokers may not be interested in working for a share of an already small commission.

Agent has a buyer at hand: You pay less: the agent won't have to advertise, hold open the property or split the commission.

The purchase contract or settlement is at risk: An agent may be willing to make concessions to hold onto a piece of a deal that's on the verge of getting away.

For example, take a situation where the seller is dealing directly with a buyer whom the seller found; if that buyer's offer—which might net more for the seller—is accepted, the seller's listing agent won't get any commission on the sale. To compete against that buyer, an agent may have to present a considerably higher contract from another buyer and also shave the sales commission, to make the second contract net at least as much as the first one.

Another reason for a shaved commission might be a problem that develops on the way to settlement—say, the seller finding out he has to pay more mortgage discount points than he expected. If the deal is at stake, the agent might offer to make up the difference out of his or her own commission.

Condition of Property and What's for Sale

The listing agreement should describe the general condition of the property. It should show what is being sold "as is" and what, if anything, will be repaired, removed, substituted or altered prior to settlement. The agreement should list every fixture that will be sold with the house, and those that will not.

Make the agent aware of problems or defects in the property. If the listing agreement doesn't adequately spell out the current condition of the structure, the appliances and the electrical, mechanical and plumbing systems, have it corrected or write a letter to the agent setting out the information.

Marketing Plan

Get the proposed marketing plan in writing as an addendum to the listing contract. It can serve as documentation should you feel the agent is not fulfilling his commitments. Arrange for weekly progress reports.

Know your target market. Ask the listing agent to give you a profile of your home's most likely buyer or buyers. Will they be first-time buyers, retirees or corporate transferees? What kind of income will they have?

The marketing strategy your agent proposes should be designed to reach those potential buyers. A comprehensive plan should include these elements:

Advertising: How often and where will your home be advertised? When your home is not being advertised, will the firm be advertising a comparable home so that interested buyers can also be referred to your property?

Open houses: What efforts will the agent make to bring interested buyers to your home? For example, will agents who deal with likely clients be sent an information sheet describing the property and date of the open house? Will ads and signs be used?

Multiple listing service: How promptly will your property be placed in the MLS? Ideally, it should go into the computer very quickly, and you should specify a deadline in the listing contract; some MLSs require their members to enter new listings within 24 hours of the signing of the contract.

Some brokers will try to keep a new listing out of the MLS computer for several days or more; that gives their own agents a first shot at selling the property "in house," so that the whole 6% commission is kept within the firm. Once agents at other firms see the listing in the computer and bring prospective buyers in to see the home, the odds increase that the listing broker will have to split the eventual commission with another broker (called the "co-op" broker or agent). You'll pay only the full commission in any event, and your interests are served by a fast sale.

Agent tours: An organized tour for other agents in the office should be arranged soon after you sign the listing. An open house for other agents from other firms is another useful sales tool.

Spreading the word: Will your agent inform your neighbors that you are selling? What other networks will he or she use?

Financing: Will your agent be able to work with interested buyers to locate financing?

GET READY TO SELL

Your agent will set about the task of selling your house as soon as the ink is dry on a listing contract, so you had better be ready, too.

Ideally, your home will be ready to show immediately, but if it isn't, now is the time to do all the last-minute touch-ups and clean-ups described in Chapter 18.

From now until a sales contract is accepted, your home has to be ready to show on a moment's notice. It's difficult living in a home that's for sale, but its tidiness during an appointment or open house will have a lot of bearing on how fast it sells and for how much.

Try to have everyone out of the house when your agent brings a prospect to inspect it, even if that means gathering up the kids and your elderly parents and taking them all for a drive. This will enable the agent and house hunter to talk more candidly than if you're there, and the buyer will be able to visualize his or her lifestyle more easily if your kids aren't running around or making sandwiches in the kitchen.

Most importantly, you should be emotionally ready to deal with serious buyers. The signing of the listing contract and presentation of the first buyer's contract is not the time to discover that you have misgivings about selling or qualms about the asking price.

C H A P T E R 2 1

SETTING THE RIGHT PRICE

◆

TO SET THE right price on a home, sellers should combine objective evaluation of the property with a realistic assessment of current market conditions.

In good markets and bad, a seller is more likely to benefit by determining a fair value and sticking close to it than he is by asking an unrealistic figure and waiting for buyer response to sift out the "right" price. And when there are more sellers than buyers, setting the right price from the outset may be the only strategy that will work.

Underpricing deprives you of the full value you deserve. Unless you are in a frightful hurry, try to get full market value. Avoid over-eager or unethical agents who may suggest a price that will assure a quick and easy sale—one that won't require lots of advertising and showing.

DANGERS OF OVERPRICING

If you wish, you could set a very fair price and refuse to bargain, but that is ill-advised. It would deter people who hate to pay full price for anything and like to think they're "getting a deal."

It's better to leave a little room for negotiation, by asking slightly more than you expect to get. How much more? Certainly not more than 5% to 10% above appraised value. If sales are brisk in your area, you might just be able to get top dollar.

What many sellers don't realize is that overpricing can result in their getting *less* for their house than if they priced it right to begin with. The reason is this: knowledgeable agents and buyers won't even put in a contract on a severely overpriced house. By the time the seller wises up to the overpricing, many of those qualified buyers will have bought other houses, decreasing market demand for the now properly priced property. The overpriced house may end up selling for less than it might have fetched a few months earlier.

Occasionally, an agent agrees to list a property for far more than it is worth—usually at the owner's insistence. The agent knows that, if the owner is serious about selling, the price will have to come down sooner or later. But sometimes an agent who is competing against other agents for a sales listing will give a seller an unrealistically high estimate of value, to ensure getting the listing. After the house sits on the market a while, the agent will suggest a new, lower price that is more in line with what the other agents suggested in the first place.

Some sellers who don't have to sell by any particular deadline ("unmotivated sellers," they're called) will cling for a long time to their overly high asking price—say, 15% higher than it should be. They probably won't get their asking price, and even if they do manage to sell a year later for the original price, it will be because a rising market finally caught up with their price.

They might think they were smart to hold firm, but in fact they were naive, ignoring the time value of money. In the year (or even six months) they clung to their high price, the rest of the real estate market probably wasn't standing still. The next home they buy may have gone up in value by at least the same margin, and possibly more. Even if they don't buy a replacement home, they have lost the earnings they would have received on the invested proceeds of an earlier sale—at least 6% per year, if very conservatively invested, and possibly much more, if invested in tax-free bonds or a rising stock market.

STUDY THE COMPARABLES

You run the risk of either overpricing or underpricing if you settle on a price not based on solid information. Shop your competition. Whether you are using an agent or not, learn the offering and selling prices of similar properties. Find out how long each took to sell.

To be comparable, a house that sold has to be close to yours in age, style, size, condition and location. It also is important to know the terms under which a house was sold. A $100,000 all-cash-to-the-seller sale is very different from a $100,000 sale with $10,000 down and a $20,000 second mortgage taken back by the owner.

Timing is critical, too. If you are offering your home when sales are brisk and demand is high, you should be able to add something to the price.

Try to find at least three comparables no more than six months old. Information on home sales is available at the courthouse or city real estate tax office. In jurisdictions where there is a tax on the transfer of property, you can determine the price by the tax paid. For example, if the tax or fee is 0.1% of the sales price and the transfer fee is $88, then the price paid was $88 divided by .001, or $88,000. Sales prices of homes also are published in local or regional sections of newspapers.

You won't learn anything at the tax office about the terms of the sale, the style of the house or how long it was on the market. If you are going it alone, your best bet is to copy the names and contact the buyers and sellers yourself.

If you are listing your home with an agent, this kind of market research should be prepared and presented to you. Nevertheless, you owe it to yourself to ask questions and to be sure that properties being described as comparable to yours really are so.

SELLER FINANCING?

The market for mortgage money will play a major role in what you can ask—and get—for your home.

In the short run, mortgage interest rates and home prices usually move in opposite directions; when mortgage rates soar, it dampens demand for homes, and real estate prices level off or even decline. (But not always: In the late '70s, inflation and interest rates headed up at a furious pace, but so did home prices . . . until the recession of 1981–82.)

The less a buyer has to pay in interest each month, the more house he can afford to buy—or to state it another way, the more he'll be able to pay for your property.

Conversely, when interest rates zoom up, not only are there fewer people out looking for houses, but those qualified buyers will be able to drive hard bargains on price.

As a seller, your ability to get the price you want when interest rates are high will depend on whether you've got something to offer by way of financing help.

Do you have a low-rate assumable mortgage? That would be a big plus for the buyer and might justify a somewhat higher sale price. Look at your mortgage contract, or ask your lender if you're not sure. (All loans backed by the Federal Housing Administration and Veterans Administration are assumable.)

Are you willing to offer some cut-rate seller financing to assist the buyer in making a deal? If so, you can ask a slightly higher price for your house and stick to it (unless the eventual buyer doesn't need your offered financing).

Remember that most seller financing is, in effect, a discounting of the sale price, so if you're offering a cut-rate second mortgage (which you would have to discount even further to sell in the open market), you've got to get more from the buyer in nominal sale price to make up for it. (For more on seller financing, see the next chapter.)

GET AN APPRAISAL?

If your idea of what your property is worth and the listing broker's recommendation don't coincide, an appraisal may help. An appraisal is an especially good idea for owners attempting to sell their homes themselves. An appraisal will cost roughly $200 or so, but it can be money very well spent.

Real estate appraising is part art, part experience and part science. As a result, opinions always are subject to honest dispute. Nonetheless, an appraisal prepared by an experienced professional comes as close to an objective evaluation as you are likely to get. Get the names of good appraisers from real estate agents, mortgage lenders or from professional associations of appraisers. (See the list in the Appendix.)

The value of your home falls within a range of prices. An

appraiser uses education and judgment to determine that range, and should give you a market value figure based on the "most probable price which a property will bring." Appraisers should adjust the value of properties being used as comparables to reflect any creative financing, sales concessions, seller contributions or buy-downs.

If your home is in the low to moderate price range, you might want to consider a VA or FHA appraisal. VA and FHA appraisals are interchangeable. If you get a VA appraisal and then find a buyer who obtains an FHA loan, the FHA will accept your existing appraisal.

Obtaining a VA or FHA appraisal doesn't lock you into selling VA or FHA. Cost varies with the locality, but a typical charge for a single-family home is about $200; a condominium report costs slightly more. What you get with this type of appraisal is a certificate of reasonable value from the VA or a conditional commitment from FHA, rather than the more detailed report you'd expect from a private residential appraiser.

With an appraisal report in hand, you and the listing agent should be able to come to an agreement. The asking price you ultimately choose may well be higher than the appraised value. But, in most cases, it shouldn't be substantially higher. There's the rub. What is "substantially" higher in one community may be an accepted markup in another.

Go back to the comparables. How much of a spread was there between the original asking price and the actual selling price in each case? Is that the normal differential? Has anything occurred to warrant setting a higher margin?

Make your decision with confidence. You've got room to negotiate. You know your price is right.

SPECIAL ADVICE FOR FSBO'S

If you're selling your house yourself, whether the job will be a bit of hard work or a protracted ordeal depends largely on how accurately you price the property.

It's imperative that the FSBO seller study comparables closely, and it's also desirable to have a recent appraisal. If your asking price is close to the appraisal, show the document to the prospective buyer.

Some FSBOs solicit pricing opinions from real estate agents, even though they don't intend to list the house with an agent. That may strike you as a bit shady, but look at it this way: If you can't make a sale in your time frame, you'll probably turn it over to a professional. Many agents will be willing to prepare a market analysis for a probable FSBO, because it gives them an opportunity to introduce themselves and their firm—and try to persuade the seller to use their services for a commission.

The heart of the FSBO's pricing decision is the motivation for selling on your own. Do you want a fast and easy sale—by offering your home for less than you'd be willing to sell it for if you were to pay an agent a 6% or 7% commission? Or do you want to sell it for top dollar and keep all of the saved commission for yourself?

The best deal is one that's good for both parties. You don't want to give away all of the saved commission to the buyer, but you shouldn't try to hog it all for yourself either. If you can show a prospective buyer that: 1) the asking price is consistent with the market, 2) he'll save a little because there is no commission involved, and 3) you'll net a little more for the same reason—then you've both got a good deal, indeed.

CHAPTER 22

NEGOTIATING WITH BUYERS

◆

Conflict between buyer and seller is inevitable. A buyer wants the most house for his money; a seller wants the most money for his house.

If you're working with an agent, rely on this professional to direct events toward a mutually beneficial conclusion. If you are going it alone, consider hiring an attorney to help with negotiating; otherwise, study up on the fine points of negotiating.

However you are selling your house, carefully read Chapter 8, to get a sense of what an informed, well-prepared buyer wants out of this negotiation and how he will try to get it.

NEGOTIATING THROUGH AN AGENT

Buyers and sellers may find bargaining awkward and uncomfortable. Both are likely to be more frank and open when talking to a third party. For these reasons, an experienced agent often is successful where two-party, face-to-face negotiations fail.

You should be comfortable being utterly frank with your agent. Agents know sellers sometimes take positions they don't mean to hold to the end. Let your agent know what is most important to you. Be precise about what is and isn't acceptable. Make sure the agent has satisfied himself—and you—that the buyer is financially qualified to fulfill the contract offer; this can only be done by checking all the facts the buyer has submitted on a written financial-qualifications form.

Should a cooperating agent bring in a serious buyer, have the listing agent give him a briefing on your requirements as soon as possible. If that's not feasible, ask him to contact you before heading into a contract session.

As your agent should know, all serious negotiating should be done in writing, not verbally. Don't respond to trial balloons that the buyer sends up, hoping to find out your bottom limits on price and other terms. Ask that the buyer put his or her best offer in writing.

Don't jump at the first contract presented, especially if it's way below your expectations. Have the confidence that you've priced your home properly and that it's competitive with other houses on the market.

But don't regard your first offer too lightly, either—especially if it comes reasonably close to your goals. Experienced agents know that the first contracts on a well-priced house will usually be submitted by the most serious, well-qualified buyers—people who know their own needs and resources and who have studied the market carefully. A contract from this kind of buyer is well worth serious consideration and probably a counter-offer from you.

CONSIDERING THE CONTRACT

Money, people and the law are primary elements in any real estate sales contract. If you provided the contract form to a purchaser, you should already be familiar with it. If a purchaser presents an offer on another form, you will need time to study it carefully. In either situation, you need to be sure the parties to the contract are legally competent to do business with you (for example, of legal age, mental competence, etc.).

To be valid, a contract must be in writing and be freely offered by the buyer and accepted by the seller. Money or other valuable consideration must be exchanged for the title to the property.

Any contract that passes your preliminary review and is a candidate for acceptance should be reviewed by your attorney, or be made contingent upon that review. See Chapter 8 for a discussion of contingencies that are commonly sought by purchasers, and decide in advance how you will respond to these conditions.

Consider the contract as a whole. Is it slanted in favor of the buyer? If so, consult with your attorney about making changes. To do that, analyze the document as a series of paragraphs or clauses, each written to benefit one party or the other. Take them one by one and make an orderly evaluation.

For example, most completed purchase and sale contracts can require you to sell your property. But what could you do should the buyer default? In an option contract, the buyer has an option to buy. If he doesn't, he stands to lose the earnest deposit (or option money), assuming of course that the seller is not at fault. On the other hand, in a specific-performance contract—the most common form of contract used in home sales—the seller can require the buyer to purchase the property or pay damages.

A small earnest deposit accompanying an option contract may be viewed with alarm by a seller. That same deposit, tied to a specific-performance contract offered by a well-heeled purchaser, may be viewed with less concern.

Beware of the contract that binds only you. Getting a seller to accept an offer that nails down the price and terms but leaves the buyer free to escape through a number of clauses is a favorite strategy of buyers.

Examine each contingency. Is each one clear and precise? Some contingencies are reasonable; others are less so.

KEY ELEMENTS OF THE CONTRACT

Price

Is the offering price right? There is nothing that evokes such an emotional response from a seller as the price offered. Try to keep an open mind on the price until you've studied the whole deal. Be realistic and objective. Was the price based on an independent appraisal or on a broker's market analysis? How long has the property been on the market? How many written offers have you received? Has the market changed?

Most properties don't bring full price. And price, by itself, usually doesn't make or break a deal.

Condition of Home and Inspection

It is fair that the purchaser should have the opportunity to have your home inspected for soundness of construction and state of repair. Keep it fair by insisting that the person or firm to be used be named in the contract by professional designation, and set a time limit for the removal of the contingency—five or so working days. If radon is a problem in your area, having test results available on request will save everyone time.

Watch what you guarantee. Occasionally, a purchaser asks a seller to guarantee that the roof won't leak, the heating system won't go out or any number of other such assurances. Don't do it. If you do, you are not making a sale, you are taking on a partner. Do not undertake to remain responsible for your property once you have sold it.

As a rule, contract language determines what must be in working order at settlement. Have everything clearly spelled out, otherwise local law and custom may prevail. Say that only three of the four burners on your stove work, and you don't want to pay for repairs. Unless your contract states that the stove is being sold "as is"—with three burners, not four—you may end up paying for the repair at the settlement table.

Buyers often are willing to negotiate on the condition of the house. For example, if your home is a candidate for extensive upgrading, a prospective buyer who is planning renovations that include installing central air conditioning may be happy to bargain over the broken window unit, since it would be discarded anyway once work begins.

Financing

If the contract is contingent on a buyer being able to obtain an acceptable loan, does the clause spell out what actions are required by the buyer? What interest rate and number of discount points does the buyer consider "acceptable"? Is there a time limit? What will happen if no loan is secured by the agreed-on deadline? How will the seller know when the buyer gets a loan commitment? How can the contingency be removed? Generally, you'll want to leave the buyer as few escape hatches as possible.

Response Deadline

You'll be asked to respond to a contract offer within a specified period of time—say, two or three days. Try to get as long a response time as possible. If you are presented with a desirable contract containing a deadline you are unable to meet—perhaps because your attorney or spouse is out of town—counter promptly with a more suitable one . . . and an explanation.

If you think you'll have other offers coming in, you'll want to buy as much time as possible to review them and perhaps use one offer to jack up another offer. Tell other interested parties (or have your agent tell them) that you've got a good offer on the table, and if they want a shot at this purchase, they had better move fast with an attractive offer.

It may benefit you to tell other parties what the highest offering price is, to get them to top it; but in other cases, it may be better not to name a price, in case the other bidder is willing to go much higher. If you try to bluff buyers by telling them you've been offered a price or contract you don't really have in hand, it might work—or it might backfire and scare off interested parties, leaving you with nothing.

While you are studying the offer, keep the buyer informed of your progress. A buyer left hanging may have second thoughts and may even withdraw the offer before you have a chance to accept or produce a counter-offer.

Prior Sale of Buyer's Home

Should you cooperate with a prospective purchaser who must sell a home before buying yours? Maybe. But that hinges the sale of a property you know—yours—on the sale of one you don't know—his.

Any such contingency clause should be carefully constructed and reviewed—if not written—by your attorney. Before getting to that point in the negotiations, however, seek the advice of a broker familiar with the area of your potential buyer's home.

Assure yourself that the property is saleable and reasonably priced. Ask for a hefty earnest money deposit, or try for a non-refundable deposit should the deal fail.

Settlement Date and Occupancy

If you're selling your home because you already have your next home under contract, try to get a settlement date that will enable you to take your sales proceeds to the closing of the purchase; that will make it unnecessary for you to get a bridge loan. Be realistic, however; the buyer of your home will probably need at least 30 to 45 days to arrange financing.

Most sold homes are delivered to the buyer empty and clean on settlement day. If you would like to stay on in your home after settlement, make this desire known to buyers and write it into the contract, suggesting a lease-back price that just covers the new owner's out-of-pocket costs (mortgage, taxes, utilities, insurance) for the time you remain there.

Other Conditions

Other contingencies address problems or events that may happen between the time the contract is signed and the time title is passed to the buyer. If your house burns down, what happens? Does the buyer have to buy and pay the agreed-on price? Can the whole deal be called off? Can a lower price be offered? What about insurance proceeds?

TAKE BACK A MORTGAGE?

High interest rates and shortages of available mortgage money are always bad news for both home buyers and sellers. Be sure that any solution suggested to you—by whatever name—doesn't just shift the problem rather than solve it.

First of all, ask yourself whether you belong in the mortgage lending business. If you need your equity to make a down payment on another home, you may not be able to take back a mortgage. And even if you can afford to help your buyer with financing, you may not want to. Mortgage lending can be complicated. It involves two major phases: origination and servicing. Origination is setting up the loan—screening applicants, appraising the property and drawing up the papers. Servicing is collecting the monthly payments, dunning for delinquencies, sending annual statements and foreclosing when necessary.

There is considerable risk. Because seller mortgages are really worth much less than they appear, they generally are the equivalent of cutting the price. And because the interest rates and other terms of seller mortgages are almost invariably generous, these mortgages can be distinctly inferior to alternative investments.

Avoid making these mistakes, which are common among seller financing:

Too little down payment: Don't take back a mortgage if the buyer has less than 20% equity in the property. Professional mortgage lenders prefer that the buyer have at least that much equity. This insures an adequate buffer in the event of foreclosure because it increases the probability that the property can be sold for enough to cover your loan. It also gives the borrower incentive to avoid foreclosure in the first place.

No prepayment penalty: When permitted by state law, professional lenders almost always impose a prepayment penalty. Sellers almost never do. Sellers hope the borrower will pay off the loan early and don't want to discourage the borrower in any way. Mortgage investors, on the other hand, see the prepayment penalty as providing the possibility of an even higher yield. Often they will pay less for a mortgage that has no prepayment penalty.

Too low an interest rate: Sellers rarely ask enough, even on second mortgages. Lower-than-market interest rates reduce the return if you keep the loans and reduce the resale value if you sell it. In addition, the IRS requires that a minimum interest rate be charged. Check with your attorney or tax accountant for the latest information on rates.

Too long a term: Keep the length of the loan as short as possible—one or two years if you can get it. Resist going over three years. The longer the term, the deeper the discount when you sell the loan.

Skimpy credit check: Too often, laymen tend to rely on appearances. If the buyer to whom they intend to extend a mortgage seems okay, they make the loan. Prospective buyers of that mortgage, however, are likely to ask for the credit report on the borrower. A credit report is inexpensive and relatively easy to obtain.

Amateur loan documents: Generally speaking, the best-drawn documents are the ones used by professional lenders. Ask a mortgage lender for copies of mortgage forms he uses. You should also have an attorney—one who has considerable experience in putting together mortgages. Ask a local professional mortgage lender for the name of the lawyer he uses.

Allowing late payment: Pros have learned that failure to crack down on chronic delinquents often leads to costly problems. Make sure your loan documents include a late charge, and enforce it to the letter.

FORGING AN AGREEMENT

If you're selling through an agent, contracts will be presented to you through that agent, and you will counter all inadequate offers through the same agent.

Everything in the offering contract is negotiable. Decide what you want to give on and what doesn't matter that much to you. Changes can be inked in over or next to language on the contract, or a new contract can be drawn up from scratch. A draft contract can go back and forth between buyer and seller any number of times, but you'll both want to avoid an interminable negotiation, in which fatigue and disgust could jeopardize the whole deal.

When everyone has agreed to all the terms, initialed all changes and signed the contracts, you've got an agreement binding on all parties. All that remains is the removal of any contingency clauses, arranging of financing, clearing of title, and other steps on the road to settlement.

SELLING ON YOUR OWN

The sale-by-owner seller will probably be doing his or her own negotiating with prospective buyers. However, some FSBOs hire an experienced real estate attorney to do this for them, paying the attorney a flat fee or hourly rate. If you've consulted an attorney to have your sample contract drawn up or to review a contract presented by a buyer, find out if this person will also do your negotiating for you.

If you have already agreed to pay a partial commission (say, 3%) on an open listing with any agent who brings in the successful buyer, you'll probably be dealing not with the buyer directly, but with the buyer's agent. Keep in mind that it is you, not the buyer, who will be paying the agent's commission. You may feel as if you're an adversary of that agent, but in fact the agent has a legal obligation to help you get the best possible deal on the sale; if things get tense, remind the agent of this simple fact.

If you're truly on your own—one on one with the buyer—keep all your dealings as professional and courteous as possible. Don't take anything personally; remember, the buyer has a right to try to pay as little as possible for your home, and you have a right to get as much as you can. It's a business deal, so try not to be offended by a low initial offer or any other tactic the buyer may try.

If an offer is to be made, both parties must be willing to ask for what they want, voice their objections and offer alternatives. Begin negotiations by seeking out areas of agreement. Find out what is attractive about your property, and build on that. Move on to issues that don't involve anyone's ego, such as the desired date of possession. (Normally, that's not a touchy issue, though, like everything else in a real estate sale, it can be.) Get the buyer thinking about moving in; it makes the whole purchase seem more real.

Check the Buyer's Credentials

If the buyer intends to assume your current mortgage, you must be even more careful about verifying his or her financial stability and credit record. Under some circumstances, if the new owner defaults on the mortgage he assumes from you, you could be held liable.

In recent years there has been widespread mortgage fraud on FHA and VA loans assumed by crooks who purchased houses from desperate sellers with little or no money down; it has been most common in distressed local economies where home prices have fallen. The new owners often put tenants in the houses and collected rents, but made no payments on the assumed mortgages, inviting foreclosure. The FHA and VA have often tried to collect their losses from the original borrower. Both federal agencies are tightening their assumption credit checks, but the scam still poses a risk to unwary sellers.

All the legal fine print in the world can't make a good deal with a bad buyer. You could be back on square one if an impulsive or unprepared buyer is derailed by the first negative comment from a home inspector or mortgage lender. Make a judgment about a prospective buyer's commitment and financial capability before proceeding into a nitty-gritty examination of the purchase offer.

Ask for a net worth statement. How does the buyer intend to pay for the property? Has he or she been prequalified by an agent or lender? Where will the down payment come from? How knowledgeable is the buyer about market value, the neighborhood and so forth? Are the terms of the sale understood? Has the property been examined thoroughly? Ask these questions now. You have the right to know.

Keep Selling

When you sense your prospect is getting close to the contract-writing stage, keep selling. Now is not the time suddenly to begin acting the role of pleasant host or hostess, assuming the buyer will take it upon himself to do the rest. Avoid these common mistakes:

Appearing too eager: If the buyer feels you are overly eager, or too anxious to make a deal, you may lose a sale. He may become suspicious, or he may pressure you into making major concessions.

Appearing too tough: A good deal can slip through your hands if you are too rigid or unpleasant to work with. Try to be flexible and objective. If you can't agree over one point, keep pushing toward agreement in areas where you do see eye-to-eye. Try not to close the door on any one point completely; just put the matter off until later.

Failing to empathize: Try to see the buyer's side of things.

Never become defensive. Be ready with all the information needed; be confident and patient.

If you reach a point where you recognize you must compromise or make a concession, get everything else agreed on in writing. Then, when you do concede the point, the deal essentially is locked in.

Once you have an accepted contract—fully signed and all changes initialed—stop talking! Stand up, shake hands and change the subject.

You have a contract and are on your way to settlement.

CHAPTER 23

PREPARING FOR SETTLEMENT

◆

BUYERS MAY dread the arrival of closing day and the huge outlay of cash, yet still be eager to get it over with so they can move into their new home. Sellers, on the other hand, look forward to collecting their bounty, but their anticipation may be tinged with anxiety and sadness about giving up their home for good.

Most of the work between contract signing and closing falls on the buyer, who must get the house inspected quickly, arrange financing, and buy homeowner's and title insurance.

The seller has relatively little to do. If you agreed to have anything repaired, it must be done now. If a problem arises with the title, it may involve you in some paper work, legal expense and delicate diplomacy. (Carefully read Chapter 12.) If a title problem is intractable or so complicated it could threaten to delay settlement for a long time, your buyer may be tempted to try to void the contract. These anxieties might be calmed by you or a good attorney, but if the deal is on the rocks, have your attorney tell you what your rights are.

KEEP YOURSELF INFORMED

The most important thing you need to do as seller is keep

yourself informed of everything that is happening. If the buyer is having trouble getting a loan on the terms specified in the contract, you should know it; it could jeopardize the whole deal and end up putting your house back on the market. A day or so before closing, make sure all the papers are in place. The settlement agent was probably selected by the buyer, but you are free to bring your own attorney to the settlement appointment, at your expense.

Nothing is more tedious than sitting around a settlement table while the escrow officer telephones lenders, insurance companies, contractors and others for figures that should be at hand. A process that should take 45 minutes drags on for hours instead.

There should be no arguing over who pays what, because the contract and escrow instructions spell out everything. There should be no financial surprises, either. Your agent should have kept you up-to-date on what you could expect to net out of the transaction. You should have received an estimated net sheet when you signed the listing agreement, and another one along with each contract presentation. Prior to settlement, the escrow officer or settlement attorney should provide you with a copy of the settlement sheet. (See page 181 for an example of closing costs on a $150,000 home.)

If you are handling your own settlement, you can get an estimate at the time you arrange for closing, or "open escrow," whether it is with a title or abstract company or an abstract attorney.

Still, things can go wrong. Documents get misplaced or don't arrive in time, to name just two examples. Other areas where last-minute glitches or misunderstandings occur include:

◆ No-shows and too-lates: People who need to be present at closing should be kept informed of any change in the date, time or place. They should be reminded a week before closing, and again the day before.

If closing is being conducted by the buyer's attorney, and you want your attorney to be there to represent you, you no doubt cleared the initial date with him before signing the contract. However, if closing is delayed, or is changed for any reason, you'll need to clear it again. The same follow-through tactic should be used for each individual you are depending on to attend.

♦ Anyone named on the deed under which you hold title must sign the new deed by which you grant title. In many jurisdictions, if you have married since acquiring title, your spouse also will have to sign the deed. If your co-owner doesn't live nearby, allow time to have the deed signed and returned before settlement.

♦ Determine when you will be paid. Don't expect to walk away from the settlement table with a check in hand, but don't leave the question of when and how you will be paid undetermined.

Most settlement attorneys do not disburse checks until all the necessary documents have been recorded. If that's the case, when will the recording take place, and how often are checks made up? An additional delay in disbursement can occur if the lender wants to review settlement papers after it is over and then wait for the deed to be recorded before disbursing any funds.

If you are buying another property, consider having both settlements at the same office, scheduled back-to-back. That way, the timing of the disbursement is not a problem. You sign a paper authorizing the title company or attorney to assign the funds from your sale to your purchase.

THE PAPERS YOU'LL NEED

For more detail on the settlement process, read Chapter 13, "Get Ready for Settlement." Here's a checklist of what will be needed to facilitate the closing:

♦ A copy of the sales contract and any documentation needed to show that contingencies have been removed or satisfied.

♦ All documents needed to complete the transfer of title. These usually are handled by the title insurance or abstract company and your attorney or closing officer. They may include: certificate of title, deed, correcting affidavits, quitclaim deeds, survey and title insurance policy or binder. Be sure the closing officer has the necessary papers showing that all judgments, liens and mortgages have been removed or satisfied.

♦ Homeowner's insurance policy. If the buyer plans to take

over the unused portion of your hazard insurance, you'll need to make arrangements in advance so that all the paperwork will be completed on time.

◆ Prorations for on-going expenses, such as insurance premiums, property taxes, accrued interest on assumed loans, and utilities (if not shut off between owners). The proration date usually is determined by local custom but can be different if the contract so specifies.

◆ Receipts showing payment of latest water, electric and gas bills.

◆ A certificate from your lender indicating the mortgage balance and date to which interest has been prepaid. The closing officer usually obtains these figures calculated to the day of settlement.

APPENDIX

REAL ESTATE
APPRAISERS GROUPS

$$T$$here is no reliable estimate on the number of people working as appraisers; figures range from 100,000 to 300,000. Membership in one or more of the professional appraisers' organizations (which number more than a dozen) may indicate higher standards, or it may indicate little more than the ability to pay the price of membership.

The best of the appraisal groups confer certification based on continuing education requirements, ethical standards, and grievance and enforcement procedures. The following three are among those with the most rigorous standards for membership:

American Institute of Real Estate Appraisers (430 N. Michigan Ave., Chicago, IL 60611; 312-329-8559). Affiliated with the National Association of Realtors. Members use the designation MAI or RM after their names.

An appraiser using the designation MAI (member, Appraisal Institute) must have a college degree or its equivalent, at least five years appraising experience and must have submitted an income property demonstration report judged satisfactory by a committee of Institute peers. A residential member (RM) must have three years experience and also must have submitted a satisfactory report on residential property. Members using either designation must have passed written examinations.

National Society of Real Estate Appraisers (1265 E. 105th St., Cleveland, OH 44108; 216-795-3445); this group designates members as master, senior or junior (MREA, CRA, RA). Master and senior members must have at least five years experience, junior members at least two, along with demonstration reports and approved courses. The top two rankings require qualifying interviews.

Society of Real Estate Appraisers (225 N. Michigan Ave., 7th Floor, Chicago, IL 60611; 312-819-2400); SREA designates its members as senior real estate analyst (SREA), senior real property appraiser (SRPA) and senior residential appraiser (SRA). All members are certified on the basis of training, examination and performance. All are qualified to do residential appraisals, but SRPAs and SREAs can appraise income property as well.

INDEX

◆

References to tables and charts
are in boldface type.

master deed, 62
questions to ask, list, 60–62
for sale by owner, 267
sales contract or purchase
agreement, 63
*A Consumer Guide to Financing a Co-
operative Using Share Loan Financing,* 69
*A Consumer's Guide to Mortgage
Lock-Ins,* 153
Contingencies, contract, 104–109,
294, 295–296
Contracts
agreeing to terms, 299
condition of property, 295
condominiums, 63
contingencies, 104–109, 294,
295–296
counter-offer, 110–111
elements, 104–109
financing, 295–296
inclusions, 104
inspection, 295
land, 143
listing, 280–284
occupancy, 297
preprinted forms, 103, 267
presenting, 110
price, 294
prior sale of buyer's home,
296–297
property management, 228–
229
response deadline, 296
review by attorney, 293–294
for sale by owner, 267
sales, 293–294
settlement date, 297
temporary listing contract, 272
typical home inspection
clause, 108
Contract statement of condition,
105
Conventional mortgages, 22, 153
Cooperative apartments
bylaws, 67
definition, 65
documents, 67
financing options, 66–67
governing boards, 65
inspection, 118–119

and new owners, 65
questions to ask, list, 67–69
Co-ops. *See* Cooperative apartments
Council of State Housing Agencies,
149
Counter-offer, 110–111
CRA. *See* Senior real estate
appraiser
Creative financing, 30–31
for sale by owner options, 268
take-back mortgage, 141–142
Credit
evaluating, 15–16
report, 17–18, 298–299
Credit bureaus, 17–18
Credit check, 298–299
Credit life insurance, 155
Credit report, 298–299
Credit unions, 149

D

Deed, 105
Deed of trust, 167
Department of Housing and Urban
Development (HUD)
discrimination complaints, 96
mobile home standards, 72
Deposit check, 104–105
Depreciation, 198–199, 202–203, 221
deduction for, 255–256
Depreciation recapture, 221
Disbursement of checks after settle-
ment, 305
Discount agents, 273–274
Discount brokers, 275, 282
Discrimination
agents and mortgage lenders,
restrictions, 95–96
forms of, 94–96
Distance test, 256
Double score, 282
Down payment
maximum, figuring, 13
minimum, 14
second-trust loans, 14–15
worksheet, **13**

I

O

P